GORBACHEV'S RETREAT

GORBACHEV'S RETREAT

The Third World

Melvin A.ˡⁱᵃⁿ Goodman

PRAEGER

New York
Westport, Connecticut
London

Library of Congress Cataloging-in-Publication Data

Goodman, Melvin A. (Melvin Allan), 1938-
    Gorbachev's retreat : the Third World / Melvin A. Goodman.
       p.   cm.
    Includes bibliographical references (p.   ) and index.
    ISBN 0-275-93696-1 (alk. paper)
    1. Developing countries—Foreign relations—Soviet Union.
    2. Soviet Union—Foreign relations—Developing countries.   3. Soviet
    Union—Foreign relations—1985-   I. Title.
    D888.S65D65   1991
    327.4701724—dc20   90-23421

British Library Cataloguing in Publication Data is available.

Library of Congress Catalog Card Number: 90-23421
ISBN: 0-275-93696-1

First published in 1991

Praeger Publishers, One Madison Avenue, New York, NY 10010
An imprint of Greenwood Publishing Group, Inc.

Printed in the United States of America

(∞)™

The paper used in this book complies with the
Permanent Paper Standard issued by the National
Information Standards Organization (Z39.48-1984).

10 9 8 7 6 5 4 3 2 1

To my mother and the memory of my father

Contents

Preface

This study describes and analyzes President Mikhail Gorbachev's strategic retreat from the Third World. The Gorbachev years have marked an era of tumult and change in Soviet domestic and foreign policies, particularly in the Third World. Gorbachev's decisions are directly responsible for the decline in Soviet military presence in every major region of the world and the reduction of Soviet military aid and advisers in every key Soviet client state. Gorbachev has worked closely with the United States to resolve crises in Afghanistan, Angola, Cambodia, Nicaragua, and the Persian Gulf. The Soviets have taken significant steps to improve relations with Israel, South Korea, and South Africa, and have signaled their client states to improve relations with these states as well.

Gorbachev deserves the major share of credit for these changes in Soviet behavior. From the outset, he recognized Moscow's inability to project power into the Third World and to continue to extract scarce resources for foreign and military policy goals. His willingness to allow communist regimes to collapse in Eastern Europe, to withdraw Soviet forces from Central Europe and the Sino-Soviet border, and to retreat from the Third World is a direct response to the "imperial overstretch" of the Brezhnev era. It is an even more incredible achievement that he has taken such a weak diplomatic hand and, having played his cards so well since 1985, improved the Soviet international position. Gorbachev perhaps is a student of Talleyrand, who remarked two hundred years ago that, "France can no longer be great if it is merely powerful."

This book acknowledges Gorbachev's recognition that the Soviet Union lacked the basic requirement of power, that is, to make sure that other countries took Moscow's interests into account in their decision making. The United States had a freer hand in the Third World than it realized in the post-war period, and U.S. clients were not really inhibited by Soviet behavior. Even Soviet clients who were dependent on Moscow for military and economic assistance pursued their own policies and took numerous actions that were at odds with Soviet national interest. Indeed, Gorbachev and Shevardnadze realized that, in the Third World, the tail was clearly wagging the dog. Moscow's economic weakness, moreover, made it difficult to capitalize on its arms relationships with key regional states. The Soviet model of development and Communist ideology became irrelevant, as Third World states turned to the United State, Western Europe, and Japan for assistance.

The resignation of Foreign Minister Eduard Shevardnadze in December 1990, saying he could not stand to watch the Soviet Union lurch toward dictatorship, should have no effect on the retreat from the Third World. In the wake of the resignation, Moscow continued to coordinate efforts to resolve the Persian Gulf crisis and to mediate confrontations in Cambodia and El Salvador. The Soviets have been particularly helpful in identifying Soviet-manufactured surface-to-air missiles, which had been smuggled from Nicaragua to guerrillas fighting in El Salvador. Further tests will take place during talks to end the civil war in Angola between the pro-Soviet government and pro-American guerrillas, and discussions to settle the confrontation in Afghanistan. The Afghan talks stalled prior to Shevardnadze's resignation over the timing of elections, Soviet and U.S. arms shipments, and the future political role of President Najibullah.

The selection of Aleksandr Bessmertnykh in January 1991 as the new foreign minister is a strong indication that Moscow wants to preserve the improvement in Soviet-U.S. relations as well. Bessmertnykh was deputy foreign minister and first deputy foreign minister from 1988 to 1990, responsible for Soviet-U.S. relations, before becoming ambassador to the United States. As first deputy foreign minister, he traveled to Iran, Iraq, Syria, and Turkey. He has spent nearly twenty years at the embassy in Washington, specializing in bilateral issues and arms control in such posts as first secretary, counselor, and minister-counselor. Bessmertnykh has attended nearly every Soviet-U.S. summit meeting since 1985 and, in the 1960s, attended several sessions of the United Nations General Assembly as an aide to then Foreign Minister Andrey Gromyko.

Bessmertnykh's swift and overwhelming approval as foreign minister by the Supreme Soviet in the wake of the violent crackdown in Lithuania also indicates that the Soviet leadership remains sensitive to the international reaction to Moscow's hard-line domestic policies. Bessmertnykh is a veteran diplomat with a reputation as a reformer within the foreign ministry; upon confirmation, he immediately pledged to continue the "new thinking" of his predecessor.[1] He is probably Moscow's leading expert on the United States, and his appointment signals continued cooperation with the United States and West Europe on bilateral and Third World matters.

Gorbachev's retreat from the Third World and particularly from competition with the United States raises many questions for readers of this book. In demonstrating enormous interest in resolving regional disputes, what are the limits to Soviet reliance on the United Nations and the Security Council for conflict resolution? There appear to be domestic opponents of Gorbachev's retreat from Central Europe and the Sino-Soviet frontier, but is there evidence of opposition to the retreat from the Third World? Is Soviet-American cooperation in the Third World replacing arms control and disarmament as the centerpiece of detente in the 1990s? Is Gorbachev's retreat irreversible, and will the "civil crisis" in the USSR threaten the stability in Moscow's behavior in the International arena? Did the United States exaggerate Soviet influence and power in the Third World even before Gorbachev's strategic surrender? Finally, will Shevardnadze's dramatic resignation have any effect on Soviet policy in the Third World? I suggest answers to some, but not all, of these questions, and hope I have shed some new light in the field of Soviet foreign policy in doing so.

I have received assistance from many people in writing this book. My first thanks go to Dr. Robert Ferrell of Indiana University, who helped me to complete a dissertation twenty years ago and was still willing to encourage and guide this effort. Several other individuals deserve special thanks: Dr. Amin Banani of UCLA is responsible for my interest in Soviet studies; Dr. Alvin Rubinstein has patiently argued with many of the ideas in this book over the past ten years; Ms. Carolyn McGiffert Ekedahl was an informal adviser and perceptive observer along the way. Finally, and most importantly, I should especially like to thank my family—Ann, Suzanne, and Michael— for being supportive in every possible way.

NOTE

1. David Remnick, *The Washington Post*, January 16, 1991, p. 16, "Envoy to U.S. Succeeds Shevardnadze." Bessmertnykh was approved by an overwhelming vote of 421 to 3, with ten abstentions; Victor Pugo, a former KGB official and a

hardliner, was confirmed as Interior Minister by a vote of 315 to 75, with forty abstentions. Pugo has been the official spokesman for the bloody army action in Lithuania on January 13 that left 14 people dead; Bessmertnykh stated that Moscow "must work out ways to prevent and avoid such things and keep in mind the foreign policy aspects as well."

GORBACHEV'S
RETREAT

Introduction

We cannot use our military power as a means of stopping imperialist intervention in the affairs of other countries. We must search for other ways.

General V. Varennikov
Deputy Minister of Defense

Since Mikhail Gorbachev's rise to power in 1985, Western analysts have made a series of fundamental errors regarding this new leader's domestic and international behavior. His consolidation of power has been underestimated, his dramatic international maneuvers unanticipated. From the beginning he was assessed as no different than his predecessors. "He has no new ideas," Dmitri Simes assured us. In many respects he is "more dangerous," warned Zbigniew Brzezinski. Seweryn Bialer wrote that the "main thrust of Gorbachev's Eastern European policy is to strengthen the Soviet hold on its empire and to control the satellite parties more tightly" and added two years later that he had "no intention of transforming the major national institutions." Jerry Hough of Duke University wrote that Gorbachev believed the United States "more valuable as an adversary than a partner" and that an anti-U.S. faction was dominating Soviet foreign policy.

All of these views were incorrect and ignored the compelling motivations for Gorbachev's efforts to change Soviet society and provide a legitimate place for the USSR in the international arena. Admittedly, Gorbachev's inheritance could not have been more bleak. The economy faced the prospect of negative growth; any solution required major infusions of capital. Nor was Moscow a player in the international economic arena. The Soviets lacked membership in the World Bank, International Monetary Fund, and the General Agreement for Trade and Tariffs. They had never played more than a minor role in trade markets and relied on Eastern European states for manufactured goods and machine tools. The Eastern European states, of course, had their own economic problems.

Military modernization was also a problem. The Soviet military faced U.S. weapons systems that included Pershing-II and cruise missiles in Western Europe with a capability against command and control facilities around Moscow. The prospect of U.S. Stealth technology for aircraft and cruise missiles created additional problems for Soviet air defense. The Strategic Defense Initiative posed an additional challenge to strategic forces, and technological spinoffs of SDI in deep penetration weapons systems threatened Soviet forces in Europe.

The USSR's international position in 1985 was no more promising than its military-industrial situation. Every important bilateral relationship was either at an impasse or in disarray. Soviet-U.S. relations were dead in the water because of Moscow's walkout from Strategic Arms Reduction Talks and Intermediate-range Forces negotiations in Geneva and Washington's ideological opposition to dealing with the Soviets. The Sino-Soviet relationship was stagnant, with little economic activity and continuing polemics. Soviet-Japanese relations were hampered by the hostility of Foreign Minister Andrei Gromyko, and no noncommunist government in Asia was interested in dealing with a Soviet Union that could not come to terms with the two major Asian powers. The Soviets faced the prospect of increased military and intelligence cooperation between the United States, China, and Japan.

Relations with European members of NATO were similarly idle, as the Soviets had gone too far in trying to force the West German government to refuse Pershing-II deployments. Bonn, London, and Paris were becoming increasingly conservative in foreign policy. West Germany was in front of the United States in encouraging modernization of NATO's missile systems. The "special relationship" that Brezhnev had developed with de Gaulle and France had eroded.

The Soviet position in the Third World was no better than in other areas. Many students of foreign policy argued that the Soviet position in Angola, Ethiopia, and South Yemen demonstrated a robust regional policy and that Gorbachev would pursue strategic advantage in the Third World against the interests of the United States and the other Western powers.[1] In fact, the Soviet situation in most areas of the Third World was embarrassingly bleak. The invasion of Afghanistan in 1979 had significantly worsened prospects throughout the Middle East and Southwest Asia. Moscow had never been successful in Asia and could not find a solution to the Sino-Soviet rift. It was unlikely that any noncommunist Asian state would embrace Soviet policy that was prominently anti-Chinese. The Soviet military presence in Vietnam made Moscow additionally unattractive to the states of Southeast Asia.

From the outset, Gorbachev was forced to address a series of regional problems. Moscow's problems in the Mediterranean dated from the ouster of military advisers and technicians from Egypt in 1972. Moscow played no role in the agreements between Israel and Egypt or between Israel and Syria, which took place from 1974 to 1979 under three American presidents.

The Soviet position in Africa reached a peak in the late 1970s with the successful use of Soviet military equipment and a Cuban proxy army on behalf of governments in Angola and Ethiopia. By 1985 the cost was getting notably greater and the rewards smaller. Moscow had lost naval and air facilities in Somalia to position itself in Ethiopia, but the wretched security situation in the latter country prevented access to the Ethiopian coast.

In Central America, Nicaragua offered no more than nuisance value against the interests of the United States; Gorbachev had no apparent interest in base rights or military facilities in the region. The Soviet-Cuban relationship appeared on an even keel, but there were signs that Fidel Castro was becoming restless with Moscow's unwillingness to provide a security guarantee against Washington.

It now appears that Gorbachev decided at the outset on fundamental change in foreign policy to achieve a more stable international arena and a less threatening Soviet image that would allow Moscow to concentrate on its economic morass. He adopted "perestroika" or restructuring, both economic and political, and moved the United States to the top of the foreign policy agenda. He hoped that improving the strategic environment would lead to improved ties to Western European states as well as China and Japan.

Gorbachev swept aside Foreign Minister Andrei Gromyko in the summer of 1985 and rapidly changed policies associated with Gromyko. One arms control proposal followed another in the wake of Gorbachev's major disarmament address in 1986. The Soviet grip on Eastern Europe was relaxed after a major statement in 1987, allowing Hungary and Poland to evolve in new political directions. The decision to withdraw from Afghanistan was announced in 1988 and, during that same year, the Soviets began to cooperate privately with the United States to reach a cease-fire agreement in Angola that included a Cuban withdrawal.

In Asia, the Soviets have withdrawn their own forces from Mongolia and along the Sino-Soviet border, and pressured Vietnam to leave

Cambodia. Soviet relations with China have improved significantly as a result and overtures to Japan could have similar results. Gorbachev has made efforts to improve relations with North Korea and has established diplomatic relations with South Korea. Former Foreign Minister Eduard Shevardnadze visited the key states of the Association for Southeast Asian Nations and, as a result, the USSR is no longer "odd man out" among the noncommunist states of Southeast Asia.

The Soviet president has recognized that actions in the Third World during the Brezhnev period brought few rewards; excluded the Soviets from negotiations in Africa, Asia, and the Middle East; and vastly complicated Soviet relations with the United States. After fifteen years the Soviets were finally willing to accept Henry Kissinger's idea of linkage in which improved ties between the United States and the USSR were dependent on stability in the Third World. Gorbachev conceded that Brezhnev's fishing in troubled waters in the Third World, particularly Angola and Ethiopia in the 1970s and Nicaragua and Cambodia in the 1980s, had prevented détente and that the invasion of Afghanistan had ended any possibility for ratification of SALT II.

Gorbachev's interest in diminishing the Soviet military position in the Third World was part of another interest of the Soviet leader— demilitarization. From 1985 to 1990 there was a decline in the status of the military, a reduced role in decisionmaking, and a reduction in defense spending and modernization. Top military leaders were reshuffled—the defense minister, first deputy defense ministers, commanders of theater forces, chiefs of military districts, and the chief of the Main Political Directorate of the Army and Navy. The latter position is particularly important because it is within the defense ministry but subordinate to the central committee of the party.

In addition to cutbacks in strategic forces, including the principal nuclear submarine (Typhoon), the most threatening intercontinental ballistic missiles (SS-18 and mobile SS-24), the most sophisticated strategic bomber (Blackjack), Gorbachev has ordered a delay in construction of the first 65,000–ton carrier and made no effort to improve logistics systems for airlift and sealift in noncontiguous areas.[2] Delay of the carrier of course prolongs uncertainty over whether this new platform will introduce high-performance aircraft rather than helicopters and vertical takeoff and landing aircraft.

There has been a decline in the operational tempo and presence of naval forces and naval aviation in the Third World, which suggests that security concerns there will remain secondary or even tertiary. Naval exercises have been cut, joint exercises with Third World navies made more infrequent, reconnaissance from Third World airfields in

Angola and Cuba reduced, and military advisers withdrawn from Ethiopia and Mozambique.[3] Agreements in Angola and Cambodia presumably will mean a reduction in Moscow's advisory presence in southern Africa and Southeast Asia. By the time of the Malta summit, Gorbachev had slashed naval deployment in the Mediterranean by more than half, leaving a handful of warships, one or two submarines, a few auxiliaries.[4]

Military assistance to the Third World has dropped sharply, in part due to decline in Third World purchases of weapons systems and emphasis on less expensive spare parts, ammunition, and support.[5] The increase in Third World debt and the ceasefire between Iran and Iraq are also factors in decline of weapons agreements with client states.[6] In 1989 the Soviets stopped military assistance to Nicaragua, presumably as a signal to the new administration in Washington.[7]

Gorbachev maintains that the Soviet Union has no interest in contesting U.S. superiority in power projection. Michael MccGwire may be correct in arguing that the Soviets once sought use of the political and physical infrastructure in the Third World to meet their requirements in case of worldwide war, but the current leadership surely is reducing any military role for forces in South Asia and the Middle East.[8] The Soviets are showing no interest in extended deployments in distant areas and appear to favor reducing the size of their navy and limiting the mission in out-of-area waters to reconnaissance. Older ships are being scrapped and modernization curtailed.

Gorbachev is showing no interest in replacing bases lost in Egypt and Somalia in the 1970s or even upgrading the poor facilities that naval vessels use in Angola, Ethiopia, Yemen, and Syria. These facilities are no longer important, as traditionally thought, for protecting sea lanes between the western and eastern USSR. Reduced operations by the Soviet Navy depreciates the importance of the Mediterranean and Indian Ocean. The Soviets are withdrawing from Cam Ranh Bay and, in general, Soviet naval forces are spending less time at sea, particularly outside home waters. Interest in negotiating naval confidence-building measures with the United States and including naval forces in both strategic and conventional arms control negotiations strongly suggest that the Soviets are going to rely on disarmament agreements to blunt the superiority of the U.S. Navy and cannot afford a naval competition.

The Soviets, in other words, are making no attempt to rival the U.S. concept of forward deployment. Instead, their navy is relying on repair and support facilities in Angola, Ethiopia, Syria, and Vietnam to support a reconnaissance mission in the Third World. These facilities are extremely vulnerable, and Moscow presumably requires the permission of the host country before entering these ports. In several years, therefore, Gorbachev has challenged the policies of Brezhnev that brought the first permanent Soviet naval presence into the Mediterranean in 1964, the Indian Ocean in 1968, West African waters in 1970, and the South China Sea in 1979.

In addition to reducing military deliveries to the Third World and military activity in noncontiguous areas, the Soviets are warning Third World clients to expect less economic assistance. The escalating costs of aid to Third World economies as well as the large foreign debts of Third World states have caused them to become impatient with poor economic performance. They have been particularly critical of Third World leaders for expecting socialist states to finance efforts to "force" socioeconomic change through industrialization.

A Soviet Politburo member told the Supreme Soviet in 1989 that the government was considering a decrease in aid to the Third World and an economist with ties to Gorbachev told the Congress of People's Deputies that it was necessary to cut assistance to such states as Cuba and Nicaragua so as to balance the budget[9] The ambassador to Syria, during a press conference in Damascus in 1989, predicted military assistance to the Syrians would be reduced because of economic difficulties and military cutbacks in the USSR as well as the debt problem in Syria. In a *Pravda* article in June 1990, Shevardnadze wrote that the state of the Soviet economy will "restrict" Moscow's efforts on behalf of Third World states.[10]

All this is consistent with Gorbachev's position at the twenty-seventh Soviet party congress in 1986 rationalizing a closer relationship with the United States and encouraging greater attention to regional security in the Third World. Gorbachev repeatedly stated afterward that a resolution of the war in Afghanistan might bring increased effort to settle regional conflicts and defuse sources of tension with the United States. Shevardnadze was openly critical of Brezhnev's "confrontational spirit."[11] At the United Nations General Assembly in December 1988, on the anniversary of Pearl Harbor, Gorbachev made an unexpected announcement of a unilateral troop reduction and reminded his audience that the "bell of every regional conflict tolls for all of us."[12] He used the occasion to gather support for cooperation with the United States and progress toward regional settlements. He has advocated such settlements in Angola, Cambodia, Ethiopia, and Mozambique.

Since 1985, there is evidence of disenchantment with the Soviet investment in the Third World.[13] Messages to heads of state as well as Soviet slogans issued on the anniversary of the October Revolution (November 7) have advertised this disenchantment. Gorbachev has communicated directly with the Western and Chinese leadership, but Third World leaders are beginning to receive collective greetings from the Soviet government. Slogans published in the late 1980s did not include the once standard call for proletarians of all countries to unite and even dropped reference to strengthening communist solidarity.[14] These slogans do not, of course, predict policy decisions, but are indicators of the current consensus for "deideologization" of policy, the search to remove friction with the United States.

The only friendship treaty that Gorbachev has signed with a Third World country—the Soviet-Cuban Friendship Treaty of 1989—contained no reference to military cooperation, no provision for consultation in case of an attack, no mention of the revolutionary struggle in the Third World, and no reference to building communism—all standard items in treaties of friendship and cooperation from 1971 to 1985. The treaty affirms Cuban support for Gorbachev's foreign policy as outlined in his address to the United Nations in December 1988 and calls for rechanneling resources from military purposes to "meet the economic and social development of the countries."[15]

The current turmoil in Eastern Europe represents a direct challenge to all the USSR's radical allies and clients in the Third World. Willingness to allow the political unraveling of the Soviet bloc, particularly encouraging the removal of party leaders Erich Honecker in East Germany and Todor Zhivkov in Bulgaria, is an indication of an isolationism that does not augur well for the interests of Soviet clients. It certainly does not represent an end to military and economic assistance, but Third World leaders can only conclude that a Soviet Union unwilling to challenge revolutionary change in Eastern Europe on its western frontier and a pro-Soviet, Marxist government in Afghanistan on its eastern border will do even less in areas far from Soviet territory. The decision of North and South Yemen to merge in 1990, and reform efforts in Angola and Mozambique are a response to expectations of less Soviet assistance.

Finally, in the summer of 1990, the Soviets demonstrated for the first time that they would engage in active cooperation with the United States in challenging the policies of one of their own clients in the Third World. Following the Iraqi invasion of Kuwait in August, Moscow condemned the attack, announced an arms embargo, voted with the United States in the Security Council, and agreed for the first time to issue a joint statement with the United States in a regional crisis. Presumably Gorbachev's predecessors would have shielded Iraq from Western criticism and continued arms shipments; Gorbachev, however, has supported the first joint crisis management exercise with the United States and, in so doing, used a Third World crisis to establish a firmer basis for détente with Washington. Moscow's decision in December 1990 to agree to U.S. use of force against a former Soviet client marks a major turning point for bilateral Soviet-U.S. relations and Soviet-U.S. policy toward conflict resolution in the Third World. The Soviets have signaled that Shevardnadze's sudden resignation will not change the pattern of cooperation.[16]

NOTES

1. See Alvin Z. Rubinstein, *Moscow's Third World Strategy*, Princeton, NJ: Princeton University Press, 1988; Francis Fukuyama, *Moscow's Post-Brezhnev Reassessment of the Third World*, Santa Monica: Rand Corporation, 1986.

2. *The Washington Post*, October 22, 1989, p. 1.

3. *The Washington Post*, October 17, 1988, p. 1.

4. The normal presence of the Soviet Mediterranean Squadron consists of 5 to 7 submarines, 6 to 10 surface warships, and 14 auxiliary ships.

5. The Soviet Union registered a substantial decrease in its share of Third World arms transfer agreements in 1988, falling from 50% in 1987 to 33% in 1988. The total value of the Soviet Union's agreements also fell dramatically in 1988, from $19 billion in 1987 to $10 billion. See Richard F. Grimmett, "Trends in Conventional Arms Transfers to the Third World by Major Supplier, 1981–1988," Washington, DC: Congressional Research Service, 1989.

6. The Soviets supplied no arms to Iran between 1985 and 1990 and delivered more than $10 billion in arms to Iraq during the same period; the USSR was responsible for nearly one-third of the arms delivered to the principals in the Iran-Iraq war since the start of fighting in 1980. Western Europe's share of deliveries to Baghdad and Tehran is nearly 25% and China's share is more than 15%. The Iraqi invasion of Kuwait in August 1990 led to resumption of Soviet military supplies to Iran.

7. Although the Soviets have at least temporarily ended direct military deliveries to Nicaragua, they remain Cuba's principal supplier, making more than $12 billion in weapons deliveries over the past ten years. Cuba, of course, is Nicaragua's major supplier of military weapons.

8. Michael MccGwire, *Military Objectives in Soviet Foreign Policy*, Washington, DC: Brookings Institution, 1987, p. 220. MccGwire's book usefully identifies key decision points in Soviet strategic thinking but, in general, exaggerates the importance of the Third World to Soviet military and geopolitical interests.

9. *The New York Times*, June 9, 1989, p. 3, "Radical Plan to Balance Soviet Budget" by Bill Keller; *The Washington Post*, December 14, 1989, p. 1, "Soviet to Accelerate Output for Consumer," by Michael Dobbs.

10. *Pravda*, June 26, 1990, p. 3.

11. *Vestnik Ministerstva Inostrannykh Sel SSR*, August 1988, Speech by Foreign Minister Shevardnadze to the USSR Ministry of Foreign Affairs, pp. 27–46.

12. *The New York Times*, December 8, 1988, p. 1, General Secretary Gorbachev speech to the UNGA.

13. Kremlinology relies on an interpretation of Soviet public statements and propaganda as a means of making inferences about Soviet actions and policies.

Kremlinologists maintain that Soviet media and official statements continue to be the best indicators of Soviet behavior on most internal and external decisions.

14. *Pravda*, November 1, 1989, p. 1.

15. *The New York Times*, April 7, 1989, p. 3.

16. *The New York Times*, December 29, 1990, p. 1.

1

Soviet Policy and the Third World

There can be no doubt that President Mikhail Gorbachev has made extraordinary changes in policy toward the Third World. Nothing, surely, resembles the crude behavior of his predecessors. Everything seems in flux, with changes almost daily—for which Western observers, especially U.S. officials, can be truly grateful.

Consider what has happened within a bare few years. The USSR's withdrawal from Afghanistan has decreased the possibility of military operations in Southwest Asia, including Soviet–U.S. confrontation. Now political solutions to regional problems are at the top of the Soviet agenda, including unprecedented Soviet–U.S. cooperation to end the conflict in the Persian Gulf. The Soviet stance comes despite the existence of a treaty of friendship and cooperation and the Soviet role as Iraq's main weapons supplier.

Gorbachev and his assistants have shown no interest in replacing bases lost in Egypt and Somalia during the dark old Brezhnev era—as if anything associated with the superannuated general secretary of long ago must, by itself, be bad. He has shown no concern about the poor facilities for Soviet naval vessels in Angola, Ethiopia, Yemen, and Syria, apparently believing that to sink money in such ports is useless. Cam Ranh Bay, so long an embarrassment to the United States (which indeed did sink several hundreds of millions in that distant base), is now virtually abandoned, and Foreign Minister Shevardnadze promised withdrawal from other facilities in the Third World as well. Soviet arms transfers are down, and Soviet advisers—so long evident in Ethiopia and Mozambique—are returning home.

All in all, the disappearance of Soviet presence in many client states, the turning of those nations to other sources, and, for the most part, the limited availability of alternative sources for military and economic largesse, constitute one of the minor miracles of recent history. It is a most gratifying change from what has been one of the most worrisome developments of the past generation and more.

SOVIET THIRD WORLD POLICY BEFORE GORBACHEV

How then did we get from there to here? First an examination of the "there."

In the years after the Second World War no one, of course, could doubt that the Soviet Union had become not merely a superpower in the Soviet–U.S. confrontation but a power with worldwide naval deployments, the ability to monitor Western naval forces, especially those of the United States, and access to naval and air facilities in strategically located client states. This was a direct challenge of the United States. It has been a factor in any regional crisis or conflict. Nevertheless, the Soviets have rarely been willing to lend military support to Third World clients in engagements with U.S. allies. A confidant of high-level Egyptian leaders, Mohamed Heikal, has cited Soviet reluctance to give military assistance to the Arabs during the 1956 Suez Crisis and the 1967 June War. In the case of the Suez War, Heikal has written:

> Immediately on arrival in October 1956 Kuwatly [president of Syria] asked to see the Soviet leaders. He insisted that Egypt must be helped. "But what can we do?" asked General Secretary Khrushchev.
> Zhukov [Soviet defense minister] produced a map of the Middle East and spread it on the table. Then turning to Kuwatly, he said, "How can we go to the aid of Egypt? Tell me! Are we supposed to send our armies through Turkey, Iran, and then into Syria and Iraq and on into Israel and so eventually attack the British and French forces?
> Khrushchev folded up the map and told Kuwatly, "We'll see what we can do. At present we don't know how to help Egypt, but we are having continuous meetings to discuss the problem."

The Soviet attitude had changed little ten years later, during the Six-Day War:

> It was when Badran [Egyptian defense minister] and his party were leaving in June 1967 that the real misunderstanding took

place. Marshal Grechko had come to the airport to see them off, and he was chatting to Badran at the foot of the aircraft steps. He said, "Stand firm. Whatever you have to face, you will find us with you. Don't let yourselves be blackmailed by the Americans or anyone else." After the plane had taken off, the Egyptian ambassador to Moscow, Murad Ghaleb, who had heard Grechko's remarks, said to him, "That was very reassuring, Marshal," Grechko laughed, and said to him, "I just wanted to give him one for the road."[1]

Unwillingness to intervene in support of beleaguered Arab clients was repeated in the October War in 1973 and the Israeli invasion of Lebanon in 1982.

The USSR's Third World policy since the mid-1950s has been based on its broader national interests and demonstrated ability to capitalize on international developments. Reluctance to become involved in military engagements in the Third World prior to Afghanistan reflected caution and a realistic assessment of its limited projection capabilities. The dominant, and lower risk, Soviet activity has been provision of military assistance and advisory support and, on occasion, air defense support to Third World clients as it sought to enhance its presence and leverage. Moscow only recently acknowledged operational control over Hanoi's surface-to-air missile defense in the 1960s; the Soviets manned Egyptian air defense in the 1970s, Syrian defenses in the 1980s.

Although ideology shaped Moscow's world view in the pre-Gorbachev years, it was not a factor in determining Soviet interests or behavior in the Third World. And though its policy was keyed to competition with the United States, Moscow did not allow concern for relations with the United States to deter it from regional interests.[2] Success in achieving many objectives—a military position in every region of the world, challenging the West and China, influencing governments of key states—was accomplished with military policy. Through use of military assistance and surrogate forces, the Soviets served the security needs of Third World countries and obtained many benefits.[3]

Over the past thirty years, the Soviets made military and political gains in most regions of the world. Friendship treaties were signed with thirteen Third World states in every region, and thousands of military advisers and technicians were stationed in many states as part of their military infrastructure. Military deliveries increased dramatically in the mid-1970s. The average annual value of arms agreements was $500 million from 1955 to 1965, $5 billion from 1965 to 1975, and $10 billion from 1975 to 1985.[4] These arms allowed clients such as

Cuba, Syria, and Vietnam to take a more active part in regional policies that often complemented Soviet interests.

The USSR experienced its greatest success in the 1970s, when pro-Soviet regimes came to power in Angola, Ethiopia, Grenada, Nicaragua, and Afghanistan. U.S. setbacks in Vietnam and Iran during this period contributed to the view that the balance of power had shifted in Moscow's favor, as the Soviets were then claiming.[5] Collapse of the Portuguese empire presented opportunity in southern Africa, and the Sandinista revolution in 1979 introduced Moscow to Central America. In the Middle East, one of the USSR's top priority areas, the Soviets benefitted from the effect of the OPEC cartel on Western economies after the war in the Middle East in 1973 as well as the ongoing Arab-Israeli conflict.

Moscow developed close relations with Syria through weapons transfers: Following the war in Lebanon in 1982, the Soviets installed SAM-5 missile batteries manned by six thousand Soviet troops, as part of an air defense that limited Israel's ability to attack Syrian targets.[6] Moscow received political and military benefits as a result. While access to facilities at Tartus and Latakia for reconnaissance flights provide a modest support facility for the Soviet Navy, Syria has supported Moscow's political position by blocking any possible U.S. effort to advance a peace process without Soviet acquiescence.

In Africa, the Soviets demonstrated they would intervene to determine the outcome of a civil war in Angola and introduce forces to protect internationally recognized borders in Ethiopia. In return they received facilities on Dahlak Island in the Red Sea off the coast of Ethiopia, which expanded capabilities in the Indian Ocean. In western Africa, they use Angolan facilities as well as naval facilities in Guinea, bolstering Moscow's ability to project force in southern Africa.

In the Caribbean, Moscow enjoys port and air facilities in Cuba, as well as intelligence capabilites relative to U.S. activities in the North Atlantic, allowing Moscow to project power into international waters near the United States, threaten shipping lanes, and apply power to offset the U.S. threat close to Soviet borders. Until the defeat of the Sandinistas in 1990, military aid to Nicaragua worked in a similar manner—strengthening a regime whose activities divert U.S. attention and resources to the Caribbean basin, away from regions more important from the Soviet perspective.

During the Brezhnev era, Moscow did not seek to extend détente or "peaceful coexistence" to the Third World. Soviet actions suggested that rivalry between the superpowers could be safely pursued in the Third World as Moscow extended its influence in Africa, the Middle East, and Southeast Asia at the expense of the United States. The Soviets emphasized solidarity with progressive regimes, but exploitation of anti-Americanism was central to their actions. A typical example of Soviet behavior was Moscow's efforts to exploit the Islamic revolution in Iran in 1979, ignoring anti-Soviet aspects of Tehran's behavior.

The U.S. retreat from the Third World in the mid-1970s after the debacle in Vietnam served to whet Moscow's appetite. The Soviets became more active in the Middle East and Africa, encouraged Cuban and East German activity in conflicts in these areas, and tried to consolidate regimes on the basis of the Soviet model. Angola, Ethiopia, and Mozambique became particularly dependent on the Soviet Union for assistance and advice; Cuba and Vietnam received billions in military and economic aid; Syrian and Libyan adventurism went unchallenged. The military slant of Soviet policy and the backward Soviet economy meant that military assistance would become the core of relations with Third World states, with Soviet weaponry allowing Egypt and Syria to invade Israel in 1973, Vietnam to invade Cambodia in 1978. India signed a friendship treaty with the Soviet Union in 1971 to guarantee military deliveries before invading Pakistan; Vietnam did the same in 1978.

Third World conflicts increased dependence of Moscow's clients and worsened their economies. These states, as a result, made greater demands for support. But by the 1980s Moscow's "allies" were impoverished. It is not by accident that the largest recipients of Soviet military aid are some of the poorest states in the world. The Soviet Union became identified with their instability, authoritarianism, and economic collapse; conversely, the successful states of the Third World became suspicious of Soviet motives.

THE EFFECT OF GORBACHEV

Reexamination of policy began with Gorbachev's accession and the decision to withdraw from Afghanistan. From the outset, Gorbachev had expressed his intention to change policy, particularly in the Third World. Recognizing that his ability to do so required sweeping personnel and organizational change, he replaced the top decision makers in the field of foreign policy and reorganized party and government institutions dealing with national security. He changed leadership of the foreign ministry and the central committee's International Department and created a new foreign affairs department under Aleksandr Yakovlev to report directly to the Politburo.[7] The changes indicated that Gorbachev was giving high priority to improved relations with the United States and the West, and political rather than military solutions to Third World problems. The Soviets no longer brusquely dismissed U.S. demands that more conciliatory behavior in the Third World was a condition to more stable Soviet–U.S. relations.

At the twenty-seventh Soviet party congress in 1986, Gorbachev showed disillusion with military power in the Third World. He stressed that Moscow "would like in the nearest future to bring the Soviet force {in Afghanistan} back to their homeland" and that a "schedule has been worked out with the Afghan side for a step-by-step withdrawal."[8] This marked the first time a Soviet leader revealed a plan for a phased pullout. One year later the Soviets had withdrawn more than one hundred thousand combat forces.[9]

In addition to withdrawal from Afghanistan, the Soviets helped arrange a ceasefire and Cuban withdrawal from Angola. They helped stabilize the Persian Gulf (before the Iraqi invasion in August 1990) and Southeast Asia, to improve relations with the United States and China. United States officials have acknowledged that Moscow moderated the position of the Palestine Liberation Organization, which led to a dialogue with Washington.

The Soviets encouraged the Sandinista decision to hold Nicaragua's first free election in 1990.[10] Prior to the election, Gorbachev signaled that Moscow was ready to stop exploiting Washington's vulnerability in Central America by ending military deliveries to the Sandinistas. On the eve of Secretary of State Baker's departure for Moscow in May 1989 for his first meetings with Soviet leaders, Gorbachev informed the United States that, to "give diplomacy a chance," Moscow was no longer sending weapons to Nicaragua.[11] Moscow finally had agreed that "productive Soviet–U.S. engagement on regional questions would lead to a growing potential of goodwill in Soviet–U.S. relations," accepting the policy of linkage that Secretary of State Kissinger had encouraged twenty years earlier.

In subsequent months the Soviets pressed Cuba to stop deliveries to the guerrillas in El Salvador, and interrupted delivery of their own Mi-17 helicopters to Nicaragua. Moscow denied a Sandinista request for emergency funds during this period, and apparently pressed Nicaraguan President Daniel Ortega to call for the Salvadoran guerrillas to "immediately and effectively cease hostilities and join the process of dialogue."[12]

Soviet–U.S. cooperation in Central America led to a more cooperative dialogue on a variety of Third World matters. The Soviets have urged Ethiopian President Mengistu Haile Miriam to find a political solution to the civil war with Eritrea that has gone on for decades, and have agreed to cooperate with the United States in delivering food to tribes isolated by the conflict. In response to pressure from Moscow and Washington, Mengistu has stopped attacks on the port city of Massawa to allow food to be unloaded.

Gorbachev's speeches in Vladivostok in 1986 and Krasnoyarsk in 1988, calling for an end to foreign bases in Asia and reduced naval activity in the Pacific, were designed to limit competition with the United States and improve relations with China. The removal of forces from Cam Ranh Bay and along the Sino-Soviet border helped persuade the Bush administration to withdraw 15,000 of the 135,000 U.S. troops stationed in Japan, South Korea, and the Philippines. The Pentagon acknowledged in 1990 that "traditional threat perceptions are changing" and that the U.S. presence in Asia is "seen as less relevant" because of the Soviet retreat.[13] The meeting between Gorbachev and the South Korean president in June 1990 added to this perception.

Moscow's moderation toward the Third World and Gorbachev's emphasis on creating stable Soviet–U.S. relations has caused concern among Soviet allies. Speaking at the Soviet party congress in 1986, Cuban leader Fidel Castro reminded Gorbachev that "blood had been spilled" in the Third World and the task of economic development was just as important as avoiding nuclear war.[14] Mengistu urged the Soviets not to give the issue of regional conflict a lower priority than nuclear matters and warned that Third World allies continued to expect support. Angolan President José Eduardo dos Santos called for more assistance and reminded his audience that Angola suffered not only from effects of war but deterioration of the international economic situation.[15]

All these leaders were concerned about Moscow's possible retreat from international obligations and correctly believed that Gorbachev's focus on the United States rather than the Third World would weaken Moscow's commitment to countries of "socialist orientation." Soviet–U.S. cooperation on the ceasefire in Angola, and size and cost of the United Nations peacekeeping force for Namibia, convinced African leaders that the superpowers intended to cooperate on matters that reduce the risk of flashpoint situations. High rates of Soviet Jewish emigration and U.S. efforts to liberalize Soviet emigration angered Arab states. Soviet backpedaling in Central America convinced Castro that he was isolated. As a result, various Soviet clients including Castro, dos Santos, and Mengistu signaled the United States that they too were interested in improved relations.

DISILLUSION WITH THE THIRD WORLD

Along with Gorbachev's remarks at the party congress and the decision to withdraw from Afghanistan, authoritative articles have documented Moscow's disillusionment with the Third World and noted the effect of Soviet actions on Soviet–U.S. relations. In the party journal *Kommunist*, three members of the Soviet Union's USA and Canada Institute (Deputy Director Vitaliy Zhurkin, section head Sergey Karaganov, and senior researcher Andrei Kortunov) argued that, while the threat of nuclear aggression is decreasing, the "threat of war may be increasing due to the struggle in regional sectors."[16] They warned that any state relying on military means "sets its own security against international security" and that security requires negotiations and compromises with adversaries.

These views reflect positions taken by Gorbachev and former Foreign Minister Eduard Shevardnadze since the party congress in 1986. Gorbachev has urged repeatedly that resolution of the war in Afghanistan should resolve conflicts in the Middle East and Persian Gulf. The argument for Afghanistan as a model for resolution of regional confrontation was made in *Izvestia* in 1988 by Konstantin Geyvandov: the Soviet Union and the United States, "as mediators and official guarantors of the Afghan settlement, have set a precedent for constructive collaboration to improve international relations."[17]

When the Soviets began withdrawing from Afghanistan in 1988, Vyacheslav Dashichev of the Institute of the Economics of the World Socialist System wrote that Moscow's aggressive policies had undermined its security and provoked formation of rival coalitions seeking to counter Soviet expansion.[18] He charged that Moscow had created the impression that the USSR was a dangerous power, seeking to eliminate bourgeois democracies and establish communism throughout the world. He accused Brezhnev of squandering opportunities created by attainment of strategic parity with the United States. Dashichev condemned past Soviet policy in the Third World, arguing that Moscow had no clear idea about Soviet interests when it embarked on Third World policy, and had wasted resources in the "pursuit of petty gains."

Months later, then deputy chief of the foreign ministry's International Organizations Administration, Andrei V. Kozyrev, wrote a serious critique of Soviet policy, emphasizing errors in the Third World.[19] He argued that Moscow's "direct and indirect involvement in regional conflicts" had led to "colossal losses by increasing international tension, justifying the arms race and hindering establishment of mutually advantageous ties with the West." He charged that military aid to Third World regimes contributed to "protracted conflicts with an opposition that depends on outside support," without returns to Moscow from its large economic assistance. Kozyrev concluded it made no sense to build relations with Third World regimes on the basis of their "opposition to Western influence" and called for "mutually advantageous economic and technological cooperation."[20]

Much of Kozyrev's message was repeated in 1988 at a foreign ministry meeting, where Shevardnadze described the "Soviet confrontation spirit" as "too strong" and emphasized withdrawal from Afghanistan as a model for resolution of differences in Cambodia, southern Africa, Cyprus, and the Koreas.[21] He faulted the ministry for not trying "everything" to prevent confrontation with China and failing to warn the Kremlin that prolonged war between Iran and Iraq could lead to a "massive U.S. presence in the Persian Gulf."[22]

At the United Nations General Assembly in December 1988, on the anniversary of Pearl Harbor, Gorbachev reminded his audience that the "bell of every regional conflict tolls for all of us" and reaffirmed Moscow's commitment to remove forces from Afghanistan. In his speech to the USSR Supreme Soviet in October 1989, Shevardnadze referred to the decision to invade Afghanistan as "gross violation of our legislation and intraparty and civic norms and ethics."[23] He and Gorbachev, who had been nonvoting members of the Politburo in 1979 when the decision was made, apparently had learned of the invasion from the Soviet media. In his speech, the minister castigated the decision as having been made "behind the party's and people's backs . . . a *fait accompli*." As Gorbachev's point man on foreign policy, he urged *glasnost* for future military issues, making it more difficult to use force.

Shevardnadze's call for legislative oversight could further erode the cult of secrecy in the Soviet Union, pressing the secretive Soviet defense establishment on such issues as defense spending, weapons procurement, and power projection. Aleksey Arbatov, son of the director of the USA Institute and a department chief at the Institute of World Economy and International Relations (IMEMO), has complained that secrecy inhibits the ability of experts to provide analysis for policymakers, especially with regard to calculating military cuts that will meet the requirements of Gorbachev's "reasonable sufficiency."[24]

GORBACHEV AND SOVIET MILITARY POLICY IN THE THIRD WORLD

The decline in Soviet presence in the Third World is consistent with Gorbachev's policy of demilitarization since 1986. There have been reductions in status of the military, the military's part in decision making, military spending, and procurement. The top echelons of the military have been reshuffled; the defense minister, first deputy defense ministers, commanders of forces, chiefs of military districts, and chief of the Main Political Directorate of the Army and Navy all have been replaced. The latter post is particularly important because it is within the defense ministry but subordinate to the Central Committee of the party.

Gorbachev has retired or overseen resignations of senior marshals inherited from the Brezhnev era—notably defense minister Sokolov, chief of the general staff Akhromeyev, and Warsaw Pact commander Kulikov, the latter one of nine generals and marshals purged from the central committee in April 1989 in a formidable display of Gorbachev's power. The purge included former chief of the general staff Nikolai Ogarkov, the top career military officer in the early 1980s.

Gorbachev won debates with the military in getting acceptance of a unilateral test moratorium in 1986, intrusive on-site inspection in the INF agreement of 1987, and unilateral cuts of Soviet forces in 1988 and 1989. The outline of the START treaty signed at the summit in 1990 ignored military objections to Soviet concessions on range and verification of U.S. cruise missiles and limits on mobile ICBMs.

Gorbachev announced defense cuts of 14 percent and procurement cuts of 19 percent by 1991, and there have been slowdowns in modernization of strategic forces, including the powerful nuclear submarine, the Typhoon; threatening intercontinental ballistic missiles, the SS-18 and mobile SS-24; and sophisticated strategic bomber, the Blackjack.[25] The Typhoon program has been terminated after production of six submarines, although U.S. defense experts had projected eight by the early 1990s. The SS-24 program will be halted at fifty to seventy-five missiles instead of 150 to 200, and modifications of SS-18 silos have been halted. Only ten Blackjack bombers have been deployed, although Western experts predicted fifty to seventy-five before 1990, and the program has been heavily criticized in the military press.[26]

Gorbachev agreed at the 1990 summit to reduce ICBMs and strategic bombers to make a first strike less possible and ban new types of heavy ICBMs, including mobile launchers. The Soviets signaled willingness to limit the range of the Blackjack by limiting its refueling capability. Secretary of Defense Richard Cheney conceded in 1990 that his decision to defer construction of U.S. fighter aircraft was based on delays in production of new Soviet fighters and attack planes.[27]

As part of the military drawdown in the Third World, Gorbachev has cut resources for missions abroad, believing costs of forward-deployed forces are not justified. There has been a lower operational tempo to naval activity in support of out-of-area missions and Third World clients and a drawdown of the advisory presence.

The USSR sent no naval task force to the Caribbean in 1986 and 1987, and the task force in 1988 stayed for a shorter period than usual and did not enter the Gulf of Mexico. Soviet reconnaissance flights out of Cuba and Angola have been reduced, particularly TU-95 Bear deployments to Cuba.[28] Naval operations are being conducted closer to the Soviet mainland, and out-of-area naval deployment has dropped everywhere.

Fewer naval maneuvers are part of budget cuts for the Soviet navy that include reduced submarine production, fewer operations in the Pacific, and more time in port. The director of naval intelligence, Rear Admiral Thomas A. Brooks, reported to Congress in 1989 that the Soviet Navy took more surface ships out of service in 1988 than any other year in recent history and had begun selling large combat ships for scrap on the world market.[29] The process of scrapping ships and submarines reached new heights in 1989, when a soft drink company took a cruiser, destroyer, frigate, and seventeen submarines as scrap in partial payment for products sold in the Soviet Union.[30] Admiral Chernavin, commander-in-chief of Soviet naval forces, reported that seventy-three ships would be withdrawn from the Pacific fleet in 1989 and 1990, and the new 65,000–ton Tbilisi-class aircraft carrier would not be assigned to the Pacific Fleet as expected by Western military analysts.[31]

A less active navy and emphasis on introducing naval limitation to arms control talks suggests that Moscow wants to end its naval competition with the United States in the Third World. Marshal Sergey Akhromeyev, who retired as chief of the general staff on the day of Gorbachev's statement to the UN in 1988, proposed limiting missions of the U.S. Navy, particularly aircraft carriers, and Defense Minister Marshal Dmitri Yazov in 1989 called for ending asymmetries in Soviet and U.S. naval and marine forces. Naval commander-in-chief Admiral Vladimir Chernavin displayed a particular sensitivity to U.S. "sea strike forces" and "amphibious assault" forces, referring to aircraft carriers and Tomahawk cruise missiles on nuclear submarines.[32]

The United States may hold a significant edge over Soviet forces in naval and air power abroad, but Moscow has an advantage in supplying military weapons systems to the Third World. The source of Moscow's advantage is large stockpiles of surplus equipment because, as one Western military official observed, "the Soviets never throw anything away. They just upgrade weapons and provide them to client states."[33] There has been a decline in arms transfers to the Third World since 1988, particularly to the Middle East and Africa, and reference to the liberating mission of the Soviet armed forces has disappeared from military writings. Economic and political factors have played a part in the decline of arms sales to the Middle East, the location of seven of the ten leading Third World arms importers.[34]

Cuban and South African troop withdrawals from Angola in 1989 led to a significant reduction in Soviet military assistance.[35] And among the top ten recipients of Soviet military aid in the 1980s, only Afghanistan continues to receive increasing amounts of weaponry, and these are primarily such obsolescent equipment as T-55 tanks and BTR-60 armored personnel vehicles.[36] Any Soviet–U.S. agreement on Afghanistan would lead to a reduction in Soviet military aid to the government in Kabul.

The Soviets still earn a considerable amount of hard currency from sales to the Middle East, particularly to Libya, but the ceasefire between Iran and Iraq, the Soviet embargo against Iraq following Baghdad's invasion of Kuwait, Libyan military setbacks, and Syria's need to invest in its economy have reduced opportunities. It is unlikely that deliveries to Iraq in the 1990s will come close to matching the tens of billions in arms transfers that took place in the 1980s.[37]

In addition to political causes for declining arms transfers, economic problems in Angola and Ethiopia have led to reduced transfers to Africa as well. Deliveries to Vietnam in 1988 were down from 1987, and the Vietnamese withdrawal from Cambodia, as well as Vietnam's economic morass, should further the decline. There was a decrease in military deliveries to Nicaragua in 1987 and 1988, and Gorbachev in 1989 ended supplies of weapons systems to the Sandinistas.[38] Cambodia reportedly is receiving less military and economic assistance from the USSR and Eastern European states, which will provide an incentive for improved relations with the United States.[39] The Phnom Penh government is dependent on Moscow for oil and gasoline, and nearly all electricity in Cambodia comes from oil-burning generators. An associated problem is the USSR's request for assistance from the International Monetary Fund, which prohibits loan recipients from providing aid to third countries.

The decline in arms deliveries is consistent with Gorbachev's efforts to reduce military spending and broaden political oversight over the military. At a Foreign Ministry conference in July 1988, Shevardnadze called for more political supervision of the military, strengthening the presidency and the Supreme Soviet in deciding military policy, force structures, and budget allocations.[40] Outspoken reform advocates, including Vyacheslav Dashichev and *Izvestia* political observer Aleksandr Bovin, have written commentaries on Shevardnadze's report, indicating that he and Gorbachev are determined to broaden discussion of security issues, if only to outflank critics and create a more open society.

GORBACHEV AND SOVIET FOREIGN POLICY IN THE THIRD WORLD

Shifts in the foreign ministry have signaled Gorbachev's commitment to political solutions for regional rivalries. The replacement of Andrei Gromyko as Foreign Minister in 1985 marked the "passing of the torch" for foreign policy. Gromyko's "promotion" to the presidency in 1985 was followed by improved Soviet–U.S. relations as well as gains in relations with China, Japan, and such moderate Arab states as Egypt, Jordan, and Saudi Arabia. Gromyko, who died in the summer of 1989, had given no support to the Soviet decisions to withdraw from Afghanistan, improve relations with Israel, and accept intrusive on-site inspection in the INF agreement with the United States.

Less than a year after Gromyko's removal as foreign minister, Gorbachev removed the Central Committee's International Department chief Boris Ponomarev, who had led the department for twenty-five years and promoted "progressive socialist forces" in the Third World. Ponomarev's successor was Anatoly Dobrynin, long-time ambassador to the United States, who immediately staffed his department with former colleagues from the embassy in Washington. His former minister-counselor in Washington, Aleksandr Bessmertnykh, was named ambassador to the United States, and another protégé, Yuly Vorontsov, became Permanent Representative to the United Nations in 1990.[41] The appointments of Vorontsov and Bessmertnykh, formerly First Deputy Foreign Ministers, reflected the pattern of placing more capable diplomats in important overseas positions. In addition to reshuffling their foreign affairs departments, Shevardnadze and Dobrynin upgraded representation in Soviet–U.S. expert-level talks on regional issues. Bessmertnykh's appointment as foreign minister in January 1991 indicates that these trends will continue.

Since his election as president of the Supreme Soviet in 1989, Gorbachev has distanced himself from Third World clients by sending personal messages to Western leaders and greetings from either the Supreme Soviet or the Council of Ministers to Third World counterparts. In 1989 and 1990, heads of state in the United States, France, and the United Kingdom received personal greetings; leaders from Cuba, Egypt, India, and Iraq received collective greetings from government institutions.

CRISIS PREVENTION IN THE THIRD WORLD

Gorbachev and Shevardnadze supported disengagement from the risks and costs of Third World involvement on behalf of "progressive" states and are seeking ties to nonsocialist states to expand Moscow's international position. Their actions tacitly concede that Soviet military power has not produced corresponding political influence in the Third World and that competition with the United States has not brought any advantage. In an interview in 1987, Deputy Foreign Minister Vladimir Petrovsky disavowed the notion of a "zero-sum" game between the superpowers in the Third World and remarked that Moscow could not "achieve a victory for itself by destroying someone else."[42] As part of a more pragmatic approach, the Soviets are emphasizing regional settlements and Soviet–U.S. cooperation. In the military newspaper *Red Star*, Soviet–U.S. cooperation in the Persian Gulf was described as "remarkable," with special attention given to the Soviet arms embargo against Iraq.[43] The embargo was described as a "difficult step," which could be an indication of leadership disagreement.

In their efforts to settle confrontations in Africa, Soviet officials have tried to arrange settlements between Luanda and the National Union for the Total Independence of Angola (UNITA), Maputo and the Mozambique National Resistance (Renama), and Addis Ababa and the Eritrean People's Liberation Front (EPLF). Gorbachev sent a message to Zaire's President Mobutu in 1989, praising his sponsorship of ceasefire talks for Angola, expressing satisfaction with accords between Luanda and UNITA.[44] Not long after, *Izvestia* political observer Aleksandr Bovin validated UNITA's demand for talks and stated that UNITA had been "legalized and recognized as a negotiating party to be included in the government."[45] Soviet and American officials are acting as observers at Angolan-UNITA talks.

The Soviets endorsed talks between Addis Ababa and the Eritreans in 1989, the government's first statement on any African issue other than South Africa.[46] The statement indicated willingness to press Mengistu on resolving rebellions in the northern provinces of Eritrea and Tigre, where the regime has suffered serious setbacks. Deputy Foreign Minister Anatoly Adamishin went further in meetings with the EPLF in London in the summer of 1989, when he stated that "both sides seem ready" to begin talks.[47] The Soviets have even threatened to reduce military deliveries to Ethiopia if Mengistu were unwilling to solve the Eritrean problem. Thus, after playing a behind-the-scenes role in negotiations for a ceasefire in Angola and Cuban troop withdrawal, Moscow appears willing to get out in front to arrange a negotiated settlement on the Horn of Africa. If so, Gorbachev may be prepared to give up naval access to facilities on Dahlak Island, which supports the Soviet presence in the Red Sea and the Indian Ocean, and rely on facilities in Yemen.

During Secretary of State Baker's visit to the USSR in May 1989, Shevardnadze indicated that Moscow was prepared to compromise on regional issues that divide the United States and the USSR, referring to "new elements" in the U.S. position as a "reasonable basis for productive cooperation."[48] He credited the United States with sharing Moscow's goal of a "genuinely all-embracing settlement" in the Middle East and Africa. Weeks later Adamishin met with his U.S. counterpart and stressed that negotiations on Angola and Namibia in 1988 had become the model of cooperation in the Third World. Thirteen years earlier Soviet intervention in Angola had become the symbol of failure of Soviet–U.S. détente for many U.S. officials, including Secretary Kissinger.

A Soviet official conceded in 1990 that the Soviet Union does not have vital interests in the Third World and that "large-scale arms deliveries are in no way a guarantee of firm influence, as shown by the example of Egypt and other countries."[49] Unlike Czechoslovakia, the Soviets cannot be expected to renounce the export of weapons on principle. Economic and military factors will demand a Soviet role in weapons transfers. But it is likely that Moscow will be more willing to limit weaponry in areas of conflict, apply the test of "reasonable sufficiency" to arms agreements, and reduce transfers of sophisticated weapons. The Soviets appear willing to negotiate such limits with the United States and, on their own, may apply limits to states not solvent or in debt to the USSR.

Moscow will promote economic development in the Third World without offering any solution to the debt problem, and rail against military confrontation while earning hard currency from military transfers. Shevardnadze remarked in 1990 that the idea of abandoning all military commitments to Third World countries was a "primitive approach," although he acknowledged that cutbacks were on Moscow's agenda.[50] The Soviets will maintain interests connected to security, such as positions in Cuba and Vietnam for intelligence collection, as well as India and Syria for regional influence, but defensive deployment of the Soviet Navy could lead to less use of littoral states for access, and satellite technology could supersede requirements for intelligence assets in distant locations. Gorbachev has acknowledged that security concerns will be limited by domestic political and economic problems and the importance of relations with the United States and Western Europe. His objectives are political in the Middle East, where the Soviets have reduced military sales to Iraq, Libya, and Syria, while improving relations with Egypt and Israel. He did nothing to defend Libya from U.S. raids in 1986 or help Qadhafi in Chad in 1987; he warned Libya and Syria that terrorism was counterproductive and could lead to another round of hostilities. He reduced commitments to Marxist and radical states in Africa and brokered an Ethiopian-Somali agreement against further hostilities. In 1990, Gorbachev supported U.S. efforts to condemn the Iraqi attack against Kuwait and issued an unprecedented joint statement with Washington to rally international support.

On balance, "new thinking" has produced success in Afghanistan, Angola, Cambodia, and Ethiopia and greater stability for the Middle East and Persian Gulf. Gorbachev has promoted an expanded role for the United Nations in peacekeeping for the Third World and, unlike his predecessors, is no longer using the Security Council merely to take rhetorical swipes at the United States. He has called for revival of the UN Military Staff Committee and suggested stationing of UN observation points in explosive areas and UN naval forces in the Persian Gulf.[51] For the first time since the end of the Second World War, the Soviet Union and the United States have entered a genuine dialogue on the Third World, with vast implications for regional politics.

NOTES

1. Mohamed Heikal, *The Sphinx and the Commissar*, New York: Harper and Row, 1978, pp. 70–71, 179–180.

2. See Robert Donaldson, ed., *The Soviet Union and the Third World: Successes and Failures*, Boulder, CO: Westview, 1981; Carol Saivitz and Sylvia Woodby, *Soviet Third World Relations*, Boulder, CO: Westview, 1985.

3. See Uri Ra'anan, Robert Pfaltzgraff, and Geoffrey Kemp, *Power Projection*, Hamden, CT: Archon, 1982.

4. W. Raymond Duncan and Carolyn McGiffert Ekedahl, *Moscow and the Third World under Gorbachev*, Boulder, CO, Westview Press, 1990, p. 34.

5. Harry Gelman, *The Brezhnev Politburo and the Decline of Détente*, Ithaca: Cornell University Press, 1984, pp. 26–27.

6. *The New York Times*, March 16, 1983, p. 1.

7. *The New York Times*, October 21, 1988, p. 3.

8. The speeches and proceedings of the party congress were received from daily reports on the Soviet Union of the United States Foreign Broadcasting Information Service (FBIS) for the period February 25–March 4, 1986. They were taken in most cases from TASS reports on Radio Moscow. General Secretary Gorbachev spoke to the Congress on opening day.

9. *The New York Times*, February 23, 1989, p. 1.

10. *The Washington Post*, April 22, 1989, p. 9.

11. *Time*, June 4, 1990, p. 39, "Anger, Bluff—and Cooperation," Michael Kramer.

12. Ibid., p. 45.

13. *The New York Times*, June 4, 1990, p. 2.

14. FBIS, February 25–March 6, 1986, TASS reports on Radio Moscow.

15. Ibid.

16. V. Zhurkin, S. Karaganov, A. Kortunov, "Challenges of Security: Old and New," *Kommunist*, No. 1, January 1988. (Zhurkin is currently head of the Institute of Western European Studies.)

17. *Izvestia*, April 22, 1988, p. 5.

18. Vyacheslav Dashichev, *Literaturnaya Gazeta*, May 1988, p. 17. Dashichev is from the Institute of the Economics of the World Socialist System, and the head of the institute—Oleg Bogomolov—published a letter in *Literaturnaya Gazeta* on March 16, 1988, in which he stated that his institute argued against intervention on the grounds it would undermine détente and damage the USSR's international stature. In the first authoritative account of the high-level military debate on the invasion, General of the Army Valentin I. Varrenikov, a deputy defense minister, stated in an interview with the weekly magazine *Ogonyok* that the General Staff opposed the invasion but was overruled by Defense Minister Dmitri F. Ustinov. Varrenikov was the senior defense ministry official in Afghanistan for the last four years of the war and, after the Soviets completed the withdrawal of forces, was named commander of ground forces. Varrenikov added that Marshal Nikolai Ogarkov, then chief of the general staff, and Marshal Sergei F. Akhromeyev, who later became chief of the general staff, also opposed the intervention. (Article in *The New York Times*, March 19, 1989, p. 27, by Bill Keller. Also see *Washington Post*, March 20, 1989 regarding the same topic.)

19. *International Affairs* (*Mezhdunarodnaya Zhizn*), Summer 1988, Andrey V. Kozyrev.

20. Ibid.

21. *Vestnik Ministerstva Inostrannykh Sel SSR*, August 1988, Speech by Shevardnadze to the USSR Ministry of Foreign Affairs, pp. 27–46.

22. Ibid.

23. *Pravda*, October 24, 1989, pp. 2–3.

24. *Mezhdunarodnaya Zhizn*, March 1989, p. 121. My discussions with Soviet military and civilian experts in Moscow and Leningrad in 1989 indicated that Gorbachev's efforts to force the sharing of sensitive security information and encourage debate on issues of national security has contributed to the current tension between party and military officials in the Soviet Union.

25. *The Washington Post*, November 12, 1989, p. 1, "Soviets Slow Strategic Weapons Program," by R. Jeffrey Smith; *The New York Times*, November 13, 1989, p. 8, "U.S. Says Moscow is Braking on Some Arms," by Michael R. Gordon.

26. *The New York Times*, June 5, 1990, p. 23, "U.S. Says Soviets Will Field Fewer of Its Latest Bombers," by Michael R. Gordon.

27. *The New York Times*, June 4, 1990, p. 23.

28. *The Washington Post*, October 18, 1988, p. 1. Also see unpublished paper by Wayne P. Limberg, "Moscow and Regional Conflicts: Linkage Revisited" (American Political Science Association, Washington, DC, 1988).

29. *Washington Post*, February 17, 1989, p. 7, Testimony of Rear Adm. Brooks to the House Armed Services Committee Subcommittee.

30. *London Times*, April 16, 1990, p. 4, "Russians Like to Scrap 100 Warships, MoD Says," by Michael Evans.

31. *Washington Times*, August 13, 1990, p. 2.

32. *Moscow News*, May 17, 1989, p. 4; *Morskou Sbornik*, June 11, 1989, p. 3.

33. *The New York Times*, March 15, 1987, p. 16, "U.S. Reports New Iranian Missiles; Threat to Hormuz Oil Traffic Seen," by Bernard E. Trainor.

34. Egypt, Syria, Iraq, Libya, Jordan, Saudi Arabia, and Israel are seven of the ten largest recipients of military assistance; India, in fourth place, is the only country outside the region in the top five with purchases from the Soviet Union that include MiG-29 fighter aircraft, TU-142 Bear ASW aircraft, and the leasing of a nuclear submarine. See Richard F. Grimmett, "Trends in Conventional Arms Transfers to the Third World by Major Supplier, 1982–1989," Washington, DC: Congressional Reference Service, 1990.

35. *The Washington Post*, June 18, 1990, p. 17, "U.S. Seeking More Aid for Angolan Rebels" by David Ottoway. U.S. officials estimated that Soviet military aid to Angola in 1989 was $800 million, down 40% from the $1.2 billion provided in 1988.

36. The list includes Cuba, Syria, Vietnam, India, Angola, Ethiopia, Iraq, Afghanistan, Libya, and Algeria, according to ACDA's *World Military Expenditures and Arms Transfers*, Washington, DC: U.S. Government Printing Office, 1989.

37. Richard F. Grimmett, *Trends in Conventional Arms Transfers to the Third World by Major Supplier, 1980–1987*, Washington, DC: Congressional Reference Service, 1988, p. 5.

38. Testimony to the House Arms Services Committee, February 22, 1989, Rear Adm. Thomas A. Brooks.

39. *The New York Times*, August 12, 1990, p. C3, "Cambodians Face Loss of Eastern Trade and Aid," by Steven Erlanger.

40. *Pradva*, July 28, 1988, p. 3.

41. *New Times* (Moscow), May 7, 1990, pp. 44–45. Vorontsov had a major role in drawing up agreements for Afghanistan that led to the Soviet withdrawal in 1988–1989, and was a "shuttle" diplomat between Tehran, Islamabad, Geneva, and Moscow during that period. Bessmertnykh was head of the U.S. department in the Soviet foreign ministry from 1983 to 1986.

42. *The Washington Post*, May 27, 1987, p. 5.

43. *Krasnaya Zvezda (Red Star)*, August 10, 1990, p. 3, "The World Today: Problems and Views: 'In the Beginning Was the Word . . . '," by Manki Ponomarev.

44. *Izvestia*, July 9, 1989, p. 5.

45. *Izvestia*, July 27, 1989, p. 5.

46. *Izvestia*, June 15, 1989, p. 1.

47. *Izvestia*, July 14, 1989, p. 5.

48. *Pravda*, May 12, 1989, p. 5.

49. *Mezhdunarodnaya Zhizn*, April 1990, No. 4, "Reexamining Policy in the Third World," Andrey Kolosov, pp. 37–45.

50. *Pravda*, March 27, 1990, p. 5.

51. *Pravda*, September 17, 1989, p. 1.

2

Decision Making Under Gorbachev

Since Gorbachev's rise to power in 1985 there has been fundamental change in key institutions, particularly the Politburo, Foreign Ministry, and the Central Committee's International Department. These institutions are now run by individuals who support the general secretary's "new political thinking," are more capable than their predecessors of making changes in policy, and who are improving analysis at all levels. The Politburo has been virtually disenfranchised as a central party apparatus and will have no major role in areas of national security.

Personnel changes reflected the demands of Gorbachev, Aleksandr Yakovlev, and Eduard Shevardnadze—the three key members of the leadership from 1985 to 1990—and involved the party and government in "democratizing" the foreign policy process. Gorbachev and Shevardnadze were critical of the exclusivity of decision making during the Brezhnev era and particularly the failure of the apparatus to warn about negative aspects of decisions.[1] The party's influence in the military has been seriously weakened.

Gorbachev apparently decided at the outset that, to alter Soviet policy, there would have to be changes in Soviet institutions at the highest levels. No institution has escaped scrutiny, beginning with the foreign ministry in the summer of 1985 (when Shevardnadze replaced Andrei Gromyko), the Central Committee's International Department in the winter of 1986 (when Anatoly Dobrynin replaced Boris Ponomarev), the defense ministry in the spring of 1987 (when Dmitry Yazov replaced Sergey Sokolov), and finally the KGB in 1988 (when Vladimir Kryuchkov replaced Viktor Chebrikov). In every case except the KGB, these moves were followed by purges of the top echelons, with younger supporters of Gorbachev replacing cadres appointed in the Brezhnev era.

Gorbachev in 1988 created six policy commissions ostensibly to streamline decisions, guarantee support for new thinking in domestic and foreign policy, and ensure innovative thinking. Two of the commissions—the Ideological Commission and the International Policy Commission—are now part of the national apparatus and originally were led by Gorbachev allies—Vadim Medvedev and Aleksandr Yakovlev, who became party secretaries in March 1986, a year after Gorbachev's accession. They support a conciliatory line toward the United States, Eastern Europe, and the Third World. Yakovlev held responsibility for propaganda, ideology, and foreign policy; Medvedev is an economic theoretician and drafter of Gorbachev's speech in 1987 that signaled willingness to allow the non-Soviet members of the Warsaw Pact to pursue reform. The two commissions are now headed by weak political figures, suggesting further decline in the status of the Politburo and Secretariat in foreign policy and national security.

The depth of Gorbachev's changes in the apparatus says that the general secretary believed that cadre change had to be institutionalized to make shifts in foreign policy. Gorbachev is the only member of the Politburo or Secretariat appointed before Brezhnev's death in 1982. Regional party leaders now hold the balance of power in the Politburo, and day-to-day decision making has been transferred to state institutions.

The Presidential Council, a key group of civil and military officials that vets national security decisions and reports to Gorbachev, shared responsibility with the Defense Council, which reports to the Politburo. The Presidential Council was designed to enhance government authority in security decision making, until it was replaced by the National Security Council in November 1990. Defense Minister Yazov was the only military member of the Presidential Council, which downgraded the role of the military.

To strengthen the government in decision making, Gorbachev has assumed greater power in foreign policy as the Soviet Union's first executive president. He presided over the Presidential Council that functioned as his cabinet, including Shevardnadze, Kryuchkov, Yakovlev, and Yuri Maslyukov, head of the State Planning Committee, or Gosplan. Gorbachev will have the right to declare war, command the armed forces, veto legislation, and appoint and remove ministers. In his first speech as president, Gorbachev took credit for "new foreign policy" and emphasized that the armed forces could no longer fight outside the USSR "without sanction from the Supreme Soviet," except in the case of "surprise attack."[2]

Gorbachev now chairs the National Security Council, whose membership includes Kryuchkov and Yazov. The Council will deal with foreign policy and military issues, and probably will monitor the Defense Council. A separate institution will deal with domestic security.

Gorbachev has established a more prominent foreign affairs role for the Supreme Soviet, so the USSR's legislative body has more than a rubber stamp for security policy. The Supreme Soviet has two committees with responsibility for policy and military affairs—the Committee on Defense and State Security and the Committee for International Affairs. Membership includes deputies from both the Supreme Soviet and the more liberal Congress of People's Deputies, and their behavior indicates a more active role. They appear to be permanent bodies with full-time staffs, modeled after the committee structure of the U.S. House of Representatives and Senate.

Shevardnadze's speeches over the past years indicated he believed decisions to invade Afghanistan, deploy SS-20 medium-range missiles, continue to manufacture chemical weapons, and build a radar in violation of the Anti-Ballistic Missile Treaty would not have been made if the Supreme Soviet had debated the decisions of the Politburo. Oversight responsibilities for the Supreme Soviet address Shevardnadze's criticism of secrecy and ideologization of past decisions and overreliance on the military. The International Policy Commission, which includes such Gorbachev supporters as Georgi Arbatov, Yuri Primakov, and Anatoly Chernyayev, will debate national security issues.

Gorbachev's selection of advisers reflects the priority of East-West affairs and downgrading of the Third World and national liberation movements. Six of his seven personal advisers are experts on national security and foreign policy; three of them have extensive knowledge of the United States and East-West relations and accompanied Gorbachev to the Malta summit in December 1989. Yakovlev, ambassador to Canada for nearly ten years, was appointed to the Politburo in 1987, and when chairman of the International Policy Commission was presumably responsible for carrying out Politburo decisions on foreign policy. Anatoly Chernyayev, long-time member of the International Department, has become Gorbachev's personal foreign affairs adviser, comparable to the U.S. president's National Security Adviser. Yakovlev no longer has an official position in the government, but Chernyayev has the most seniority of the advisers and probably is the most influential, accompanying Gorbachev to summit meetings with U.S. presidents in Reykjavik in 1986, Washington in 1987, and Malta in 1989.

Anatoly Dobrynin, who spent nearly twenty-five years as ambassador to the United States and is the only ambassador who has ever been returned from a post to become a member of the Politburo or Secretariat, was former head of the Central Committee's International Department and is now foreign policy adviser to Gorbachev. He has been at the President's side during summit meetings in Moscow.

Other advisers are Marshal Sergey Akhromeyev for military affairs and arms control, Vitaly Gusenkov for Europe, Vadim Zagladin for Germany, and Georgy Shakhnazarov, who accompanied Gorbachev to Beijing in 1989. Akhromeyev, a member of the Central Committee, International Policy Commission, and Supreme Soviet, is extremely influential. Zagladin is a member of the Central Committee, and Shakhnazarov is a member of the Congress of People's Deputies and the only non-Slavic adviser close to Gorbachev. In an interview in 1989, Shakhnazarov emphasized that Gorbachev makes his own decisions and is not directed by his advisers.[3]

SOVIET DECISION MAKING AND FOREIGN POLICY

One of the problems in deciphering roles and responsibilities for Soviet policy has been the traditional silence of Soviet leaders on key issues. Stalin had little to say about disputes with Tito; Khrushchev did not use his memoirs to record differences with Mao; Brezhnev and Kosygin were virtually silent on confrontations in the Middle East; and the entire Soviet Politburo refused to comment on political destabilization in the late 1970s. Only recently, under the policy of glasnost, or openness, have there been statements and commentaries revealing differences between policy makers and institutions. Until Gorbachev and Shevardnadze began to refer to problems for policy that stemmed from the invasion of Afghanistan, the Islamic revolution in Iran, and the war between Iran and Iraq, students have had to rely on Kremlinological interpretations of doctrine and politics to describe decisions. Gorbachev's candid discussion, his reshuffling of personalities conducting diplomatic and political relations in the Third World, and encouragement of debate among policy experts have made it easier to speculate on decisions. Glasnost has not been fully extended to media coverage of international issues, but Soviet officials and journalists are increasingly testing the Kremlin's tolerance of discussion.

THE POLITBURO AND SOVIET FOREIGN POLICY

Events in the Third World over the past three decades have demonstrated that, until recently, party institutions—not government organizations—dominated the Soviet policy process. Soviet documents claim that party congresses and central committee plenary sessions determine the line in foreign affairs, and the Politburo exercises day-to-day responsibility.

In fact, the party congress and central committee plenum have done little, and the focal point has been the Politburo. Politburo meetings used to be weekly, normally on Thursdays, and lasted from three to six hours. The Politburo will now hold monthly meetings, which is one of many indicators of lost influence and even participation in matters of national security.[4] In view of the regional composition of the new Politburo, it is inconceivable that a full meeting of the group could be gathered together on a timely basis to discuss matters of state security.

Brezhnev told the twenty-fifth Party Congress in 1976 that, in the five years since the previous congress the Politburo had held more than two hundred sessions and that foreign policy had taken precedence over other state matters.[5] Several years earlier he told a group of Western reporters that he normally chaired meetings of the Politburo and in his absence this task passed down the line to members of the Secretariat who were members of the Politburo.[6] The Politburo member currently responsible for foreign affairs is without experience, the former head of the trade union movement, Gennady Yanayev, who became Gorbachev's vice president in December 1990.

Memoirs of Egyptian officials reveal the former role of the Politburo in Third World affairs, particularly in the "war of attrition" between Egypt and Israel in 1969 and 1970. Following deep aerial attacks by the Israeli air force, Egyptian leaders made several trips to Moscow to appeal for military support. On each of these occasions, according to memoirs of the late president Anwar Sadat and his confidant Mohamed Heikal, a key Egyptian official held secret talks with members of the Politburo; the talks were followed by a meeting of the Politburo, and finally a decision on introduction of a sophisticated Soviet weapons system to the Egyptian armed forces.[7]

In December 1969, a visit by then–vice president Sadat was followed by a Politburo meeting and introduction of surface-to-air missiles manned by Soviet air defense forces. The following month, President Gamal Abdel Nasser traveled to Moscow and several months later the Soviets shipped MiG-21 fighter aircraft. Another visit by Nasser led to an emergency Politburo meeting and subsequent delivery of TU-16 fighter bombers.[8] (Presumably the Politburo approved the delivery of sophisticated weapons systems to Third World countries, such as

MiG-29 fighter aircraft to Cuba and Syria in 1988 and 1989, and SU-24 fighter bombers to Libya in 1989.)

Memoirs reveal that Nasser and Sadat met for the most part with only three leaders of the Soviet hierarchy—Brezhnev, Premier Kosygin, and President Podgorny—and that Defense Minister Grechko was consulted only on technical military issues. Nasser and Sadat stated that the International Department of the Central Committee played a peripheral role and that the Ministry of Foreign Affairs was subordinate to the Ministry of Defense. It is noteworthy that the Egyptians believed Kosygin uneasy with the level of risk Brezhnev was willing to take with Soviet-manned weapons systems and that all the top leaders were angry upon learning that Nasser and Sadat had accepted a U.S.–inspired ceasefire without consultation with the Soviets.[9]

It is almost certain that Politburo meetings have accompanied decisions during international negotiations and crises. Raymond Garthoff has written that during the five days of intensive bargaining on an arms limitation agreement at the first Soviet–U.S. summit in Moscow in May 1972, the Politburo met four times.[10] This pattern was repeated during talks between Secretary of State Kissinger and Brezhnev in 1974 and Secretary of State Shultz and Gorbachev in 1987. Gorbachev remarked in a speech to the Central Committee that the shift in tactics that led to the decision to withdraw from Afghanistan began in April 1985, only one month after he took power, when the "Politburo conducted a hard and impartial analysis of the position and started even at that time to see a way out of the situation."[11] There was no announcement of such an Afghanistan review at the time.

There was no indication until recently that the role of the Politburo has weakened, and there is reason to believe that—like his immediate predecessors—Gorbachev continues to rely on close allies within the leadership. Shevardnadze, Yakovlev, and Medvedev are no longer members of the Politburo, and, because of differences over domestic policies, are no longer close to Gorbachev. Vladimir Kryuchkov and Yazov have been critical of Gorbachev in certain areas of national security and have been removed from the Politburo, but have gained influence because of the internal fragmentation that threatens the Soviet Union.

THE PRESIDENTIAL COUNCIL AND SOVIET FOREIGN POLICY

In 1990, Gorbachev announced a Presidential Council to assume tasks in national security and supervise domestic policy and economic reform. In composition and responsibility the Council resembled the U.S. president's cabinet and the National Security Council; membership included such Politburo officials as Shevardnadze, Yakovlev, and Council of Minister's Chairman Nikolay Ryzhkov as well as Defense Minister Dmitry Yazov and KGB Chief Kryuchkov. Other members with understanding of national security issues included former Minister of Internal Affairs Vadim Bakatin and Gosplan Chairman Yuri Maslyukov. The most notable omissions from Council membership were former Politburo members Yegor Ligachev and Lev Zaykov; Ligachev was Gorbachev's most influential critic within the Soviet leadership until he lost his Politburo seat at the twenty-eighth party congress in July 1990, and Zaykov became deputy chief of the Defense Council in 1989.

The Council marked a shift in responsibility for foreign policy from the Politburo and the Party to the office of the presidency under Gorbachev, who will have powers in the field of foreign policy that resemble those of a U.S. president. Unlike his predecessors, Gorbachev will be liberated from the need for consensus within the Politburo but will have to operate under the constraints of his Council as well as legislative debate in the Supreme Soviet.

In a press conference in March 1990, Gorbachev emphasized that the Presidential Council would operate in a fashion similar to the Defense Council.[12] He explained that a "considerable portion of those people who were involved in the work of the Defense Council will continue to take part and assist the president." Gorbachev indicated that the Presidential Council would "exert influence" over him, but he abolished the group in November 1990 and turned over responsibility for national security affairs to the Security Council.

THE DEFENSE COUNCIL AND SOVIET FOREIGN POLICY

Until the formation of the Presidential Council and the Security Council, the Defense Council was the highest peacetime body in the USSR dealing with political-military matters and presumably looked into Third World military issues brought to the attention of the Politburo, such as the invasion of Afghanistan or the provision of Soviet-piloted aircraft to Egypt. The 1977 Soviet constitution placed the Defense Council under the Presidium of the Supreme Soviet, although the group remained subordinate to the Politburo. The draft constitution announced in 1988, however, stipulated that the President of the Supreme Soviet was to head the Defense Council, suggesting an effort to shift responsibility in national security to the government. Key military and defense industrial officials who were on the Defense Council but not on the Presidential Council include Zaykov, Chief of the General Staff Mikhael Moiseyev, and Military-Industrial Commission head Belousov.

The role of the Defense Council remains uncertain but the deputy chairman, Zaykov, told a *Pravda* reporter in 1989 that the group discusses "all the state's main military-political initiatives."[13] He cited the unilateral test moratorium of 1985, Gorbachev's arms control speech in 1986, and the decision to withdraw from Afghanistan and unilateral troop reductions in 1988. He named some but not all members of the council, including Ryzhkov, Shevardnadze, Yazov, and First Deputy Minister Maslyukov who is head of the State Planning Committee or Gosplan. In addition to Gorbachev, who is chairman of the Defense Council, it is believed that KGB Chairman Kryuchkov and Military-Industrial Commission head Belousov are permanent members.[14] Western sources believe that the head of the defense industry department of the Central Committee Secretariat, and the chief of the Defense Ministry's general staff, attend on a regular basis.[15] Among this group only Kryuchkov was on the Presidential Council.

At the twenty-eighth Soviet party congress in 1990, Zaykov told the members that the council adopted and confirmed all major strategic military programs.[16] He explained that the council "approved" the weapons program and then "forcibly" got the money, thus "expanding" the military-industrial complex. Zaykov added that the communist party "must not retreat" from its responsibility for major questions of security, but the "center of gravity" for decision making must move toward the president and the Supreme Soviet.

Virtually nothing is known of inner workings of the Defense Council, but Kremlinologists believe the meetings of the group are "highly regularized affairs, with agendas set in advance and lists of invitees agreed upon."[17] The council probably has no independent staff but relies on information provided by the KGB, the defense ministry, and party organizations.[18] Zaykov compared the Defense Council to the National Security Council under the U.S. president, citing such functions as elaboration and adoption of national security decisions and preparation of daily reports for President Gorbachev.[19]

The Defense Council provides institutional memory essential to decisions in, say, the Middle East, particularly during crises. The decisions to mount airlifts of military equipment to Egyptian and Syrian forces during the wars of 1967, supply Soviet-manned equipment to Egypt during the war of attrition of 1969–1970, and provide surface-to-air missiles to Syria in the wake of the Israeli invasion of Lebanon in 1982 presumably had the imprimatur of the Defense Council.

There are ad hoc committees or investigatory commissions that have examined crises in Czechoslovakia, Afghanistan, and Poland before decisions have been made at the Politburo level, but the Defense Council presumably also checks on military appointments, arms control, and Soviet military forces in the Third World. When SA-5s were deployed in Syria in 1982, Soviet personnel maintained control over the missiles until Syrian troops were trained to operate them, which presumably was a decision by the Defense Council.[20] That Soviet pilots and air defense units have rarely operated in noncontiguous areas, that Soviet naval forces have never engaged in combat in out-of-area waters, and that Soviet combat ground forces have not appeared in confrontations in noncontiguous areas points to the cautious nature of the Politburo and Defense Council.

THE SECRETARIAT AND SOVIET FOREIGN POLICY

The Secretariat is the Party's executive body responsible for coordinating information and recommendations to the Politburo for final decision. The Secretariat has a staff organized into departments responsible for monitoring policy. Government ministries and other agencies are subject to control by one or more of the departments. In foreign affairs, the departments traditionally were the International Department, the Department for Relations with Communist and Workers' Parties of the Socialist Countries (often referred to as the Bloc Department), and the Department of Cadres Abroad.

Gorbachev has weakened the Secretariat by placing commissions between the Politburo and the Secretariat that report to the General Secretary, and ending references to the unofficial "second secretary" on the Secretariat, which usually designated the heir apparent to the general secretary. The second secretary was also responsible for chairing meetings of the Politburo in the absence of the general secretary. Foreign affairs departments now report to the International Commission rather than the Secretariat.

The commission, one of six commissions created by Gorbachev in September 1988, reports to the Politburo. It is too early to determine the workings of any of the commissions, but it appears that Gorbachev is trying both to simplify authority at the politburo level as well as exercise more personal control.

Yanayev's role as head of the International Commission indicates a weak role for that party body as well; his speech to the party congress in 1990 ignored foreign policy. The Ideology Commission is now headed by Aleksandr Dzasokhov, a specialist on the Middle East and former ambassador to Syria. Yanayev and Dzasokhov, who were named to their new positions at the party congress in 1990, are far less influential than their predecessors.

In 1988, Dobrynin was replaced as Chief of the International Department by Valentin Falin, who had been director of the Novosti press agency and ambassador to West Germany; he is a candidate member of the central committee.[21] Falin is deputy to Yanayev and his International Department is the most important body under the International Commission.

Under Gorbachev, the International Department has been less concerned with Third World issues than East-West issues, particularly arms control. Dobrynin's predecessor was Boris Ponomarev, a party secretary and candidate member of the Politburo since 1972, who led the international department for twenty-five years and was expert on Third World issues, particularly national liberation movements. According to Arkady Shevchenko, adviser to Gromyko and the highest-ranking Soviet official ever to defect, Ponomarev's ability to influence policy was limited by his acrimonious relations with Gromyko.[22] Nevertheless, Moscow's role in the Third World grew during Ponomarev's leadership of the International Department. Dobrynin and Falin are far more interested in East-West issues.

THE FOREIGN MINISTRY AND SOVIET FOREIGN POLICY

The party apparatus still has authority over the foreign ministry, as the International Commission now exercises general oversight over Politburo decisions by the foreign ministry and other nonparty institutions. From 1973 to 1990, the foreign minister held voting membership on the Politburo and acted as adviser to the general secretary. Gromyko, foreign minister from 1957 to 1985, was the first diplomat to be named to the Politburo; his promotion seemed to increase his authority, particularly in American and Third World relations. Shevardnadze became a full member and foreign minister in 1985, and conducted the reorganization of the foreign ministry.

Gorbachev's effect on the foreign ministry began in July 1985 with the appointment of Shevardnadze, the first of many surprises by the general secretary in foreign policy. It was probably not coincidental that announcement of Gromyko's "promotion" to the presidency and Shevardnadze's to the foreign ministry was followed by the terse announcement of the first summit meeting between Gorbachev and President Ronald Reagan. Since then there has not only been remarkable improvement in Soviet–U.S. and Sino-Soviet relations, but major departures in Soviet policy on issues that deal with the Third World. Gromyko probably was responsible for restoring the role of the foreign ministry in decisions, but Shevardnadze has become influential as a shaper of policy.

Many personnel changes took place after an unusual meeting of the foreign ministry in Moscow in 1986 to discuss "implementing the decisions of the twenty-seventh Soviet party congress in the field of foreign policy."[23] Gorbachev, Shevardnadze, and Dobrynin attended the meeting in addition to Yakovlev and Medvedev, then new members of the Secretariat. Shevardnadze, Yakovlev, and Medvedev lost their political positions in 1990, but Gorbachev is committed to pursuing their foreign policy adgenda.

Gorbachev criticized the foreign ministry in a speech that Soviet media portrayed as a critical examination of policy delivered with "party-style exactness."[24] He emphasized that the ministry would have the same standards of accountability and anti-corruption that Gorbachev was putting in place in the rest of Soviet society. Emphasis on corruption suggested that Shevardnadze may have come to Gorbachev's attention as minister of internal affairs in the Georgian Republic, where he exposed serious corruption and became first secretary of the Georgian communist party.[25] Gorbachev and Shevardnadze became candidate members of the Politburo in the late 1970s.

One of Shevardnadze's first changes was reorganization of the Near East department under Vladimir Polyakov, an expert on Arab-Israeli affairs for more than twenty-five years and one of the most visible figures in diplomacy in the region.[26] For the past two decades Polyakov has traveled to the Middle East on a regular basis and in 1988 became the first official to visit Saudi Arabia in more than fifty years. Like Karen Brutents, his counterpart in the Central Committee's International Department, Polyakov has argued for more flexible policy and like other regional specialists has spent time at the embassy in Washington.[27] In view of the lack of Third World expertise on the part of Shevardnadze and his deputies—Anatoly Kovalev, Aleksandr Bessmertnykh, and Yuly Vorontsov—Polyakov occupied an influential position. Bessmertnykh was named foreign minister in January 1991, which suggested continuity in East-West matters and a continued retreat from the Third World.

In addition to replacement of personnel in the ministry, Shevardnadze installed a ministry official, Boris Pyadyshev, as editor of the foreign policy journal *Mezhdunarodnaya Zhizn* (*International Affairs*) and confirmed the links between the monthly and the ministry. The journal has dealt with foreign affairs and frequently carries articles by ministry personnel, but had not been acknowledged as an organ of the ministry.

THE SUPREME SOVIET AND SOVIET FOREIGN POLICY

If the Secretariat has lost power under Gorbachev in foreign policy, the Supreme Soviet has moved into the vacuum. The general secretary appears to believe that mistakes of the Brezhnev era could have been prevented if there had been debate of controversial moves in the Supreme Soviet. He has created two new foreign policy departments under the aegis of the Supreme Soviet. These committees, one for international affairs and the other for defense and state security, are to have a role in legislative oversight, a new aspect of Soviet decisions.

Thus far these committees have played a part in choosing ministers of defense and foreign affairs, as well as the chairman of the KGB. They are supposed to recommend approval of budgets of the ministries, which points to a possible part in monitoring the defense budget. The Soviets have published membership of the committees but not named a permanent chairman for the committee for international affairs.[28]

The committee on defense and state security was originally led by Vladimir Lapygin, a career defense industrialist and specialist on ICBM guidance systems and space technology. He was replaced by Leonid Sharin at the party congress in 1990, who is a longtime party official without specific ties to the military-industrial complex. Most of his career was spent in Vladivostok, where he graduated from the Naval Academy.

The committee is one of twenty-five standing committees and commissions of the Supreme Soviet and the first legislative body with oversight of the military-security apparatus. Sharin and his deputy, an Air Force colonel, administer more than forty Supreme Soviet deputies as members, including six military officers, three representatives from the KGB, and several defense industry managers. The committee has subcommittees for the armed forces, defense industry, and state security, and has begun to scrutinize the defense and KGB budgets. In open hearings the subcommittees have discussed defense conversion, the role of KGB border guards, and social conditions of the military.

In his *Pravda* interview, designed in part to extend glasnost to foreign policy, Zaykov confirmed that the committees would make decisions on defense spending and on regulation of the military and the KGB.[29] Statutes would clarify functions of the committees, and he compared the committees to the Foreign Affairs and Foreign Relations Committees of the U.S. House and Senate. These groups presumably will examine such Third World issues as military and economic assistance, military power abroad, and intervention of Soviet forces in regional crises. Just as the foreign ministry and international department employ "consultants" from research institutes, Supreme Soviet committees will need guidance on policy. The consultants may not play an institutionalized part in foreign policy but could become responsible for inputs on an ad hoc basis. A former consultant, Yevgeny Primakov, moved from the Institute of World Economy and International Relations to become a candidate member of the Politburo where he was the leading authority on the Third World until he lost his seat at the twenty-eighth party congress. He is a senior adviser to Gorbachev and played a major role in the Persian Gulf crisis of 1990.

CRISIS MANAGEMENT AND SOVIET FOREIGN POLICY

Crisis management is well known to Soviet leaders who have had to make decisions about the Third World, particularly the Middle East and Southwest Asia, where proximity has compensated for disadvantages in power projection. There is no indication that any crisis management group or staff exists or that the Soviets are engaged in any programmatic effort to correct deficiencies in force projection.[30] They have no forces for use in the Third World and, unlike the United States, little historical or military experience with rapid deployment forces or carrier task forces. They have no operating responsibility for overseas bases in the Third World, with possible exception of Cam Ranh Bay in Vietnam from 1979 to 1989, and continue to deemphasize out-of-area naval deployments in noncontiguous areas.[31] Naval support to Third World clients has been confined to symbolic uses or, as before the October War, evacuation of military personnel and dependents.

According to Egyptian memoirs, key Soviet leaders in times of crisis have been the general secretary, chairman of the Council of Ministers, and chairman of the Presidium of the Supreme Soviet.[32] The defense minister has played a key role in Arab-Israeli crises when military advice was needed, and it was noteworthy that the foreign minister and chief of the International Department took only peripheral parts, with the foreign ministry secondary to defense.[33] When Third World leaders have been brought to the Presidium in the Kremlin in situations short of crisis proportions, other officials have been present, including the chairman of the Committee for State Security (KGB), and the politburo member responsible for ideology and propaganda.

In former crisis and noncrisis situations, the Politburo has played the key role, with the Moscow-based members of the Politburo being the most important actors. The general secretary has had to proceed cautiously and even slowly in crises because of the collective nature of decision making, but the same collectivity has provided bureaucratic protection when Politburo decisions have been criticized. Presumably Gorbachev will now have a freer hand as executive president, but the Security Council will play a key role. The draft union treaty, published in *Pravda* in November 1990, preserves Gorbachev's primacy in conducting foreign relations.

After the Six-Day War, Moscow party boss Nikolai Yegorychev reportedly attacked Brezhnev for failing to provide greater military support for Egypt and Syria.[34] Several months later Yegorychev lost his post as first secretary of the Moscow city committee of the Party. Five years later Ukrainian party chief Petr Y. Shelest criticized Brezhnev's decision to proceed with a summit meeting with President Nixon after the increased bombing of North Vietnam.[35] The following year Shelest lost his position on the Politburo.

Gorbachev has enhanced his power over the Politburo and remains first among equals. His efforts to reduce Soviet visibility in the Third World and promote political solutions to regional problems appears to have wide support within the leadership but there is no assurance the general secretary will continue to have support if he encounters difficulties in either domestic policy such as economic reform or foreign policy such as German reunification or troop withdrawal from Eastern Europe. Republic representatives are getting more active in foreign policy, and a high-level official at the Foreign Ministry has resigned to become foreign minister of the Russian Republic.

THE THIRD WORLD AND SOVIET FOREIGN POLICY

The change in personnel under Gorbachev and Shevardnadze has contributed to flexibility and dynamism. Shevardnadze reorganized the Near Eastern and North African Countries Administration and named department chiefs for sixteen Arab countries. Yevgeniy Primakov, expert on Arab affairs and former director of the Academy of Science's Oriental Institute, works closely with Gorbachev and met with President Bush on several occasions in 1990 to coordinate Persian Gulf policy. Yuliy Vorontsov, chief negotiator of the Intermediate Nuclear Forces Agreement (INF) in 1987–1988 and ambassador to Afghanistan during the period of withdrawal, returned to Moscow in 1989 as First Deputy Foreign Minister with special responsibility for the Middle East. He was named ambassador to the United Nations in 1990. Aleksandr Zotov, a leading Arabist, was named ambassador to Syria in 1988 and, upon arrival in Damascus, began making tough statements on the limits to assistance and Moscow's unwillingness to accept Syrian strategic parity with Israel.

Presumably these officials are responsible for the flexibility in policy over the past years, which has included conciliation in Arab-Israeli peace efforts, more contacts with Israel and moderate Arab states, and cooperation with the United States to arrange political solutions. The Soviets have encouraged the Palestine Liberation Organization to enter a dialogue with the United States and have tried to mediate the differences between Iran and Iraq. Shevardnadze's successful tour of the Middle East in February 1989, including high-level discussion in Egypt, probably can be attributed to these policymakers. Under Shevardnadze, the Soviets established full diplomatic relations with all six conservative Arab states in the Persian Gulf.

The Soviets have shown flexibility toward the Asian states and reshuffled the Asian departments of the ministry. Removal of Mikhail Kapitsa as deputy minister with responsibility for Asia and Sino-Soviet consultation marked the end of the long tenure of an opponent to dialogue with China and Japan. His replacement, Igor Rogachev, is far more flexible. The chiefs and deputy chiefs of the Pacific Ocean Countries Department and the Socialist Countries of Asia Administration are new to their positions.[36] They deserve some credit for improvement with China, Japan, and South Korea.

Shevardnadze named six ambassadors-at-large to deal with such issues as Eastern and Western Europe and arms control and a new function bureau for arms control and disarmament. The former chief of the Soviet START and INF delegations, Viktor Karpov, was named director of the Problems of Arms Control and Disarmament Administration. Karpov has been involved in arms control negotiation with the United States since the beginning of SALT I in 1969, and his two deputies are experienced negotiators.

GORBACHEV AND THE FOREIGN POLICY MACHINERY

In several years, Gorbachev has established control over policy and reshuffled the leadership. Shevardnadze reorganized the foreign ministry, including the appointment of two new first deputy ministers, seven deputy ministers, seven ambassadors-at-large, and a reorganized Near Eastern and North African Countries Department, which reflects emphasis on that part of the world. Dobrynin enhanced the role of the International Department from 1986 to 1988 and brought in first-rate "Americanists" from the ministry. The Supreme

Soviet is getting oversight function on national security for the first time. Accountability is being introduced at the legislative level.

Gorbachev has enhanced his power by creating the USSR's first executive president with power to chair the security council, conduct negotiations, and sign treaties. The Soviet president will be able to nominate decision makers for policy who will, in turn, receive confirmation from the Congress of People's Deputies. Gorbachev will have the privilege of veto but subject to majority vote in the Supreme Soviet. He has the power to declare war, but the decision to commit Soviet forces, except if the USSR is under attack, must be submitted to the Supreme Soviet. Presumably Gorbachev could be removed as general secretary of the party but retain his presidency.

Gorbachev brought Medvedev into the Politburo, author of the more moderate doctrine toward the non-Soviet members of the Warsaw Pact; he replaced the conservative Ligachev as chief ideologist of the Party. After promotion in 1988, Medvedev told a gathering of political scientists from communist countries that communism is in crisis around the world and that the notion of class struggle is no longer a determinant of policy.[37] Medvedev's remarks were clear refutation of the orthodox positions taken by Ligachev and Viktor Chebrikov and provided the best indication that a more moderate element had taken over. Chebrikov was dismissed as chairman of the KGB, which meant that for the first time in twenty years the KGB chief was not a member of the Politburo. Politburo decisions on sensitive policy issues were taken without a vote from two major pillars of the national security bureaucracy, the KGB and defense ministry, until September 1989, when KGB chief Kryuchkov was named to the Politburo as a full member. Kryuchkov lost his Politburo post in 1990.

Gorbachev has established control over the military, reducing its influence in national security and foreign policy and making cuts in the budget and procurement. He has reshuffled the leadership of the military, including the defense minister, first deputy defense ministers, and ten of sixteen deputy defense ministers. The new defense minister, Dimitri Yazov, upon appointment, was a junior officer with a background in personnel.

Gorbachev has changed all the theater-level commanders-in-chief and chiefs of military districts, and many members of the general staff. The new chief of the general staff, General Mikhail Moiseyev, stated in 1989 that the number of military districts would be reduced.[38] The military continues to oppose unilateral cuts and creation of an all-volunteer force, but Gorbachev and the Supreme Soviet have outmaneuvered the military on most matters.

Personnel moves have been accompanied by a series of steps to strengthen Moscow in the Third World, particularly Africa, the Middle East, and Asia, by gaining a place at the Arab-Israeli bargaining table, enhancing the USSR as a responsible superpower intent on constructive solutions to regional disputes.[39] Initiatives on the Third World have not been as sweeping as Gorbachev's approach toward the United States or his arms control proposals, but are based on similar perception that the USSR's military position has not produced political and military gains.[40]

Unlike Khrushchev, and Brezhnev before him, Gorbachev seems less concerned with Soviet military and political influence in the Third World vis-à-vis the United States. He is responsible for a new willingness to recognize a link between larger East-West relations and regional conflict, willing to recognize the U.S. interest in the Middle East.[41] He has ended the "blank pages" in Soviet diplomacy, improving and expanding contacts with such countries as Israel and South Africa, and establishing relations with South Korea.

Invigoration of Soviet policy towards the United Nations appears to be part of a broad effort to demonstrate desire for constructive solutions to regional conflict in the Third World. Gorbachev laid the groundwork in 1986, when he unexpectedly agreed to pay Moscow's assesment for the United Nations Interim Force in Lebanon (UNIFIL), present in southern Lebanon since 1978 without Soviet support. The following year the Soviets announced they would pay $225 million to the United Nations to cover dues for the year as well as assessment for past peacekeeping operations—including those in the Golan Heights.[42]

In a statement of policy in *Pravda* in September 1987, Gorbachev made an eleven-point proposal for strengthening the United Nations, including creation of a multilateral center to manage conflicts that would incorporate a UN hotline to capitals of the five permanent members of the Security Council.[43] U.S. officials have acknowledged that, when President George Bush referred to some states as no longer "silent or ambivalent" about American hostages in the Middle East, he was referring to the USSR and its role in pressing Iran and Syria to help release hostages.[44] Deputy Foreign Ministers Yuly Vorontsov and Vladimir Petrovsky have been active in touring Arab states to convince leaders that improved Soviet-American relations are central to peace in the Middle East.[45] Petrovsky also visited Iran in 1990 to discuss an earlier Soviet proposal to sponsor a meeting of Iranian, Iraqi, and Soviet foreign ministers in the USSR, taking pains to stress that Moscow was not trying to circumvent mediation by the UN secretary general as mandated by Security Council Resolution 598.[46]

Gorbachev's policy changes are consistent with efforts to stress nonmilitary aspects of security and defuse regional conflicts that carry the risk of compromising Soviet–U.S. relations. Personnel shifts have clarified East-West relations and arms control and deemphasized the Third World. Emergence of key government institutions, such as Supreme Soviet committees, indicates the debate on national security will become broader and more intense and that there will be greater scrutiny of issues involving forces and weapons. Nearly every Soviet republic has called for the right to conduct foreign relations independently.

When Yakovlev visited Japan in November 1989 he was careful to describe himself as head of a Supreme Soviet delegation—a body that had recently acquired powers in "actively formulating" policy, according to Soviet commentary.[47] Soviet journalists informed Japanese counterparts that the Supreme Soviet (the Soviet parliament) differed from other Soviet institutions and held radical positions on returning "northern territories." The following year, a leading Soviet commentator, Vsevolod Ovchinnikov, suggested that the territories could be put under UN trusteeship and turned into a Soviet-Japanese economic zone, the first important sign of Soviet flexibility on the issue.[48]

Gorbachev's cadre policy hence has resolved a debate within Soviet circles over the past twenty years dealing with the Third World. Officials have been arguing since the 1960s about whether "socialist progress" could be reversed in states of socialist orientation and whether military institutions played a role in revolution.[49] Soviet academic writings are becoming more sophisticated and such experts as Georgi Mirsky are becoming more critical of the military bureaucracy in Third World states.[50]

Gorbachev has been careful to place skilled politicians at the helm of the foreign ministry and International Policy Commission to ensure loyalty to "new political thinking." Shevardnadze and Yakovlev were two close supporters and, along with Medvedev and Ryzhkov presumably supported the president on most security issues. Extensive personnel changes within the ministry and the International Department probably make it less likely there will be institutional rivalries between state and party instruments of security decision making. Bessmertnykh favors a reformist course in foreign policy, but lacks Shevardnadze's political influence.

Although there is evidence of serious differences within the leadership on East-West relations and arms control, there is no sign of significant controversy on policy toward the Third World and regional settlements. Prior to the party congress, former Politburo member Ligachev and several lesser party figures were critical of Gorbachev's laissez faire policy toward the collapse of communism in Eastern Europe and German unification; others complained about the absence of a "positive response" from the West to Gorbachev's initiatives and issued alarmist views of the balance of power in Europe.[51] Shevardnadze, Yakovlev, and Zaykov defended Gorbachev on all these issues.[52] The discussion of retrenchment and retreat in the Third World has been less polemical and controversial, and does not suggest a leadership debate. Therefore, Shevardnadze's resignation and Yakovlev's fall should not lead to changes in policy toward the Third World.

The diminished role of the military contributes to easier consensus on cutting back presence in the Third World. The military may have doubt about the unilateral test moratorium of 1985 and 1986 and unilateral troop reductions of 1989 and 1990, but there is no evidence of opposition to cutting back assistance and operational deployments in the Third World. Progress toward a chemical arms ban and a strategic weapons agreement in 1990 indicates a continuation of the trend of declining military influence under Gorbachev. Moscow also withdrew thousands of tanks, armored vehicles, and artillery from East Europe in 1989 and 1990.

The president's revamping of the Politburo in July 1990 leaves the major party body as well as the Secretariat without a role in foreign policy decision making and separates the party hierarchy from the government. Only Gorbachev as President of the USSR and General Secretary of the Communist Party will hold top posts in both organizations. The Politburo itself has doubled in size and the regional focus of that body has made it largely irrelevant on matters of national security.

NOTES

1. See Foreign Minister Shevardnadze's foreign policy report to the Supreme Soviet on October 23, 1989, as reported in *Pravda*, October 24, 1989, pp. 2–4; his report to the foreign ministry on the 19th All-Union Conference as reported in *Vestnik Ministerstva Inostrannykh Sel USSR*, No. 15, August 1988, pp. 27–46; and his report to the foreign ministry on May 3, 1987 as reported in *Vestnik Ministerstva Inostrannykh Sel USSR*, No. 1, August 1987, pp. 17–22.

2. *Pravda*, March 15, 1990, p. 1.

3. TASS, August 17, 1989.

4. *The Washington Post*, July 15, 1990, p. 1, "New Soviet Politburo Excludes Senior Figures" by David Remnick.

5. *Documents and Resolutions, 25th Congress of the Communist Party of the Soviet Union*, Moscow, 1976, p. 40.

6. *The New York Times*, June 15, 1973, p. 5.

7. Mohamed Heikal, *The Sphinx and the Commissar*, New York: Harper and Row, 1978, pp. 203–214; also see Anwar Sadat's memoirs.

8. Heikal, *The Sphinx and the Commissar*, pp. 203–214. It must have been particularly embarrassing for General Secretary Brezhnev and the Soviet Politburo in 1972, when Sadat's sudden and surprising decision ordering the removal of the Soviet military advisory presence included the withdrawal of most Soviet-controlled military equipment that had been introduced as a result of decisions made by the Soviet leadership. This equipment included Soviet-piloted MiG-25 interceptors and TU-16 reconnaissance aircraft that had been used to surveil Israeli military positions and had never before been introduced into the Third World.

9. The fact that Brezhnev was willing to undertake significant political and military risk in the "war of attrition" in 1969–1970 is particularly important because only two years earlier, during the Six-day War, he was criticized by the leader of the Moscow party apparatus for failing to take significant steps on behalf of these same Egyptian clients against an Israeli military onslaught. See Harry Gelman, *The Brezhnev Politburo and the Decline of Detente*, Ithaca, NY: Cornell University Press, 1984.

10. Raymond L. Garthoff, "SALT and the Soviet Military," *Problems of Communism*, Vol. XXIV, January–February 1975, p. 29.

11. *Pravda*, March 16, 1989, p. 5.

12. *Pravda*, March 17, 1990, p. 3.

13. *Pravda*, November 27, 1989, p. 2, "At the Defense Council" by V. Izgarshev. Zaykov, who supervises the USSR's military-industrial complex, was the first publicly announced deputy chief of the Defense Council; his absence from the Presidential Council suggests that he is not an ardent supporter of Gorbachev's national security policies.

14. Department of Defense, *Soviet Military Power, 1981*, Washington, DC: U.S. Government Printing Office, 1981, pp. 16–17.

15. Jerry Hough and Merle Fainsod, *How the Soviet Union is Governed*, Cambridge, MA: Harvard University Press, 1979, p. 384.

16. *Pravda*, July 4, 1990, p. 3. Speech by Lev Zaykov to the 28th CPSU Congress at the Kremlin Palace of Congresses in Moscow on July 3, 1990. Reported in Foreign Broadcast Information Service, Soviet Daily Report, July 5, 1990, p. 2.

17. Mathew P. Gallagher, "The Soviet Military Role in Soviet Decision Making," in Michael MccGwire, Ken Booth, and John McDonnell, eds., *Soviet Naval Policy: Objectives and Constraints*, New York: Praeger Publishers, 1975, pp. 40–58.

18. Jeffrey T. Richelson, *Sword and Shield: The Soviet Intelligence and Security Apparatus*, Cambridge, MA: Ballinger Publishing Co., 1986, p. 49.

19. *Pravda*, November 27, 1989, p. 2.

20. *The New York Times*, March 16, 1983, p. 1.

21. *The New York Times*, October 21, 1988, p. 3.

22. Arkady N. Shevchenko, *Breaking with Moscow*, New York: Alfred A. Knopf, 1985, pp. 188–191.

23. TASS, May 23, 1986.

24. *The New York Times*, May 24, 1986, p. 1.

25. Shevardnadze is still held in high regard in the Georgian Republic and traveled to Tbilisi as Gorbachev's personal emissary in the spring of 1989 to

investigate the military attack on a Georgian demonstration that resulted in the deaths of 20 young people, mostly women.

26. Polyakov entered the diplomatric service in 1956 after graduating from Moscow's Institute of Oriental Studies. He was ambassador to South Yemen from 1972 until 1974, and served as ambassador to Egypt from 1974 to 1981, when he was expelled following accusations of meddling in internal politics.

27. Under Gorbachev and Shevardnadze, more prominent roles at both the foreign ministry and the international department are being awarded to such "Americanists" as Georgy Korniyenko, Yuly Vorontsov, Aleksandr Bessmertnykh, and Vadim Loginov.

28. *Izvestia*, July 13, 1989, p. 5.

29. *Pravda*, April 11, 1990, p. 5.

30. Melvin A. Goodman, "The Soviet Union and the Third World: The Military Dimension," in *The Soviet Union and the Third World*, edited by Andrzej Korbonski and Francis Fukuyama, Ithaca, NY: Cornell University Press, 1987, pp. 46–66.

31. The former U.S. chairman of the Joint Chiefs of Staff, Admiral William J. Crowe, recently remarked that "there is no question that we have seen less forward naval deployment" in out-of-area waters, which seems to reflect a pattern in Soviet naval deployment since Gorbachev's accession to power in 1985. The Soviets also did not send a naval task force to the Caribbean for the first time in nearly ten years and have reduced the number of naval reconnaissance aircraft flights to Cuba and Angola. See *The New York Times*, July 17, 1988, p. 1.

32. Mohamad Heikal, *The Road to Ramadan*, London: Collins Publishers, 1975, pp. 165–184.

33. Mohamad Heikal, *The Sphinx and the Commissar*, New York, 1978, p. 11.

34. Jon D. Glassman, *Arms for the Arabs: The Soviet Union and War in the Middle East*, Baltimore: Johns Hopkins University Press, 1975, p. 59.

35. Harry Gelman, *The Brezhnev Politburo and the Decline of Detente*, Ithaca, NY: Cornell University Press, 1984, p. 157.

36. *Directory of USSR Ministry of Foreign Affairs Officials*, Washington, DC: Central Intelligence Agency, July 1987.

37. *The New York Times*, October 6, 1988, p. 3.

38. *Red Star*, March 27, 1989, p. 3.

39. It is noteworthy that in the wake of the Soviet decision to withdraw from Afghanistan, there has been progress on resolving disputes in which Soviet allies have a role, including Angola, Cambodia, and Nicaragua.

40. Melvin A. Goodman and Carolyn McGiffert Ekedahl, "Gorbachev's 'New Directions' in the Middle East," *The Middle East Journal*, Fall 1988, pp. 571–586.

41. Mikhail S. Gorbachev, *Perestroika: New Thinking for Our Country and the World*, New York: Harper and Row, 1987, pp. 173–177.

42. *The New York Times*, September 18, 1987, p. 1. The USSR has vetoed only one UN peacekeeping mission, the United Nations Emergency Force in Israel and Egypt, established after the Camp David agreements in 1978. For the most part, Moscow has resorted until recently to nonpayment of its assessments to demonstrate opposition to such operations.

43. *Pravda*, September 17, 1987, p. 1.

44. *The Washington Post*, August 10, 1989, p. 1, "Bush Offers 'Goodwill' If Hostages Are Freed," by David Hoffman.

45. *Pravda*, March 19, 1988, p. 3; TASS, March 19, 1988.

46. *Pravda*, May 16, 1990, p. 5.

47. TASS, November 13, 1989.

48. *The Washington Post*, July 2, 1990, p. 17, "Soviet Suggests Compromise in Territorial Dispute with Japan" (Reuters).

49. See Elizabth Valkenier, *The Soviet Union and the Third World: An Economic Bind*, New York: Praeger Publishers, 1983; Jerry F. Hough, *The Struggle for the Third World: Soviet Debates and American Options*, Washington, DC: The Brookings Institution, 1986.

50. Georgi Mirsky, *Mirovaya Ekonomiki I Mezhdunarodnyye Otnosheniya*, No. 7, July 1989, pp. 44–54, in Foreign Broadcast Information Service, *Soviet Union Daily Report*, August 22, 1989, pp. 19–26.

51. *Krasnaya Zvezda*, (*Red Star*), June 13, 1990, p. 5.

52. *Pravda*, June 26, 1990, p. 3.

3

Afghanistan

The Soviet invasion of Afghanistan in 1979 and its protracted, painful aftermath were catalysts for change in policy toward the Third World. Military failure was demoralizing; international isolation was a setback to prestige. Moscow's preoccupation with Afghanistan distracted the Kremlin from the unexpected rise of Solidarity in Poland in 1980, a challenge that ultimately led to collapse of the Soviet empire in Eastern Europe.

The USSR's decision to withdraw from Afghanistan in 1988 marked acknowledgment by Moscow that it was impossible to suppress the insurgency, that the Soviet Union could not establish a government that could win even grudging support from the mujahideen. Withdrawal was also an acknowledgment that Afghanistan was an obstacle to Gorbachev's "new thinking" in foreign policy, both East-West relations as well as to long-term objectives in South and Southwest Asia, where a Soviet military presence threatened to leave a permanent scar on Soviet relations. Gorbachev presumably believed withdrawal would improve relations with Pakistan and Iran, benefit those with China and the United States, remove an irritant with India. Indeed India was the key to Moscow's position in the region.

The invasion itself had been carried out with full brutality, whatever the initial behavior of the Kabul regime toward the huge superpower on its border. Rumor had it that the Afghans had killed a high official of the Soviet secret police. Admittedly a small power should behave cautiously in proximity to a large power. But the Soviets chose to execute Prime Minister Hafizullah Amin. Soviet troops participated in the storming of Amin's palace. The full details of what happened have never been disclosed, but they can be imagined, and were imagined, by leaders of all governments in the region. The subsequent effort to destroy the Islamic insurgency was likewise ruthless. . . .

THE INVASION

Most Third World states, physically and psychologically removed from Afghanistan, were impressed by the brutality of the Soviet takeover—particularly the execution of Amin.[1] The ruthless effort to destroy the Islamic insurgency in Afghanistan had repercussions on states in the Middle East and South Asia. Even Soviet clients that had accommodated a Soviet military presence and concluded friendship treaties with the USSR had doubt about the desirability of involvement with Moscow.[2] States bordering the USSR and Afghanistan were suspicious of Soviet objectives in the region. The invasion also compromised relations with the United States and added an obstacle to any improvement in ties with China.

IMPACT ON IMMEDIATE NEIGHBORS

Iran

Soviet presence in Afghanistan was a source of friction, hampering dialogue and feeding suspicion. The Shah opposed the Communist takeover in Kabul in April 1978, and the Khomeini regime condemned intervention in December 1979. Iran eventually took in a million refugees and called for both a Soviet withdrawal and an Islamic solution. Tehran voiced support for the insurgents, permitted groups to operate from Iranian territory, and—according to Soviet media commentary—trained and equipped some of those groups.

Until the departure of Andrei Gromyko as foreign minister in 1985, Soviet media frequently criticized Iran and argued that the insurgency was a creature of the United States, alleged to be simultaneously supporting counterrevolution in Iran. In late May 1983, for the first time, *Izvestia* charged that Iran was allowing insurgents to use its territory as a base of operations.[3] An *Izvestia* article in July contained a detailed indictment of Iranian support for the insurgents and claimed support had been increasing.[4]

At the outset of the intervention, Moscow responded to Iran's activity on behalf of the mujahideen by stepping up military operations on the Afghan-Iranian border. An incursion of Soviet forces into Iranian territory occurred in April 1982, the same month Moscow signed an arms agreement with Iraq and a month after an article in

Pravda revealed frustration with Iran.[5] While the incursion may have been inadvertent, Soviet willingness to operate in proximity to the border revealed increasing sensitivity to Iranian-supported insurgents and decreasing concern about damage to bilateral relations.

Prior to the invasion of Afghanistan the Soviets had used the crisis in U.S.–Iranian relations to strengthen ties to the Khomeini regime and improve their image as defender of "anti-imperialist" revolutionary causes. Ties never became close, and the invasion and occupation revealed latent anti-Sovietism in Iran's new leadership. Not even Moscow's unwillingness to honor its arms agreements with Iraq in the first two years of the Iran-Iraq war persuaded Tehran to seek better relations.

Circumspection toward Moscow is part of Tehran's awareness of the history of Soviet intervention in Iran in this century. In 1920, Soviet forces occupied Gilan—the northernmost province of Persia—to rid the area of British forces. The following year, when Soviet policy shifted from promotion of revolution to collaboration with national governments, the Soviets withdrew. During the Second World War the Soviets occupied all of northern Iran and, along with British forces, secured Iran and the Persian Gulf corridor as an important supply line. The Azerbaijan Democratic Republic was formed in 1945 with Soviet support, but pressure from both the United States and the United Kingdom compelled Soviet forces to withdraw the following year. The Republic collapsed when Iranian troops reentered the area on the pretext of supervising national elections.

The Soviets invoked the 1921 Russian-Persian Treaty to justify occupation of Iran during the Second World War, and would undoubtedly cite it again if they intervened militarily.[6] Article Six of the agreement gave the USSR the right to introduce troops into Iran if a third party should try to carry out a policy of usurpation through intervention or should seek to use Iranian territory as a base against the Soviet Union. The article provided that the Soviets would withdraw if the danger to the USSR were removed. (Article Five of the treaty committed both sides to prevent presence on their territory of forces or organizations that might menace the other side.) The region continues to be a source of instability in the Soviet Union and a potential source of friction in Soviet relations with Iran.

Immediately after seizure of the United States embassy in Tehran in November 1979, the Iranian government announced abrogation of Articles Five and Six of the treaty. The Soviets have not responded to the Iranian action, but Moscow's continuing public affirmation of these articles provides a possible—albeit superficial—rationalization should it choose to intervene in Iran.

The Soviets could persuade themselves of the need to take action against Iran to preempt or respond to U.S. action, in response to a request from a leftist government, or in reaction to a breakup of Iran. There are incentives for such a move—access to energy, ability to press the Gulf states, control of security problems on the border, or ending Iran's aid to Afghan insurgents. As a result, the Pentagon's planning document, the Defense Planning Guidance, for years has outlined a scenario in which a full-scale conflict between the United States and the Soviet Union would begin with a Soviet attack on Iran, intended to extend the Soviet reach to the Persian Gulf.[7]

The disincentives for such an attack are more impressive—confrontation with the United States and European members of NATO, problems of occupying and pacifying Iran, U.S.–West European–Chinese rapprochment. Soviet withdrawal from Afghanistan reduces the possibilities for confrontation between the Soviet Union and Iran and provides opportunities for improved bilateral relations, which both sides appear anxious to pursue.

Pakistan

Moscow's policy in Afghanistan undermined relations with Pakistan, which used the Soviet occupation to move closer to both the United States and China. Pakistan has received three million refugees, served as the staging area for insurgent operations, and moved to the fore of Islamic nations demanding withdrawal of Soviet forces, particularly after Iraq's invasion of Iran in 1980 meant that Baghdad would play a lesser role on behalf of the mujahideen. The invasion of Afghanistan worsened Pakistan's security and increased fear of the USSR. The Soviets tried to play on fear, as well as Pakistan's internal difficulties, to pull that country into accommodation with the new Afghan regime. Overflights of Pakistani territory as well as occasional bombing of mujahideen camps in western Pakistan never threatened Pakistani security; they did cause problems for Pakistan, creating differences in Islamabad over support to the majahideen.

During the Soviet occupation from 1979 to 1989, the Soviets combined blandishment and pressure to encourage Pakistan to limit assistance to the insurgents. Political and military pressure was used to persuade Islamabad that it was "not too late" to cease all aid to the rebels. Moscow increased economic assistance to Pakistan, notwithstanding Islamabad's refusal to consider a settlement to the Afghan problem without early withdrawal of Soviet forces.

Soviet pressure tactics during this period took advantage of the weak central authority in Pakistan, which continued until the death of President Mohammed Zia ul-Haq in 1988 in an apparent assassination. The USSR had threatened "hot pursuit" against Afghan rebels, and there were reports of violations of Pakistani airspace and bombing of refugee camps by Soviet and Afghan aircraft. Soviet commentaries and propaganda broadcasts supported anti-regime elements within Pakistan, particularly the Movement for Restoration of Democracy. Soviet commentary implied that Pakistan's position would be difficult if it did not stop supporting the insurgency, and the apparent explosion on Zia's aircraft fostered conspiracy theories.

Despite accusations, there was no evidence that Moscow's tactics included a campaign to eliminate Zia, heat up the issue of an independent Pushtunistan, or encourage such anti-Pakistani tribal groups as the Baluchis.[8] Pakistani Baluchistan has been in rebellion against the central government for decades, and some Baluchis are willing to probe for Soviet willingness to secure an independent Baluchistan. There was the more farfetched concern that the Soviets would exploit their presence in Afghanistan to try to acquire a port on the Indian Ocean at some Baluchi harbor like Gwadar. In any event, Soviet presence in Afghanistan increased tensions between Afghanistan and Pakistan.

IMPACT ON ADDITIONAL NEIGHBORS

India

India has been one of the most important targets of Soviet attention in the Third World, both as a partner in containing China and as a base of Soviet influence with the nonaligned movement, and Moscow was careful to make sure its presence in Afghanistan would never become more than an irritant in relations. Return of Indira Gandhi to power before the Soviet invasion of Afghanistan was reassuring, for they were confident of her interest in ties and opposition to policies of the United States. The Soviets scheduled high-level visits to India in the 1980s, including the late Defense Minister Dmitri Ustinov in 1984 and former defense minister Marshal Sergei Sokolov in 1986. They continued large-scale shipments of military equipment. Dependence on the Soviet Union for economic and military aid was considerable during this period, matching U.S. military deliveries to Pakistan. Although never comfortable with the Soviet military presence in Afghanistan, India muted its criticism.

India has been far more sensitive to any signs of change in U.S.-Pakistani relations as a result of the Soviet invasion than to the occupation itself. India has opposed greater superpower involvement in South and Southwest Asia and is concerned that U.S. arms sales to Pakistan, including sophisticated F-16 fighter aircraft, would increase prospects for regional instability. Indian media remained almost silent with regard to the Soviet military in Afghanistan but expressed opposition to delivery of U.S. arms to Islamabad and their potential use against India. Moscow played to this concern by highlighting U.S. sales of "sophisticated" arms to Islamabad and charging Pakistan with a buildup of forces and exacerbation of tension along the Indo-Pakistani border. In fact there was no evidence of Pakistani deployments on its western border with Afghanistan during the Soviet occupation of its neighbor, and ample evidence of increased Pakistani military presence on its eastern border with India.

During the Soviet military presence in Afghanistan, India was concerned that Soviet pressure on Pakistan could threaten the status of Islamabad as a buffer between the USSR and India. Presumably the Soviet leadership was well aware of this Indian view and shared New Delhi's belief that Soviet-Indian relations were best served by distance between Soviet and Indian forces. India remains convinced that, over the long run, Pakistan should be preoccupied more with the threat from India than a threat from the Soviet Union, which would lead to loss of leverage for India in Pakistani national security decisions. Any Soviet presence at the Khyber Pass would be worrisome to India as well as Pakistan, and presumably lead elements of the Indian political elite to explore alternatives to dependence on the Soviet Union.

Although Indian concerns with the Soviet presence in Afghanistan did not drive New Delhi to the United States, the Rajiv Gandhi government did try to improve dialogue with both the United States and the People's Republic of China. Soviet presence in Afghanistan as well as increased superpower involvement in the Indian Ocean appeared to convince Gandhi of the importance of reducing tensions with Pakistan and Bangladesh. In 1988 he made his first trips to China and Pakistan. The Indians made fewer public references to their friendship and cooperation treaty with the USSR, signed in 1971, perhaps as a result of the Soviet Union's use of a similar treaty with Afghanistan to justify the invasion in 1979.

Alternatively, it is possible that Rajiv Gandhi's opening to China and Pakistan, which coincided with the "new thinking" in the USSR, was a reflection of interest in matching improved Soviet relations with China and anticipation of Soviet military withdrawal. In any event, Gandhi saw the need for flexibility.

The Islamic Community

The Islamic community was virtually unanimous in opposition to the Soviet presence in Afghanistan, and Soviet relations with Iran, Pakistan, Saudi Arabia, and the conservative states of the Persian Gulf became more difficult. Most Arab states either signed the initial request for a Security Council meeting to condemn the Soviet presence or expressed indignation in some form. Each year for nearly ten years the Islamic Conference Organization condemned the Soviet presence and demanded unconditional withdrawal.

Only Libya, South Yemen, and Syria—all of which were dependent on the USSR for military assistance—refused to support the resolutions; only South Yemen and Syria recognized Kabul before the withdrawal in 1989. Syria's diplomatic isolation, unpopular involvement in Lebanon, and dependence on Soviet military support tempered reaction to Afghanistan. Libya's preoccupation with the U.S. "threat" offset what might have been a natural empathy for Islamic insurgents in Afghanistan. The war between Iran and Iraq forced Baghdad to moderate opposition to the Soviet action, although the invasion reinforced Iraq's mistrust of Moscow and strained an already cool relationship.

Moscow's oppression of Islamic forces in Afghanistan reinforced fear of communism in the region and did damage to the USSR. The invasion and occupation drew international attention to the drama in Southwest Asia, distracting attention from the Arab-Israeli conflict. Conservative Arab states, particularly Saudi Arabia, contributed hard currency and military assistance to the mujahideen, which meant that the decision to invade Afghanistan created an "alliance" between the United States, China, Israel, Egypt, and conservative Persian Gulf states against Moscow.[9]

Saudi Arabia believed that the Soviet invasion of Afghanistan was designed in part to encircle the conservative oil producing nations of the Persian Gulf and to gain access to oil. For the Saudis this was the essential explanation for Soviet military activities in Ethiopia, South Yemen, and North Yemen, and for Soviet readiness to take advantage of discord in Iran. The war on the Horn of Africa in 1977, the Camp David dialogue in 1978, ouster of the Shah in 1979, and seizure of the Grand Mosque in the early 1980s added to Riyadh's anxiety about instability in Southwest Asia and the Gulf.

The invasion of Afghanistan marked a setback in Moscow's efforts to reestablish relations with Saudi Arabia, broken in the late 1930s. Since the Arab-Israeli war in 1973, the Soviets have signaled willingness to resume a diplomatic dialogue, but the Saudis have rebuffed these efforts. Both *Pravda* and *Izvestia* have emphasized that the USSR and Saudi Arabia have never had any "irreconcilable" conflicts, and Soviet press commentaries occasionally contain long and sympathetic accounts of Saudi policies and play upon Saudi disenchantment with the Camp David accords.[10] In 1988 the Soviets and Saudis exchanged high-level diplomatic visits for the first time in fifty years.

Moscow presumably was not surprised at Saudi Arabia's hostile response to the invasion, including willingness to agree with the United States over military assistance to the Contras and hostage rescue efforts with Iran. The Soviets probably did not anticipate Saudi ingenuity in organizing the Islamic Conferences that condemned the USSR, called for assistance to the insurgents, and stamped the regime in Kabul as unacceptable. Riyadh became a more competent opponent of Soviet interests, willing to counter Soviet-supported radical regimes in the Arabian peninsula, anxious for a "special relationship" with the United States. Soviet concern appeared in Moscow's frequent view that the United States was seeking an alliance including Pakistan and the Gulf states.[11]

IMPACT ON THE UNITED STATES AND CHINA

Invasion of Afghanistan marked a turning point in policies of the Carter administration toward the USSR. President Jimmy Carter viewed intervention as a "sharp escalation" in use of force to serve Soviet interests and described his message on the hotline as the "sharpest message of my Presidency."[12] Carter was furious with Brezhnev. In off-the-cuff remarks in a televised interview he claimed the invasion had "made a more dramatic change in my own opinion of what the Soviets' ultimate goals are than anything they've done in the previous time I've been in office."[13]

Several days later Carter approved a series of measures against the Soviets that probably came as a surprise. He postponed the opening of consulates general in Kiev and New York, curtailed Soviet fishing privileges in American waters, imposed restrictions on sale of high technology and strategic items, and declared a grain embargo. The U.S.–led effort for a Western boycott of the 1980 Olympic Games in Moscow symbolized Moscow's international isolation. In keeping with his view of the invasion as the "greatest threat to peace since the Second World War" he withdrew the SALT II treaty from the Senate, increased military aid to Pakistan, and generally placed a freeze on Soviet–U.S. relations.

The invasion added another obstacle to improvement in Sino-Soviet relations and led the Chinese leaders to insist that the danger from the USSR was far greater for the United States and Europe than for

China.[14] The invasion, along with increased size of the Soviet fleet in the Pacific and beginning of deployment of SS-20 medium-range missiles, appeared as part of a Soviet strategic thrust south from Central Asia to link Soviet military capabilities in Europe with forces in Asia. The Chinese reaction was far less emotional and far more realistic than the United States', but the United States and the PRC were to cooperate in providing military assistance to the mujahideen.

THE IMPACT OF WITHDRAWAL FROM AFGHANISTAN ON SOVIET POLICY

The decision to withdraw from Afghanistan was taken by a Politburo that no longer included such supporters of the invasion as Leonid Brezhnev, Yuri Andropov, and Dmitri Ustinov. At the twenty-seventh Soviet party congress in 1986, Gorbachev stressed that Moscow "would like in the nearest future to bring the Soviet forces...back to their homeland" and that a "schedule has been worked out with the Afghan side for a step-by-step withdrawal."[15] This marked the first time that any Soviet leader had indicated that Moscow had a plan for a pullout. Several weeks before, two high-ranking members of the International Department indicated that the Soviets wanted to withdraw as soon as possible. Following the congress, Politburo member Geydar Aliyev and First Deputy Foreign Minister Korniyenko endorsed Gorbachev's remarks. As early as 1986 it appeared that Gorbachev had achieved a consensus for the beginning of withdrawal.

Friction between the Soviet and Afghan regimes on the issue of withdrawal, and the political nature of the Kabul government, indicated a Soviet decision to reduce forces had been broached and that the Afghans were resisting. No Soviet leader met with Babrak Karmal during the Soviet party congress in February and March 1986, and Karmal's speech to the congress made no mention of a withdrawal. Soviet messages to the Afghans on national day began to drop customary references to the "leading role" of the ruling People's Democratic Party of Afghanistan or "revolutionary solidarity." Later Gorbachev replaced Babrak Karmal as general secretary of the Afghan communist party and announced that six regiments (8,000 troops) would withdraw in October. The new leader, Najibullah, was encouraged to seek a compromise with the mujahideen and call for "national reconciliation."

Two years later, on February 8, 1988, Gorbachev announced the first date for withdrawal and offered several important concessions— reduction in the pullout schedule by two months and a willingness to remove a large number of troops in the early stages of the withdrawal regardless of whether the Afghanis managed an interim agreement with Pakistan. High-level Soviet negotiators began to meet for the first time with Afghan guerrilla leaders, and indirect talks between Kabul and Islamabad resumed in Geneva with U.S. and Soviet delegations standing by. Gorbachev's ability to use his first years of leadership to revamp the Politburo and Defense Council had contributed to his success in arranging withdrawal, completed on schedule in February 1989. (See Chapter 2 for Gorbachev's extensive reshuffling of Moscow's decision-making community.)

In a stunning criticism of General Secretary Brezhnev's policy decisions, Foreign Minister Shevardnadze told a plenary session of the Supreme Soviet in October 1989 that introduction of forces into Afghanistan "had violated norms of behavior, and gone against common human interests."[16] Shevardnadze charged that invasion had violated Soviet "legislation and intraparty and civic norms and ethics." The foreign minister, who has become Gorbachev's point man in a comprehensive assault on Brezhnev's policy, maintained that the Politburo's decision in 1979 was "made behind the party's and the people's back. They were presented with a *fait accompli.*"

IRAN

Withdrawal from Afghanistan, the end to the Iran-Iraq war, and the death of Khomeini in June 1989 have begun to ameliorate Soviet-Iranian differences. The succession crisis in Iran continues to be unpredictable but the emergence of Akbar Rafsanjani as president and appointment of Ali Khamenei as acting commander-in-chief of the armed forces were setbacks for the radicals and suggested an opportunity for improved Soviet-Iranian relations. The release of two American hostages in 1990 indicated that Rafsanjani was looking for ways to end Iran's isolation.

Rafsanjani and Khamenei are close and appear to agree on expanding relations with Western Europe and reducing friction with the Soviet Union. Responsibility for additional internal security measures for Interior Minister Abdollah Nuri, who is considered a moderate, suggests greater stability for the post-Khomeini era. At the least there could be more consistency in foreign policy, making it easier for the Kremlin to insinuate itself with the leadership.

Moscow's patience during the worst of Khomeini's anti-Soviet activities—stopping shipment of natural gas, closing the Soviet consulate at Rasht, and expelling embassy personnel—could pay dividends. Ever since the late Andrei Gromyko's elevation to the Soviet presidency in July 1985 and emergence of Shevardnadze as foreign minister, policy toward Iran has been more pragmatic. In 1986, First Deputy Foreign Minister Georgi Korniyenko visited Tehran, the highest-level Soviet official to visit Iran since the revolution. Prime Minister Nikolai Ryzhkov received Iranian Oil Minister Aqazadeh in the summer of 1986, which led to discussion of a resumption of natural gas shipments to the USSR and signing of an economic cooperation agreement in December.[17] Agreement to resume supplies of natural gas to the Soviet Union in 1990 was signed in November 1989 and deliveries resumed in May 1990.[18]

Iran appears interested in stabilizing the bilateral relationship. In early 1989, Khomeini wrote a conciliatory letter to Gorbachev—his only written message to a foreign leader—and later in the year, after his death, Ali Akbar Hashemi Rafsanjani made the first state visit to Moscow. Rafsanjani's insistence on proceeding with the trip suggested that the leadership in Tehran had decided to interpret Khomeini's will as an endorsement of improved relations. The will, most of it written in 1982 and sealed in 1983, is critical of Soviet history and warns heirs to remain "independent of either the atheist East or the infidel oppressor West."[19] Khomeini called for "cordial relations with those governments that are not intent on interference in the internal affairs of our country," which could provide rationalization for better relations with the Soviet Union.

Rafsanjani's visit took place from June 20 to 23, 1989, and marked improvement in relations. The sides signed an economic reconstruction agreement that will allow Tehran to purchase machinery, plants, and technology in return for deliveries of natural gas from the soon-to-be completed Kangan refinery on Iran's Persian Gulf coast near the Strait of Hormuz.[20] This marks the largest credit that Tehran has signed with a government since the revolution in 1979 as well as reversal in Tehran's policy of avoiding foreign involvement in Iran's rebuilding.

Gorbachev held two meetings with Rafsanjani and the communiqué that marked the visit described sessions as held in an atmosphere of "mutual understanding" with a "useful and constructive" exchange of views.[21] At the dinner that Gorbachev held for Rafsanjani, the Iranian leader was even more sanguine than his Soviet counterpart in describing the current bilateral relationship, and upon return to Tehran characterized the visit as "absolutely positive." Soviet commentary has been more restrained, presumably in deference to the Iraqi government as well as conservative Arab states that would look askance upon rapprochement between the Soviet Union and Iran.

In a Declaration of Principles, Moscow agreed to "strengthen" Iran's "defense capability."[22] Both sides chose to play down the possibility of Soviet military sales or assistance. They stressed progress in economic agreements, which call for credits to Iran worth $2 billion and repayment in natural gas. Soviet media have been reluctant to discuss regional issues covered during the talks, but Rafsanjani noted that Moscow and Tehran were "completely in unison" on a settlement of Iran's conflict with Iraq and in "complete agreement" on principles of an Afghan settlement.[23] Soviet commentary also had indicated that Moscow was supportive of Iran's position on negotiations with Iraq.

The following month Shevardnadze visited Tehran for two days, ostensibly to enlist Tehran's support for the Soviet-backed regime in Afghanistan in a negotiated settlement.[24] Unlike the Rafsanjani visit to Moscow, the two sides recorded their support for the ceasefire in Afghanistan and an "inter-Afghan dialogue" to establish a "broad-based government." Iran was less forthcoming responding to Shevardnadze's request for assistance in releasing Soviet prisoners captured by Afghan insurgents.

Iran has its reasons to be careful about improving relations with the USSR. Tehran will continue to need Western economic assistance to achieve reconstruction as well as a Western political dialogue to avoid becoming isolated in the region. Indeed, Iranian media have indicated interest in improving relations with the West, and an editorial in the *Tehran Times*, timed to coincide with Rafsanjani's arrival in Moscow, warned against "moving too fast" in relations with the USSR, so as not to contradict the policy of "neither East nor West."[25] In addition to Soviet caution in discussing bilateral relations, the Soviet political observer Aleksandr Bovin has questioned the wisdom of "weapons sales" to Iran, arguing that in return for minor short-term gains Moscow would be promoting "instability" by "continuing to pump weapons into the most restless region" in the world.[26] Nevertheless, the delivery of SA-5 surface-to-air missiles and MiG-29 fighter aircraft in the fall of 1990 indicates that a military aid agreement has been signed.

Moscow is particularly concerned to improve relations to ensure that current frictions between Armenia and Azerbaijan do not become problems for the USSR and Iran. Tehran thus far has shown no interest in exploiting Moscow's ethnic problems, and the Soviets have allowed increasing cross-border communications between Azeris, a key demand for Soviet Azeris. The Kremlin also has offered to mediate the dispute between Iran and Iraq, and pressed Baghdad to adopt a more constructive stance in the negotiations. The Islamic Republic News Agency (IRNA) reported in January 1990 for the first time that Tehran would "look positively" at any Soviet offer to "intercede" between Iran and Iraq.[27]

IMPACT ON IMMEDIATE NEIGHBORS

Pakistan

Even before the invasion, the Soviets found arms sales to India an obstacle to relations with Pakistan. The Soviets were neutral in the Indo-Pakistani war of 1965 and Premier Alexei Kosygin mediated the Tashkent agreement in 1966, but these developments did not lead to improvement in Soviet-Pakistani relations. The Soviets offered economic assistance to Pakistan after the 1971 war over Bangladesh, but Islamabad continued to see the Soviet-Indian military relationship as a security threat and after the invasion signed a six-year, $3.2 billion arms deal with the United States.[28] Pakistani distrust of India, and the Indo-Soviet military relationship led to a Pakistani request to purchase sixty U.S. F-16 fighters to supplement the forty F-16s in the Pakistani inventory.[29]

Withdrawal from Afghanistan leaves a Pakistan more aligned with the United States and China, more a military threat to its neighbors, and steps closer to nuclear capability. In testimony to the Senate Governmental Affairs Committee on May 18, 1989, William H. Webster, Director of the Central Intelligence Agency, publicly addressed the issue of nuclear proliferation in South Asia. He noted Pakistan was "engaged in developing a nuclear capability" and that the missile and atomic research programs of Pakistan and India had "all the earmarks of a race."[30] During her visit to the United States in June 1989, Prime Minister Benazir Bhutto of Pakistan assured President Bush that Islamabad was "not interested in making a nuclear device" and favored a nuclear test ban treaty "with other countries in the region."[31]

The invasion was responsible for reversal of the U.S. decision to stop military deliveries to Islamabad in response to the latter's nuclear program; from 1979 to 1989 the United States extended $3 billion in military and economic assistance to Pakistan. Moscow's threats against Pakistan during the Soviet occupation of Afghanistan, as well as Pakistani support for the Afghan insurgency, were the justifications for U.S. assistance.

The Soviet decision to withdraw, and the sudden death of Pakistani President Zia ul-Haq in 1988, gave Moscow reason to believe a turning point had been reached in Soviet-Pakistani relations. Zia's immediate successors, Ghulam Ishaq Kham and then Benazir Bhutto, shared Zia's opposition to the pro-Soviet regime in Kabul and the commitment to repatriate three million Afghan refugees in Pakistan. She made clear her intention to continue ties to the United States and China, and traveled to both Beijing and Washington during her first year in office.

Distrust of India and Soviet-Indian relations led her to request the U.S. F-16 fighters.[32] Moscow threatened that delivery of F-16s could lead to transfer of MiG-29 fighter aircraft to Afghanistan, along with other systems that it thus far had refrained from supplying.

Moscow and Islamabad have reasons for stabilizing relations. The USSR would favor accommodation between Islamabad and the regime in Kabul and an end to military assistance to the mujahideen. Pakistan requires stable relations with the Soviet Union so the current Nawaz Sharif government can concentrate on problems with India. Neither Moscow nor Islamabad would benefit from deterioration in Soviet-Pakistani relations and both would have difficulties with a radical Islamic regime in Kabul. A Soviet initiative to improve relations is likely, and the two sides are in agreement on avoiding controversial debates on Afghanistan at the United Nations as well as Bhutto's dialogue with Rajiv Gandhi, who in 1988 became the first Indian prime minister to visit Pakistan in twenty-eight years. Both Shevardnadze and Vorontsov visited Pakistan before the Soviets completed their troop withdrawal from Afghanistan.

India

Withdrawal will make it easier for Moscow to achieve its objectives toward India, which have remained unchanged for two decades: a stable relationship regardless of the government in New Delhi; cooperation against the United States, China and Pakistan in South Asia; and encouragement of Indian support for Soviet positions within the United Nations and the Nonaligned Movement. India's interest as the major regional power in South Asia as well as memory of wars with Pakistan over forty years provide leverage for Moscow. Indo-Pakistan relations improved after the withdrawal, but the continued dispute over Kashmir, concern over delivery of sophisticated arms from the United States and the Soviet Union, and use of foreign technology to develop ballistic missile programs in both India and Pakistan have created tensions once again.

Soviet arms transfers have been the key to Moscow's success in the Third World, evident in the case of India. New Delhi has not only received MiG-23 and MiG-29 fighter and interceptor aircraft, T-72 tanks, and BMP armored personnel carriers, but received equipment before members of the Warsaw Pact. Soviet defense minister Dmitri Ustinov agreed in 1983 to sell the MiG-29 to India before the aircraft has been delivered to the Soviet air force.[33] The Soviets allowed the Indian government to coproduce the MiG-29 to stop discussion between India and France for purchase of Mirage aircraft. India began receiving T-72 tanks before some of Moscow's Warsaw Pact allies, and entered into a coproduction scheme for this system.[34] India is the first Third World country to lease nuclear submarines from the USSR and has at least a dozen diesel submarines in its fleet.

The Soviets will have to continue these arrangements with the Indians because, as Rajan Menon has noted, Moscow is facing competition from West European states in arms transfers to New Delhi.[35] Over the past decade, India has purchased Jaguar and Sea Harrier aircraft from the United Kingdom, Type 1500 submarines from West Germany, and Mirage fighters from France. Several years ago India began producing the Franco-German Milan anti-tank missile. Moscow's willingness to sell both MiG-29 aircraft and T-80 tanks to India before introducing them into Soviet forces is the strongest indication of Kremlin concern with the diversification of Indian arms purchases. It is almost certain, therefore, that the Soviet program of giving pride of place to India in delivery of frontline weapons will continue under Gorbachev.

Arms transfers enabled Moscow to withstand uncertainty in Soviet-Indian relations that followed assassination of Indira Gandhi in October 1984. At that time her son Rajiv appeared less ideological and likely to seek more balanced relations between the Soviet Union and the United States. Moscow's willingness to supply India with sophisticated equipment at excellent prices as well as production licenses for some frontline weapons systems stabilized Soviet-Indian relations after Indira Gandhi's assassination.

Gorbachev quickly made clear in 1985 that India's position was secure as one of Moscow's most important Third World clients. His first visit to an Asian country or any Third World nation was to India in November 1986. Whereas Washington was slow to pursue a dialogue with Rajiv, Gorbachev reassured New Delhi that Soviet-Indian relations were important. He expressed Moscow's concern with India over U.S. supplies of military assistance to Pakistan and affirmed that the USSR "naturally sees the need to strengthen India's defensive capabilities."[36]

During his visit to New Delhi in 1986, Gorbachev received Indian support for many of the themes of "new thinking." He and Gandhi signed the "Delhi Declaration," setting forth principles of peaceful coexistence, and both subsequently touted the statement as the guiding document for international effort to promote peace. After Gorbachev's second visit to India in November 1988, Soviet commentary stressed the importance of India to the Soviet presence in South Asia.[37]

THE IMPACT OF SOVIET WITHDRAWAL ON THE UNITED STATES AND CHINA

Soviet intervention in Afghanistan was decisive in the decline of Soviet–U.S. relations, particularly failure of the United States to ratify the SALT II agreement in 1979, as well as worsening of the Sino-Soviet dispute. Prior to Gorbachev's accession, Soviet behavior in the Third World was not linked to Soviet–U.S. relations. At the party congress of the Czechoslovak Communist Party in 1981 Brezhnev ridiculed what he termed an attempt by the United States to set "preconditions" for negotiation between the superpowers and argued that the United States would view Soviet leaders as "simpletons" if they demanded that the U.S. abandon bases abroad or end arming of "dictatorial terrorist regimes."[38] Brezhnev, like his predecessors, viewed improved relations with the United States as an opportunity for advancing into the Third World.

After the invasion, Soviet officials began to address the need for "rules" for superpowers in the Third World, and two months before his death, during a visit to India, Brezhnev suggested that NATO and the Warsaw Pact refrain from extending operations in Asia, Africa, and Latin America.[39] Brezhnev's successor, Yuri Andropov, showed interest in containing regional conflict at the outset of his term, avoiding mention of Moscow's traditionally favored "socialist-oriented" clients in the Third World and emphasizing dire economic conditions in the Third World without indication of additional assistance from the Soviet Union.

It was not until Gorbachev, however, that Moscow began overhaul of its policy toward Asia, including withdrawal from Afghanistan. (See Chapter 2 for a discussion of the Soviet decision that led to the withdrawal in 1988–1989.) As a result, the relationship with China finally was normalized, an entrée has developed to the states of Southeast Asia, and relations with the countries of the southern Pacific have become more stable. The end to the break between the USSR and China will help end the feeling in Asia that the Soviet Union is an outsider, a European power trying to manipulate Asian politics against Beijing. The end to the Sino-Soviet rift, for which Gorbachev and Shevardnadze deserve a major share of the credit, makes it more difficult for North Korea to play the USSR against China and removes the rationale for excluding the Soviet Union from discussion of the Korean problem.

The effect of Soviet withdrawal has been improvement in Soviet-American relations. Both the Carter and Reagan administrations had held bilateral relations hostage to the Soviet presence in Afghanistan, and cooperation between Moscow and Washington prior to the completion of the withdrawal in the early part of 1989 enhanced dialogue on a variety of issues. It is possible that the Soviet–U.S. cooperation instrumental to signing of the Angolan ceasefire in 1988 could not have taken place without collaboration over Afghanistan.

Soviet articles and statements over the past several years indicate that Gorbachev has revived measures to reduce Soviet assets and commitments in the Third World as well as to arrange regional solutions, preferably in conjunction with the United States. In addition to completing withdrawal from Afghanistan, the Soviets have encouraged such clients as Cuba and Vietnam to reduce military involvements in Angola and Cambodia, and have proposed Soviet–U.S. guarantees for security in Central America. Gorbachev's patience and diplomacy in dealing with Khomeini's hostility and indifference over the past ten years should allow Moscow to capitalize on withdrawal from Afghanistan to establish more correct relations with Khomeini's successors. Moscow presumably will turn to the Middle East and South Asia where there has been concern with proliferation of sophisticated weapons systems. (See Chapter 5 for a discussion of Soviet interest in the creation of a "military risk–reduction center" and a "nuclear-free and chemical-free zone" in the Middle East.)

PROSPECTS FOR SOUTH ASIA AND SOUTHWEST ASIA

The increased pace of Soviet-Iranian relations presumably will continue over the near term. Iran will continue to require Soviet assistance for reconstruction and the USSR will require support in any regional effort to hamper assistance to the mujahideen in Afghanistan. Soviet officials have gone out of their way to contrast Tehran's "realistic approach" to an Afghan settlement and Islamabad's "obstructionist course."[40] A long-term U.S. presence in the Persian Gulf will make it easier for Tehran to justify improved relations with Moscow.

Rafsanjani's visit to Moscow in the summer of 1989 provided evidence of interests of both sides in improving relations. More than any event since the Islamic revolution and the Soviet invasion, the visit marked the end of Iran's diplomatic isolation and Moscow's ability to improve its position in Southwest Asia. Moscow may believe that improved relations would prevent Iran from exploiting the religious interest of Soviet Muslims at a time of ethnic and religious unrest in the Soviet Union. Both sides have their reasons for improved ties.

The outlook for the Soviet-Pakistani relationship is more problematic. The Soviets will benefit from Pakistan's requirement for Soviet cooperation in any effort by Islamabad to improve relations with India. After withdrawal Pakistan must concentrate on consolidating a new government that faces a complex regional situation and economic problems. As Thomas P. Thornton has argued, Benazir Bhutto was an "unproven quantity" and failed to establish a political agenda, and her successor—Nawaz Sharif—will probably resume the Zia policy.[41] Withdrawal from Afghanistan also has worsened the dialogue between the Afghan resistance and Islamabad and the Pakistani military and intelligence communities. Bhutto had no control over the worsening of relations between Pakistan and Afghanistan, and the dispute with India over Kashmir.

On the negative side there is a history of Soviet-Pakistani hostility fostered by close Soviet-Indian military relations and Soviet intimidation of Islamabad during the cross-border pursuit of the mujahideen from 1979 to 1989. Soviet economic aid to Pakistan has continued and there has been a Soviet offer to build a nuclear power station in Pakistan, but a distrust toward the Soviet Union continues. A Soviet initiative can be anticipated as part of Gorbachev's "new thinking" toward Asia as outlined in speeches at Vladivostok in 1986 and Krasnoyarsk in 1988, but Islamabad is unlikely to respond to any Soviet move that could compromise dependence on China and the United States.[42]

India will continue to be the focus of Soviet attention, for strategic and regional reasons. India is important to the USSR for containing the United States and China and expanding Soviet influence in the Third World and particularly among the nonaligned movement. India needs the Soviet Union to contain China and Pakistan and insulate the region from the United States. Soviet military assistance allows India to act as the power in the region, and Indian political and diplomatic support gives the Soviet Union entrée in South Asia. Soviet-Indian relations will remain close and relations of both India and the Soviet Union with the other states of the region will continue to be influenced by these relations.

Moscow's interest in reducing its defense budget as well as withdrawal of forces from Afghanistan, Mongolia, and the Sino-Soviet frontier indicate that Soviet leaders have redefined the threat and no longer believe that a greater military presence in South and Southwest Asia can assure security. When Gorbachev told the United Nations General Assembly in December 1988, that the "bell of each regional conflict tolls for all of us" he appeared to be reflecting disillusion with Soviet globalism as well as recognition that minor confrontations could lead to disputes among the superpowers.[43]

The Soviet decision to withdraw forces from Afghanistan, a Soviet client state with a Marxist government on the Soviet border, will send a signal to other Third World clients that Gorbachev believes there are limits to military force on behalf of these states. Presumably the Soviet withdrawal in 1989 made a contribution to the thinking of such Third World states as Cuba and Vietnam that Moscow was serious about its decision to seek political solutions to military problems and reduce deployment of Soviet forces. The decision to withdraw could prove a turning point in Soviet behavior in the Third World.

NOTES

1. It took nearly ten years for the USSR to acknowledge that Soviet troops had played a direct part in the military coup in Kabul in 1979. In an interview which appeared in *Izvestia* on May 4, 1989, the chief researcher of the Institute of Oriental Studies, Yuri Gankovsky recorded that Soviet troops had participated in the storming of Amin's palace although he did not address the issue of how Amin was killed. Over the past year, Soviet media have discussed some of the "mistakes" make in Afghanistan and have pointed to the "stagnation" of the leadership of Leonid Brezhnev as the major cause of the Soviet invasion. (*Izvestia*, May 4, 1989; *The New York Times*, May 5, 1989, p. 5.) In a speech in October 1989, Foreign Minister Shevardnadze referred to the Soviet decision to introduce troops into Afghanistan as having "involved gross violations" of Soviet legislation and "intraparty and civic norms and ethics. (*Pravda*, October 24, 1989, pp. 2–4)

2. Syria, Iraq, South Yemen, North Yemen, India.

3. *Izvestia*, May 23, 1983, p. 5.

4. *Izvestia*, July 25, 1983, p. 5.

5. *Pravda*, March 15, 1982, p. 3.

6. Alvin Z. Rubinstein, *Soviet Policy Toward Turkey, Iran, and Afghanistan*, New York: Praeger Publishers, 1982, p. 60.

7. *The New York Times*, November 26, 1989, p. 18. "Soviet Changes Mean Earlier Word of Attack," by Michael R. Gordon and Stephen Engelberg.

8. Henry S. Bradsher, *Afghanistan and the Soviet Union*, Durham, NC: Duke Press Policy Studies, 1983, pp. 254–255.

9. In the first authoritative account of the high-level military debate surrounding the decision making of the invasion of Afghanistan, General of the Army Valentin I. Varrenikov, a deputy defense minister, stated in an interview with the weekly magazine *Ogonyok* that the General Staff was opposed to the invasion but was overruled by Defense Minister Dmitri F. Ustinov. Varrenikov was the senior defense ministry official in Afghanistan for the last four years of the war and, after the Soviets completed the withdrawal of forces, was named commander of ground forces. Varrenikov added that Marshal Nikolai Ogarkov, then chief of the general staff, and Marshal Sergei F. Akhromeyev, who later became chief of the staff, also opposed the intervention. (Article in *The New York Times*, March 19, 1989, p. 27, Bill Keller.)

10. *Pravda*, June 11, 1982; *Izvestia*, October 27, 1983, p. 5.

11. *Pravda*, May 9, 1984, p. 5.

12. Jimmy Carter, *Keeping Faith: Memoirs of a President*, New York: Bantam Books, 1982, p. 472. Zbigniew Brzezinski takes credit in his memoirs for drafting

the hotline message; Secretary of State Cyrus Vance does not mention the message in his memoirs.

13. *The New York Times*, January 1, 1980, p. 17, "Transcript of President's Interview with Frank Reynolds on Soviet Reply." Carter's statements were not included in the official *Weekly Compilation of Presidential Documents* and were not reported in the memoirs of Carter, Brzezinski, or Vance.

14. Paul H. B. Godwin, "China's Defense Modernization," *Air University Review*, November–December 1981, p. 6.

15. The speeches and proceedings of the party congress were reviewed from the daily reports on the Soviet Union of the United States Foreign Broadcast Information Service (FBIS) for the period February 25–March 14, 1986. They were taken in most cases from TASS reports or Radio Moscow. General Secretary Gorbachev spoke to the congress on the opening day.

16. *Pravda*, October 23, 1989, pp. 2–4.

17. *The Washington Post*, August 26, 1986, p. 22.

18. TASS, November 4, 1989.

19. See FBIS Middle East June 7, 1989, pp. 47–53, for Khomeini broadcast by Tehran radio on June 5, 1989. Also see *The Washington Post*, June 8, 1989, p. 21.

20. *The Washington Post*, July 3, 1989, p. 1, "Rebuilding Plan to Cost $15 Billion, Tehran Says" by Patrick E. Tyler.

21. *Pravda*, June 24, 1989, p. 5.

22. *Pravda*, June 23, 1989, p. 5.

23. IRNA, June 24, 1989. Tehran radio interview with Rafsanjani.

24. *Izvestia*, August 3, 1989, p. 5.

25. *Tehran Times*, June 20, 1989.

26. Soviet television service in Russian, July 2, 1989, in *Foreign Broadcast Information Service, Daily Report: Soviet Union* (hereafter FBIS-SU) July 7, 1989, p. 25.

27. IRNA, January 11, 1990.

28. Menon, *Soviet Power and the Third World*, p. 223.

29. *The New York Times*, June 7, 1989, p. 3. "Bush and Bhutto Agree on Afghan Aid," by Bernard Weinraub.

30. Congressional testimony by William H. Webster, Director of Central Intelligence, to the Senate Governmental Affairs Committee on May 18, 1989. Also see *The New York Times*, May 19, 1989, p. 19. "CIA Chief Wary of Pakistani Nuclear Program," by Stephen Engelberg.

31. *The Washington Post*, June 7, 1989, p. 17. "Bhutto Denies Pakistan Plans Nuclear Bomb," by David B. Ottaway.

32. *The New York Times*, June 7, 1989, p. 3, "Bush and Bhutto Agree on Afghan Aid," Bernard Weinraub.

33. *The New York Times*, September 25, 1984, p. 7.

34. Andrew Cockburn, *The Threat: Inside the Soviet Military Machine*, New York: Random House, 1983, p. 83.

35. See Rajan Menon, *Soviet Power and the Third World*, New Haven: Yale University Press, 1986.

36. *Pravda*, January 5, 1987, p. 6, "A Big Step Forward: Thoughts Following M.S. Gorbachev's Visit to India," by Yevgeniy Primakov.

37. *Pravda*, November 23, 1988, p. 1.

38. *Pravda*, April 8, 1981, p. 3.

39. *Pravda*, September 18, 1982, p. 5.

40. *Pravda*, April 1, 1989, p. 5.

41. Thomas P. Thornton, "The New Phase in U.S.–Pakistan Relations," *Foreign Affairs*, Vol. 68, No. 2, pp. 142–159.

42. Carolyn Ekedahl and Melvin Goodman, "Gorbachev's 'New Directions' in Asia," *Journal of Northeast Asian Studies*, September 1989, pp. 3–24.

43. *Pravda*, December 8, 1988, pp. 1–2.

4

Limits to Power

Gorbachev's inheritance in the Third World included successes in Cuba, Syria, and Vietnam, as well as setbacks in Egypt, Guinea, Somalia, and the Sudan. More importantly, the new Soviet leadership faced problems that promised to become more intractable. Inability to train and discipline the Afghan army and Soviet-Afghan inability to limit the insurgency were reasons for troop withdrawal in 1989. Operational planning had not helped Arab client regimes against the Israelis, nor had it led to sustained success for Ethiopian forces against the Eritreans. The counterinsurgencies in Angola, Mozambique, Nicaragua, and Vietnam had created economic problems beyond Soviet capability to repair.

The Soviets had even less success translating military presence in Third World states into political and diplomatic influence. Huge amounts of military assistance to Arab clients had not led to a Soviet role in Arab-Israeli negotiations since 1973. Nor had they led to Soviet inclusion in talks in southern Africa dealing with Angola, Mozambique, Namibia, and Zimbabwe until recent ceasefire negotiations for Angola.

The Soviets have acknowledged that Soviet-style orthodox formulas for the Third World had declined in appeal. Party officials and academicians have recorded that completion of the "first stage" of the national liberation movement (a military struggle for national freedom) had been completed and that the "second stage" (economic advancement and independence) offers fewer opportunities to aid national liberation struggles and increased demands for economic assistance. Deterioration of East-West relations from 1975 to 1985 meant that increasing requests for economic aid were competing for limited resources with a Soviet military establishment trying to match the Western military buildup and with Eastern Europe's greater need for Soviet assistance.

In addition to economic problems placing limits on Moscow's ability to increase assistance to Third World clients, political factors complicated the expansion of Soviet influence. In Afghanistan, Angola, Ethiopia, Mozambique, and Nicaragua, the Soviets were backing either weak regimes without "legitimate" authority or clients facing insurgency movements. The USSR was no longer primarily a supporter of national liberation movements but had become a counterinsurgency power. This placed it in the awkward position of supervising a military process that was weakening economic development of clients.

Introduction of a Soviet military presence in a region also created problems. The invasion of Afghanistan caused diplomatic and political problems in the Middle East and Southwest Asia, and the buildup in Vietnam antagonized noncommunist leaders of Southeast Asia who, as a result, pursued closer relations with China. The new leadership inherited a series of problems in Asia because of worsening of the Sino-Soviet dispute that followed Moscow's military buildup on the Sino-Soviet border. They made no progress in South America because of backing the adventurist policies of Cuba. Ties to states associated with international terrorism, such as Iraq, Libya, and Syria, undermined Moscow's credibility in the United States and Western Europe.

In some areas, the Soviets had become victims of their own success. Since the late 1960s they had dramatically increased military agreements and deliveries in the Third World, doubled Soviet military personnel outside Warsaw Pact countries, sharply increased naval deployments through access to facilities and ports of call. Expansion had geostrategic benefits, enabling the USSR to break out of the Baltic Sea and Black Sea.[1]

Moscow's expanded presence led to contradictions and complications in Soviet diplomacy as choices had to be made between such antagonists as Iran and Iraq in the Persian Gulf, Syria and Iraq in the Middle East, Algeria and Morocco as well as Algeria and Libya in North Africa, and Somalia and Ethiopia on the Horn of Africa. Diplomatic overtures to Syria and Iran were unappreciated in Iraq, military assistance to Algeria and Libya led to closer Moroccan ties with Western states, and a tilt toward Ethiopia in 1977 led to a break with Somalia and loss of military facilities that enhanced access to the Red Sea and Indian Ocean.

The invasion of Afghanistan in 1979 stood out as an example of introduction of military power in one state that created problems for the Soviets in the region. There were military benefits from a protracted Soviet presence in Afghanistan, including placement of Soviet forces in a combat environment for the first time since the Second World War and use of Afghanistan as a testing area for fighter aircraft, armored helicopters, and rocket launchers. Soviet military writings referred to new concepts of command and control, and Soviet forces switched from tank-heavy mechanized units to small-unit tactics and helicopter operations.[2] Nevertheless, Afghanistan's difficult terrain and poor transportation made progress against the insurgency slow and costly, and ultimately the Soviets realized the strategic advantages of any "victory" could not be had without a long, expensive effort. The Soviet decision to withdraw acknowledged that terrain and the theology of the Afghan insurgency had stymied Moscow's tactics and technology.

The Soviets had learned that counterinsurgency problems in Angola, Ethiopia, Cambodia, and Nicaragua exacerbated risks of getting involved in a client state, meant sinking excessive investments into unsteady political systems, and—consequently—worsened economic problems within the world socialist system. A prominent Soviet historian wrote in 1988 that the Brezhnev leadership lacked

clear ideas of the Soviet Union's true national state interests. These interests lay by no means in chasing petty and essentially formal gains associated with leadership coups in certain developing countries. The genuine interest lay in ensuring a favorable international situation for profound transformations in the USSR's economy and sociopolitical system. However, at that time it was believed that no transformations were needed.[3]

The Afghan invasion undermined the USSR's claim to be the "natural ally" of Third World nonaligned countries. In contrast, in siding with Angola and Ethiopia the Soviets were seen by most African countries as on the "side of the angels." Perhaps as a result of the Afghan experience the Soviets came to realize limits in the Third World as well as problems created by military presence in areas of regional contention.

In the late 1980s a series of articles criticized Soviet policy in the Third World under Brezhnev and reflected awareness of Moscow's limits in exploiting opportunities. They were a harbinger of Gorbachev's reduced Soviet support for Third World radicals. (See Chapter 5 for a discussion of regional changes in Soviet policy.) Vyacheslav Dashichev, deputy director of the Institute of Economics of the World Socialist System (IEMSS), wrote that Brezhnev had been "wrong in assessing the global situation" and failed to realize the effect of events in the Third World on "détente between the USSR and the West."[4] In the magazine of the Soviet Foreign Ministry, *International Affairs*, commentators argued that the USSR did not have a "comparable material basis" to compete with the West in the Third World and that the Soviets had "bogged down in economic and military rivalry with the United States."[5]

THE POLITICAL LIMITS ON THE USSR'S PRESENCE IN THE THIRD WORLD

Even in states where the Soviets had made the greatest economic and military investment over the past twenty years, there was ample evidence of Moscow's inability to translate largesse into political influence. Cuba, Syria, and Vietnam are virtually dependent on the Soviet Union for military and economic aid, but have followed their own domestic policies and made decisions in foreign policy that have been unwelcome and even discomforting to Soviet leaders. Cuban adventurism in South America in the 1960s, Syrian involvement in Lebanon in the 1970s and 1980s, and the Vietnamese invasion of Cambodia in 1978 created regional problems. The strategy for economic development has had no positive effect on any key Soviet clients and it can be argued that the Soviet socialist model for economic development in the Third World has the same disrespect in Cuba, Syria, and Vietnam as the political model in Hungary, Poland, and Czechoslovakia.

SYRIA AS INDEPENDENT ACTOR AND DEPENDENT CLIENT

Hafez al-Assad's rule as president of Syria since 1970 has surpassed all expectations. Before his accession Syria had experienced more than a dozen attempted coups following departure of French forces after the Second World War. In addition to bringing stability to Damascus, Assad has managed to emerge from wars with Israel and a series of regional crises over the past two decades as a major force in the Middle East. Assad has made it difficult for Palestine Liberation Organization Chairman Yasir Arafat and Jordan's King Hussein to coordinate a strategy that does not take into account Syrian policies and interests. He reduced Arafat's role in Lebanon and, since the ill-conceived Israeli invasion of Lebanon in 1982, has become the arbiter of the balance of power in Beirut. Assad was the Arab supporter of Iran in Tehran's war with Iraq from 1980 to 1989 and, though isolated from the other Arabs on this issue, continues to provide political support to the Rafsanjani government. The Soviets have not supported him on most of these issues, but their military and economic support enabled Assad to pursue his independent foreign policy.

The Soviet expulsion from Egypt in 1972, not long after Assad's emergence, led Moscow to increase its ties in the Middle East and the Horn of Africa and to concentrate on Syria as the linchpin of its position in the region. The Soviets made contacts with Algeria and Morocco in the Maghreb as well as South Yemen in the Arabian peninsula, but the key overtures were to Iraq, Libya, and particularly Syria as the Soviets sought to buttress their position in the region and isolate Egyptian president Sadat.

The Arab-Israeli War of October 1973 provided an opportunity for an airlift and sealift to both Egypt and Syria.[6] In the first days of the war, the bulk of supplies went to Damascus and the Soviets seemed preoccupied with deterioration of the Syrian position.[7] Sadat wrote in his memoirs that the Soviets made an effort to arrange a ceasefire in the first days of fighting because of Moscow's concern for the Syrian-Israeli front.

Although the 1973 war dealt a blow to Soviet–U.S. détente, the Soviets did manage to improve their regional position as a result of the hostilities. Iran and Iraq reestablished relations after the war, and there was a reconciliation between the Ba'athist regimes of Syria and Iraq, improving Assad's position. The Soviets profited from solidarity of the oil-producing Arab states, which resulted in an embargo on oil to the United States. Soviet commentator Georgi Mirsky wrote that the embargo dispelled the myth of the "alleged fragility and illusoriness of Arab solidarity."[8]

The Soviets benefitted from the crisis within NATO because of Western European opposition to supplying Israel from U.S. bases in Europe. Differences over policy toward the oil embargo exacerbated tensions within the alliance, and the Common Market was strained by failure of Western European states to come to the aid of the Netherlands, afflicted with an oil embargo.

In the postwar period Moscow's concern continued to be relations with Syria. Soviet leaders went out of their way to emphasize support for Assad during his trip to Moscow in 1974, and the communiqué for the visit emphasized need to "further strengthen" Syrian defenses. The Syrians "reemphasized the importance" of Soviet participation in all stages of the peace process in the Middle East, and the Soviets supported Syria's "lawful inalienable right" to use "all effective means" to free its occupied lands.[9]

Weapons deliveries to Syria after the war were largely paid for by wealthier Arab states and provided the Soviet Union with valuable hard currency. Deliveries included more than 850 tanks and scores of

MiG-21 fighters, and eventually made Syria the second largest importer of Soviet arms in the world, with deliveries valued at over $5 billion during the 1976–1980 period. (Two other important Middle Eastern states—Libya and Iraq—were first and third in purchases during this period, according to studies by the U.S. Arms Control and Disarmament Agency.) Soviet-bloc arms supplies accounted for nearly all Syrian weapons during this period, and bloc economic assistance concentrated on projects in Syria, including railroad lines linking the port of Latakia with the industrial areas of the interior as well as oil refineries, phosphate plants, and land reclamation.[10]

But Moscow's presence in Syria coupled with Syrian dependence on Soviet military equipment has not led to influence over Syrian policy. Syrian domestic unrest and regional isolation led Assad to improve relations with the Soviets, but Damascus continued to pursue its own policy in ways that challenged and even compromised Soviet goals. The Soviets played no role in the Syrian-Israeli agreement of 1974, which returned to Damascus territory lost in the 1973 war as well as the city of Kuneitra lost in the Six-Day War of 1967, in spite of Soviet commentary warning the Arabs it was not in their interest to exclude the USSR from negotiations in the area.[11]

Soviet military assistance and military and economic advisors were not sufficient to dissuade Syria from intervening in Lebanon against the Palestinians in 1976, prevent Syrian attacks against the Palestinians in the 1980s, or prevent Syrian-Iranian cooperation against Iraq during the Iran-Iraq war. The Soviets were unable to convince the Syrians during the war to reopen the pipeline that pumps Iraqi oil to the Mediterranean.

Several years after the Syrians attacked Israel, the most serious Soviet–U.S. confrontation since the Cuban missile crisis, President Assad sent four thousand Syrian troops and 250 tanks into Lebanon in 1975 in support of President Suleiman Franjieh against defiant units of his Lebanese army and the Palestine Liberation Organization. The Syrian presence grew to more than forty thousand despite Arab opposition and Soviet criticism of Assad's efforts to plunge a "knife into the back" of the Palestinian movement.[12] In July 1976, General Secretary Brezhnev called for Assad to "take all possible measures to end its military operations against" the Palestinians.[13] Soviet pressure included delays in delivery of military equipment and spare parts and in signing a new arms agreement. In an exercise in reverse leverage, Assad threatened Soviet access to Syrian military facilities because of these delays, and the Soviets backed down.[14]

Until 1987 the Soviets could not prevent Syrian authorities from confiscating Soviet weaponry sent to the PLO through Syria. Nor could they prevent Syria from supporting the largest Shi'ite militia, the Amal, during its attack on Palestinian refugee camps in 1985 or backing anti-Arafat rebels in the internecine battles of the fragmented PLO. Syrian troops remain in Lebanon at significant political, financial, and personal cost despite criticism from Moscow.[15]

Soviet influence in the region has not progressed since Moscow's ouster from Egypt in 1972. The Soviets have been observers in the Arab-Israeli peace process since the October war in 1973 and were unable to exploit the Iranian-Iraqi war to gain ground in the Persian Gulf. A Soviet naval officer wrote in 1987 that the Gulf war was "explosively dangerous" because of risk of escalation in a conflict in which the USSR has no means to prevent armed acts near its border.[16] Former Foreign Minister Shevardnadze criticized his ministry in 1988 for failing to "predict the mass U.S. presence in the Persian Gulf" after eight years of war.[17] U.S. naval involvement in the Gulf was embarrassing to Moscow because of proximity to Soviet borders and the weakness of Soviet naval forces to project power. The Syrians have been unhelpful in Moscow's efforts to resume the Geneva conference or another international conference for a Middle East settlement, and the Soviets risk that Jordan's King Hussein could move closer to the West. The Soviets are in no better position to "deliver" Syria to the Arab-Israeli bargaining table than the United States is to deliver Israel.

The Soviets have been unhelpful in times of national peril for the Syrians. Before the October war, the Arabs claimed Moscow "deliberately" let them down by not providing equipment and supporting its clients as the United States had supported Israel.[18] The Soviets were passive during the Israeli invasion of Lebanon in 1982 and, except for a few critical statements did little until full-scale war between Israel and Syria appeared a possibility. The Soviets pressed the Syrians to accept a ceasefire and delayed resumption of supplies to the Syrians after Israel attacked Syrian military batteries in the Beka'a. The Soviets presumably realized that Syrian efforts to play a larger regional role in the Middle East complicated Moscow's goal of matching Western influence. The Soviets presumably would have reestablished diplomatic relations with Israel, unwisely broken during the Six-Day War in 1967, if it were not for Syrian opposition.

Despite differences over Arab-Israeli negotiations in the Middle East, Lebanon, and the Iran-Iraq war, Soviet-Syrian relations remain active. In credits, military cooperation, and economic assistance, Syria is the favored Soviet client in the Middle East and trails only Cuba and Vietnam as favored client in the Third World. President Assad traveled to Moscow in April 1987 and signed a communiqué that reaffirmed Moscow's willingness to upgrade Syria's military.

In addition to deliveries of advanced MiG-29 fighter aircraft in 1988, Western diplomats in the Middle East believe the Syrians will continue to receive sophisticated fighter aircraft, surface-to-surface and surface-to-air missiles, and military technicians. The Soviets have rescheduled Syria's military debt from accumulated purchases, believed to have reached $15 billion. In March 1987, the Soviets agreed to reschedule Egypt's military debt as well.[19] But as Alvin Z. Rubinstein has written: "What seems to be influence turns out instead to be the joint interests of the two parties."[20]

CUBA AS INDEPENDENT ACTOR AND DEPENDENT CLIENT

Just as Assad's presidency of Syria since 1970 has lasted longer than experts had expected, Fidel Castro's rule in Cuba is the longest tenure of any Cuban government since the island gained independence from Spain in 1898. Castro has wiped out the illiteracy that existed prior to the revolution and eradicated the sinecures that characterized the Batista regime as well as widespred administrative corruption. Still, he has engaged in costly and largely unsuccessful military activities throughout the Caribbean, Central America, and South America, and established a state-controlled economy that has created inflation and bureaucratic chaos.[21]

Castro has emerged as leader of the nonaligned movement and established a large military presence in Africa out of proportion to Cuba's resources. He sees support for revolution as part of Cuba's foreign policy, but the election defeat of the Sandinistas in Nicaragua in 1990 marked a major setback for Castro as well.[22] In the latter 1980s, moreover, Cuba removed most of its troops from Ethiopia, where rebel forces were beginning to threaten the regime, and began to remove forces from Angola, where war weariness among participants in the fifteen-year struggle (Angola, Cuba, South Africa, the USSR) contributed to acceptance of a ceasefire in December 1988. By mid-1991, there will be no Cuban combat forces in Africa.

Cuba's relations with the Soviet Union began in 1960 after a small guerrilla force toppled a U.S.–backed dictatorship with only slight support from the Moscow-oriented Communist party. Soviet ties enabled the Castro regime to consolidate its revolution and withstand U.S. efforts to weaken and isolate it.[23] Since 1960, Moscow has provided Havana with $9 billion in military equipment as well as 2,800 military advisers, at nominal cost to Cuba, emphasizing Havana's importance to Soviet planners.[24]

Military assistance has transformed the Cuban Ministry of the Revolutionary Armed Forces (MINFAR) into a modern military force staffed with officers who attend military academies in Cuba or the

Soviet Union. Under the leadership of Raul Castro, Fidel's brother, MINFAR has emerged as Cuba's strongest institutional force and repository of specialists trained along the lines of a Soviet bureaucratic system.[25] Militarization of the political ethos in Cuba is not unlike transformation in the Soviet Union after the Bolshevik Revolution.

During the 1980s the Soviets furnished Cuba with $4 billion annually in economic assistance and subsidies. Although subsidies declined in 1986 due to the declining price of oil, and financial help was not suficient to solve Cuba's hard-currency shortage, the USSR continues to provide most Cuban oil and agreed to provide Havana with 2.5 billion rubles between 1986 and 1990, an increase of half over the five-year period ending in 1985. One project that Soviet credits will support is completion of the first phase (two of four reactors) of the Cienfuegos nuclear-power station.[26] In the 1990s, however, there will be drastic Soviet cuts in aid to Cuba, and Moscow is encouraging Castro to resume relations with the United States.

Soviet-Cuban economic collaboration is coordinated through the Intergovernmental Soviet-Cuban Commission for Economic, Scientific, and Technological Cooperation, established in 1970, which held its first meeting in Havana in 1971. Cuba was admitted into COMECON the following year, entitling it to "preferential" treatment in economic cooperation and even closer coordination of the Cuban economy with commodity, trade, and planning agreements of other Soviet-directed COMECON states. As economies of the Eastern European states move from centralized economies, there could be serious consequences for Cuba, particularly if the subsidies that prop up the Cuban economy were reduced.

In return for Soviet aid, Moscow has had access to Cuban military facilities, naval and naval air. At the Lourdes complex near Havana, the Soviets have three sites dedicated to intelligence collection and targeted primarily against U.S. commercial satellites. Soviet naval task groups deploy annually to Cuba to train with the Cuban navy and establish a Soviet presence in the Caribbean. A typical task group consists of a guided-missile cruiser, a guided-missile destroyer, a submarine, and an oiler for anti-surface, antisubmarine, and anti-air exercises during a month-long presence. Since 1969, Soviet reconnaissance and antisubmarine aircraft have made more than 50 deployments to Cuba.[27]

Although Castro's ties to the Soviets have been essential to survival of his regime and his role as a regional and even world leader, there has been disharmony in the relationship, and Cuba has been far from compliant. In the late 1960s there were Soviet-Cuban differences over the role of armed struggle, capacity of commununist parties in leading revolution in Third World countries, the appropriate economic-development model for Cuba, and the level of Soviet military commitment to Cuba.[28] The Cubans viewed armed struggle as the correct way to revolution, downgraded Third World communist parties, and were not inclined to support bourgeois reform governments in Latin America.

The new leadership in the Soviet Union took a more cautious approach to the Third World and was interested in expanding state-to-state relations through trade and diplomatic ties, particularly in South America and Africa. Invasion of the Dominican Republic by the United States in 1965 was a sharp reminder of Cuba's vulnerability; invasion of Grenada in 1983 was a similar reminder and led to Soviet-Cuban strains over the role of "armed struggle" in the region.

The awkward Soviet-Cuban ties in the 1960s, because of Soviet emphasis on the "peaceful road to socialism" and Cuban commitment to armed struggle as a revolutionary strategy, was followed by cooperation in the 1970s in Soviet and Cuban ventures in Angola and Ethiopia. Cuban interventions in Angola and Ethiopia not only demonstrated Cuba's usefulness to the Soviets in the Third World but provided the Castro government with leverage for economic- and military-aid agreements with the USSR. At one time, the Cubans had thirty-five thousand forces in Ethiopia and fifty thousand in Angola; several thousand Cuban forces remain in Ethiopia, and Cuban withdrawal from Angola has begun. Soviet military assistance allowed Cuba to maintain more diplomatic missions, intelligence operatives, and military troops abroad than any other developing country.

As Robert Pastor has concluded, the Soviets are willing to fill Cuba's gap between internal resources and external capabilities "not because of altruism, but because the Soviets are assured that what the Cubans do abroad will serve their purposes."[29] Both Moscow and Havana gained notoriety in the Third World as a result of efforts in Angola and Ethiopia, but after the Cuban withdrawal the regime in Addis Ababa is threatened and the situation for Luanda remains uncertain. The Soviets have announced that their advisers would be withdrawn from Ethiopia and it is likely they will be reduced in Angola.

Cuban-Soviet cooperation in the Third World and Cuban dependence on Soviet economic and military assistance does not mean relations are without irritants. These include

- a coup attempt in Angola in 1977 against Agostinho Neto (favored by Cuba) by Nito Alves, leader of a pro-Soviet extremist faction, which suggested continuing differences between Moscow and Havana. The Soviets reportedly backed the coup and the Cubans helped defeat it.

- a second is the Eritrean independence movement, which continues to plague the Mengistu government in Ethiopia, but Cuba never permitted its forces to challenge Eritrean independence. The Soviets in the meantime wavered between support of force against the Eritreans and a negotiated settlement.
- a third is revolutionary success in Central America, extremely important to Castro but of less strategic concern to the Soviet Union. Cuba has opposed the low level of attention the Soviets have given to Nicaragua's economic and military needs, and even complained about conciliatory Soviet statements in the face of hostile U.S. pronouncements about the Sandinistas.
- the Soviets appeared to distance themselves from Maurice Bishop's leadership struggle with Bernard Coard in Grenada and kept an extremely low profile after the U.S. invasion in 1983. Cuba opposed the invasion and Castro ordered his soldiers to fight.[30]

These differences on regional matters were recorded at the twenty-seventh Soviet party congress in 1986. Gorbachev stressed East-West security matters and controlling the arms race and Castro reminded his Soviet audience that Third World issues demanded attention and that national liberation struggles were not fought without cost. As if to urge Gorbachev to meet Soviet obligations abroad despite preoccupation with economic reform at home, Castro noted that Third World countries expect they will "receive maximum solidarity from the socialist community in their struggle for just economic gains."[31]

Another indication of differences between the Soviet Union and Cuba since Gorbachev's accession was signing of a friendship treaty in 1989 that contained no reference to military cooperation, no provision for consultation in case of attack against one side or the other, no mention of revolutionary struggle in the Third World, no reference to building of communism—all standard items in treaties of friendship and cooperation between Moscow and Third World clients. The treaty affirms Cuban support for Gorbachev's foreign policy as outlined in his address to the United Nations in December 1988 and calls for rechanneling resources from military purposes to "meet the economic and social development of the countries."[32] Havana's willingness to rejoin the Organization of American States, which Castro signaled in October 1989, was another indication the Cubans must rejoin the Latin American community in response to Moscow's efforts to pursue larger East-West issues.

Possible sources of tension between the two states include Cuban unhappiness with Soviet efforts to improve relations with the United States, Cuba's overextension for the Sandinistas or criticism of reduced Soviet military aid to Nicaragua, and Cuban support of revolutionary movements in Central and South America in opposition to Soviet efforts to maintain cordial relations in the region.

One of the best indicators of Soviet-Cuban cooperation on international matters will be at the United Nations, where Cubans have received a seat on the Security Council. In an early test, in October 1989, it was noteworthy that for the first time the Soviets abstained from the annual exercise to expel Israel, whereas Cuba—along with Afghanistan, Angola, and Nicaragua—voted with the Arabs for expulsion.

The current turmoil in Eastern Europe represents a challenge to Castro as changes throughout the Soviet bloc deepen Cuba's political isolation and add to economic misery. Castro has rebuffed Gorbachev's call for reform and become testy about "betrayal" of Marxism-Leninism, referring to new leaders in Hungary and Poland as "apprentices of capitalism."[33] His brother Raul threatened to oppose any accord between the United States and the Soviet Union that altered the "ideological and military status quo in Europe," presumably fearing such an arrangement would give Washington an even freer hand in the Caribbean and Central America.

VIETNAM AS INDEPENDENT ACTOR AND DEPENDENT CLIENT

The Soviets have confronted more problems in Asia than in other regions of the world. Nearly all Asian states, including Vietnam, view the USSR as a European nation and ignore that one third of Soviet territory is east of Irkutsk in East Asia and a fifth of its population is of Asian nationality. The USSR has been excluded from the diplomacy and economic development of the region. The Soviets have had their own economic problems in the Soviet Far East because of isolation from the industrial and population centers of the USSR.

Asian nationalism has prevented the Soviets from influencing decisions in the region and Vietnam, now a regional force, has been particularly hostile to outsiders. Both Soviets and Vietnamese have endured a brutal history and both have unremitting suspicion of foreigners and general inability to trust, which reinforces strains between the two. Moscow has been insensitive in dealings with Asians, including Vietnamese, and has been at a disadvantage in the region. Hanoi would prefer no outsiders in Vietnam, Cambodia, or Laos and has never considered Soviet communism a relevant or effective model.

Soviet support against the United States in the 1960s and 1970s, and the People's Republic of China in the 1980s, made it possible for Hanoi to unify the country and consolidate influence in the region. Soviet contributions were minuscule compared to American expenditure and involved no confrontation with the United States, but were an element in Vietnam's success. As early as 1965 the Soviets were building SA-2 surface-to-air missile sites in North Vietnam, providing MiG-17 and MiG-21 fighter aircraft to the Vietnamese air force, transferring several thousand advisers to Vietnamese forces.[34]

The Vietnamese realized, however, that Moscow would make no effort to interfere with American deliveries of materials or troops to South Vietnam or interdict the U.S. Navy during the bombing of Hanoi or mining of Haiphong. Brezhnev's willingness to meet with President Nixon in 1972, against advice of members of the Politburo during one of the heaviest U.S. bombing campaigns against Hanoi, had to be a bitter pill for the Vietnamese.[35] Limits on Moscow's support for Vietnam prevented Soviet influence in Hanoi at war's end. Ironically, the Chinese invasion of Vietnam in February 1979 led to achievement of the Soviet objective in Southeast Asia, access to U.S.–built military bases on the South China Sea. Although the Soviets signaled that they would not become involved in the war against the Chinese, Vietnam gave access to Cam Ranh Bay and Da Nang to assure Soviet military deliveries in the effort against the Chinese as well as the Vietnamese presence in Cambodia.

Cam Ranh Bay was the largest Soviet naval forward-deployment base outside the USSR until withdrawal in 1990, servicing twenty-five to thirty Soviet ships routinely deployed to the South China Sea. It includes a composite air unit, a communications and intelligence collection, and logistics support. More than $10 billion in Soviet military aid and an advisory group of over 2,500 military personnel allowed Hanoi to maintain its occupation of Cambodia until 1989 and remain intransigent in negotiating the Cambodian problem.

Assistance to the Vietnamese continues to exceed $1 billion a year, with more than one third considered military aid.[36] Nevertheless, Soviet policy under Gorbachev has contributed to strains between Moscow and Hanoi. Soviet officials have openly complained that much of the USSR's assistance has been wasted by incompetent or corrupt Vietnamese, and Vietnam appears increasingly irritated by pressure to tighten management of its economy.[37] The Vietnamese, like other Soviet clients in the Third World, presumably resent being overcharged for outmoded Soviet technology and receiving below-market prices for exports.

Soviet efforts to push Vietnam and Cambodia toward reconciliation had little success until Gorbachev announced his decision in 1988 to withdraw from Afghanistan. Several months prior to the announcement, the Soviet foreign ministry issued its first statements on Indochina since the end of the Vietnam War, hailing Phnom Penh's adoption of a "reconciliation policy" and endorsing Cambodia's agreement to offer Prince Sihanouk a post in a new coalition government and to hold talks with all opposition forces except the Khmer Rouge.[38] Just as withdrawal from Afghanistan was beginning in May 1988, Moscow issued its third statement on Indochina, endorsing Hanoi's plan to withdraw fifty thousand troops from Cambodia before the end of 1988.[39]

During his meeting with Gorbachev in July 1988, Vietnamese General Secretary Nguyen Van Linh promised to withdraw the remainder of Vietnam's forces by the end of 1989 or beginning of 1990, and the Cambodian government agreed in January 1989.[40] Pressure on the Vietnamese to withdraw from Cambodia was matched by United States pressure on the Chinese to moderate support for the Khmer Rouge, and by the end of September 1989 Vietnamese forces withdrew despite failure of national reconciliation talks in the summer of 1989.

The Soviets are not likely to abandon Vietnam, and Vietnam's debt of $8 billion to the USSR and reliance on military and economic assistance gives it few options other than staying on good terms with Moscow. There is little doubt that the Soviets would like to reduce their aid package; the end to Vietnam's occupation of Cambodia weakens Moscow's leverage on Hanoi. Links between the countries have always been through circumstance than design, and it may be that Vietnamese dependence and Soviet opportunism will keep the countries close. As economic conditions worsen in both the Soviet Union and Vietnam and as both Moscow and Hanoi improve relations with China, there will be greater strains between the two states. The Vietnamese respect power and presumably believe that Gorbachev has gone too far in conciliation with the United States and China. As Vietnam becomes less vulnerable, opportunities for trouble between Vietnam and the Soviet Union will increase.

GORBACHEV CONFRONTS SOVIET LIMITS IN THE THIRD WORLD

The Soviets have expanded their influence in the Third World since the 1950s. U.S. acceptance of Soviet strategic parity as well as U.S. difficulties in Vietnam made the USSR more attractive than the United States as a patron for Third World countries. Military and economic assistance as well as an expanded military presence characterized Moscow's involvement. Soviet and Cuban military forces helped Angola to consolidate power in Luanda and enabled Mengistu Haile Mariam in Ethiopia to counter an invasion from Somalia. Soviet access to naval and air facilities in Africa, the Caribbean, and Southeast Asia raised questions about security of Western sea lanes through the Suez Canal and the Strait of Hormuz.

Nevertheless, Soviet military and political involvement in such key Third World states as Afghanistan, Syria, Cuba, and Vietnam led to problems in Southwest Asia, the Middle East, South America, and Southeast Asia. Soviet exploitation of the Arab-Israeli conflict and increased deployment of Soviet naval aviation to Syria produced a greater U.S. military presence and hesitation on the part of Arab moderates to improve relations with the USSR. The deployment of Soviet naval task forces to Cuba as well as operational roles of Soviet reconnaissance aircraft limited Moscow's efforts to obtain ports of entry in South America and compromised its efforts to expand influence.

Use of Cam Ranh Bay spoiled Soviet efforts to improve relations with the states of the Association of Southeast Asian Nations (ASEAN). Support for Vietnam's occupation of Cambodia undercut Soviet initiatives in Thailand, also in Indonesia and Malaysia. Soviet military interventions in the Third World, particularly in Angola and Mozambique, led to deterioration in Soviet–U.S. relations after 1975, when the United States completed its withdrawal from Vietnam.

In addition to regional limit caused by military support for key regional clients, the Soviets have confronted difficult choices because of Third World rivalries. In the Middle East, they had to choose between Iran and Iraq in a war that continued until a ceasefire in 1989. The Soviet tilt toward Iraq in 1982 plus the Syrian tilt toward Iran created problems in the Soviet-Syrian relationship.

Prior to unification of the Yemens in 1990, Moscow tried to ingratiate itself with both South Yemen (the People's Democratic Republic of Yemen, or PDRY), and North Yemen (the Yemen Arab Republic, or YAR). This effort was complicated by military and political rivalry between the North and the South.[41] The Soviets encountered difficulties trying to balance conservative and fragmented politics and society in the YAR with the tribal and radical politics of factionalism in the PDRY. North Yemeni ties with Saudi Arabia and the coup d'état in South Yemen in 1986 revealed Moscow's limited ability to affect major events in the region.[42] Unification will be to Moscow's advantage because Yemen will require assistance against Saudi Arabia, and the USSR is the most likely source.

The Soviets had similar problems in North Africa trying to balance their interests with Algeria and Morocco as well as Algeria and Libya. On the Horn of Africa, they failed to prevent war between Ethiopia and Somalia in the 1970s and have been unable to mediate differences between Ethiopia and the Sudan in the 1980s. Iraq will want the Soviets to balance their supply of fighter aircraft and surgace-to-air missiles to Iran in 1990–1991.

The Soviets have had the greatest difficulty trying to influence the policies of the clients that have received the greatest support. In Egypt they became deeply involved in operations of the Arab Socialist Union and key institutional agencies in the army and the secret police, but this did not prevent President Sadat's decision to expel twenty thousand Soviet advisors and technicians in 1972 and allow the United States to broker a peace with Israel under three U.S. presidents from 1974 to 1979. The Syrians have pursued their interests in Lebanon and Jordan, despite significant Soviet assistance, and Libya has confronted states large and small, ignoring Soviet advice to end Tripoli's political isolation in the Mediterranean and moderate its military tactics.

The Iraqi decision to invade Iran in 1980 was not appreciated in the Kremlin and led to suspension of military assistance to Baghdad, a sanction the Soviets rarely employ. The Iraqi invasion of Kuwait in 1990 led to an unprecedented Soviet arms embargo on military deliveries in cooperation with the United States and Soviet endorsement of U.S. use of force against Iraq. Large amounts of assistance to Libya and Iraq have provided the Soviets no assurance regarding use of these weapons and no guarantee against domestic Arab opposition and resentment when sophisticated Soviet arms are used unwisely by Arab military forces. The Soviets objected to Iraq's use of Scuds against civil targets in Iran during the war. Over the years the Soviets have been sensitive to the charge of insufficient commitment from such clients as Egypt, Syria, and Libya.

Even so, the Soviets have encountered difficulties when they have tried to expand their presence in support of beleaguered clients such as Egypt that have not appreciated Soviet heavyhandedness. Egyptian journalist Mohammed Heikal has recorded Egyptian dissatisfaction with Soviet demands for facilities at Mersa Matruh and Alexandria, Soviet exclusivity in the use of facilities at Cairo West airfield, and the self-isolation of the Soviet presence in Cairo.[43] Heikal and others have argued that the "disadvantages of having so many Soviet experts in the country had become at least as apparent as the advantages," citing Soviet insensitivity in dealing with Arabs and the virtual impossibility of establishing personal relationships with Soviet advisors and technicians. The exclusive Soviet position in Berbera led to similar problems with Somalia, including the eventual expulsion of the Soviet presence in 1977 and Siad Barre's unilateral abrogation of the Treaty of Friendship and Cooperation with the USSR.

Gorbachev's response has been to reduce Soviet dependence on the naval facilities of littoral states in the Third World. For the past several years, there has been a steady decline in the operational presence of the Soviet navy in out-of-area waters. Moscow's willingness to withdraw advisors from Mozambique and Ethiopia may be the harbinger of less Soviet use of facilities in those African states where insurgent forces have created security problems for the Soviet presence. The Soviets have made their own naval exercises less ambitious and reduced joint exercises with Third World navies. Soviet doctrine is placing less emphasis on interdiction and amphibious capabilities for the navy.

Gorbachev's policymakers have been concerned with their inability to influence the domestic plans of such client states as Cuba, Nicaragua, and Vietnam, whose economies have been in disarray. There has never been much warmth between the Soviets and their communist clients in the Third World who have found the Soviet model irrelevant in managing their economies. Soviet calls for economic reform have fallen on deaf ears in the Third World, whose economies are among the most backward.

The Soviets have provided the Cubans and Vietnamese with economic subsidies, particularly the purchase of oil from the USSR at below world market prices, both for internal use and resale for hard currency. At the same time the Cuban and Vietnamese economies have deteriorated and the Soviets have not been able to achieve efficiencies in these economies in order to ease their own "burden of empire."[44] Escalating costs of aid as well as Third World debts have caused the Soviets to become increasingly impatient.

Cuba and Vietnam have become full members of the Council for Mutual Economic Assistance (CMEA) and have received increasing amounts of Soviet aid and trade. Yet the declining growth of the Soviet economy and increased burden of the arms race with the West have hurt Moscow's ability to provide economic assistance to these states. The rigidity of central planning and the difficulty in transferring agricultural and industrial expertise and technology—particularly to tropical countries with small-scale industry—has made economic relations with such countries as Cuba and Vietnam even more difficult. The Soviets have been critical of unnamed Third World leaders for expecting the socialist states to "force socioeconomic change through rapid industrialization."[45]

GORBACHEV CONCEDES SOVIET LIMITS IN THE THIRD WORLD

The Soviets have conceded that preoccupation with developing basic industry—the traditional goal of Soviet economic aid—has been too costly for both patron and client, resulting in a decline in the standard of living and alienation of the population. Indeed, Third World leaders have tended to blame Soviet credits for large-scale projects that were beyond their capacities. Whereas Soviet military aid has led to apparently unimpeded use of facilities in Cuba and Vietnam, there is no indication that economic aid has convinced the Cuban and Vietnamese leadership to maintain traditional roles as agricultural suppliers to the USSR or to cease efforts to diversify their economies.

The Soviets have acknowledged the negative effect of actions in the Third World on East-West relations and repudiated military power in settling regional conflicts. Soviet leaders take a different view of developments in the Third World than they did in the 1970s. Officials at the Institute of Economics of the World Socialist System (IEMSS) now argue that the USSR is at a disadvantage in economic competition with the West in the developing world. The Soviets appear to recognize the need to be selective in choosing client states in the Third World and concede that many Third World states suffer from "economic mismanagement, low labor productivity...and shortages of consumer goods for the population," and are not susceptible to Soviet influence.[46] These statements concede the inability to gain influence among the socialist states of the Third World and provide a rationale for altering Soviet strategy.

At the twenty-seventh Soviet party congress in 1986, Gorbachev did not even refer to the socialist-oriented states or revolutionary democracies, or national liberation movements in the Third World. He indicated that Moscow's role in the Third World was far less important than addressing domestic economic concerns and improving relations with the United States. Other than Afghanistan, Gorbachev made only passing reference to regional conflicts that were problems for Soviet–U.S. relations.

His deemphasis of Third World issues led such Soviet clients as Castro, Mengistu, and Angolan leader Dos Santos to remind the USSR that it could not back away from its obligations. Castro reminded Gorbachev that "blood had been spilled" in the Third World and the task of development was as important as avoiding nuclear war. Mengistu urged the Soviets not to give the issue of regional conflict lower priority than nuclear matters, and put the Soviet leadership on notice that Moscow's allies continued to expect support.

Gorbachev's response has been to emphasize political means for resolution of regional disputes and greater Soviet involvement across-the-board in international politics. At a dinner for Assad in April 1987, he underscored that Soviet policy had to be based on "realistic analysis of the present-day world which has markedly changed recently" and the "diverse and conflicting forces of which world politics are comprised.[47]" He acknowledged that the absence of diplomatic relations between the USSR and Israel could not be "considered normal" and that military power in settling regional conflicts had become "completely discredited."

Following the Assad visit, Soviet officials began to criticize optimistic analyses of development in the Third World. Georgi Mirsky, a well-known Soviet expert on the nonaligned movement, acknowledged that Western experts were in front of Soviet counterparts in understanding the insignificance of class contradictions in the Third World and the importance of the military and the bureaucracy.[48] Other experts concluded that only the poorest nations in the Third World chose socialism, that most Third World states "remain linked with the capitalist world system."[49]

Gorbachev's announcement in 1988 of a phased troop withdrawal from Afghanistan emphasized that regional conflicts have the greatest risk of compromising Soviet–U.S. relations. He stated that "implementing political settlement" in Afghanistan could be an "important rupture" in the chain of regional conflicts in Africa, the Middle East, Southeast Asia, and Central America. Articles by three members of the USA Institute (the chief Soviet research establishment on the United States)—Deputy Director Vitaliy Zhurkin, section head Sergei Karaganov, and senior researcher Andrei Kortunov—have argued that the "threat of premeditated nuclear aggression was decreasing, but that the threat of war may be increasing in part due to the struggle in regional sectors."[50]

Withdrawal from Afghanistan and threat of regional conflict is a warning to the most radical Third World states that there are limits to Soviet military assistance. Y. Primakov, then director of the Institute for World Economy and International Relations and former member of the Presidential Council, wrote in 1987 that "international relations in general cannot be the arena in which the contest between global socialism and capitalism can be decided" and that the "nuclear era necessitates that the revolutionary forces are extremely cautious in deciding to wage an armed struggle."[51] Radical states have been critical of Moscow's more conciliatory stance as well as perestroika and some have begun to assert even more independent policies. Cuba and Ethiopia did not follow the USSR to the 1988 Olympic Games in Seoul; Libya and the PLO refused to join the embargo against Iraq in 1990.

Domestic turmoil in the Soviet Union and the Eastern European states will be unnerving to Third World states that have been counting on Moscow for political and economic support. These states have been willing to take strikingly similar positions on major ideological, military, and foreign policy issues and trade with Eastern European states to guarantee Soviet largesse. Moscow's willingness to allow the political unraveling of the bloc, particularly the removal of Erich

Honecker in East Germany and Todor Zhivkov in Bulgaria, will be interpreted in the Third World as indication of Soviet isolationism that will not augur well for the interests of Soviet clients.

This does not suggest that the Soviets will stop using their military assets to protect gains in Cuba, Syria, and Vietnam. Military and economic assistance will continue, but Moscow appears to recognize that military power will not resolve conflicts and not guarantee that Soviet interests will benefit from a more active world role. Third World leaders presumably can conclude that a Moscow unwilling to protect Eastern Europe and a pro-Soviet, Marxist government in Afghanistan will do even less in areas far from Soviet territory.

In an interview in May 1987, Deputy Foreign Minister Vladimir Petrovsky disavowed the notion of a zero-sum game between the superpowers in the Third World and stated that Moscow could not "achieve a victory for itself by destroying someone else."[52] Other Soviet officials have acknowledged that Moscow lacked the "material resources" to play such a game in the Third World against the interests of the United States. The leadership of Moscow client states in the Third World is being told that the USSR has made a major move to improve its relations in the West and will no longer allow its position in the Third World to become an obstacle.

NOTES

1. Daniel Papp, *Soviet Policies toward the Developing World*, Washington, DC: U.S. Government Printing Office, 1986, pp. 169–173.

2. Henry S. Bradsher, *Afghanistan and the Soviet Union*, Durham, NC: Duke Press Policy Studies, 1983, pp. 210–213.

3. *Literaturnaya Gazeta*, May 18, 1988, p. 14.

4. Vyacheslav Dashichev, "East-West: Quest for New Relations," *Literaturnaya Gazeta*, May 18, 1988, p. 14 in Foreign Broadcast Information Service, *Soviet Union Daily Report*, (hereafter, FBIS), May 20, 1988, pp. 7–8.

5. Andrei Kozyrev and Andrei Shumikhin, "East and West in the Third World," *International Affairs* (Moscow), No. 3, 1989, p. 68.

6. Many Western analysts have incorrectly referred to the Egyptian-Syrian conduct of the October war as a Soviet-style military operation. Whereas Soviet military doctrine favors deep penetration and projection of firepower through the entire depth of the opponent's military formations and his homeland, the Arabs concentrated on the area of the immediate tactical battlefield. As Jon D. Glassman argues in his *Arms for the Arabs: The Soviet Union and War in the Middle East*, the Arabs made few attempts to strike at Israel proper and no attempt to interdict in any substantial way the movement of Israel's mobilized reservists to the front.

7. Soviet AN-12 and AN-22 air transports made more than 900 flights to Egypt and Syria, delivering 10,000 tons of military equipment before the end of the war. During the same period, U.S. C-5 and C-141 air transports made more than 500 flights to Israel, delivering more than 22,000 tons of military equipment. See William Quandt, *Soviet Policy in the October 1973 War*, Santa Monica, CA: Rand Corporation, 1976, pp. 21–26.

8. Georgi Mirsky, "The Middle East: New Factors," *New Times*, No. 48, 1973, pp. 18–19. The other myths that Mirsky claimed were dispelled by the war were Israeli military superiority, Arab weapons inferiority, and the idea that détente had no value. (Mirsky said that détente had prevented an even worse "flare-up" in the Middle East, which is a noteworthy claim in view of the nuclear alert that took place in the United States following the challenge to the ceasefire.)

9. Robert Freedman, *Soviet Policy Toward the Middle East since 1970*, New York: Praeger, 1978, pp. 141–165.

10. Ibid.

11. Ibid.

12. Dmitry Volsky, "Step Toward Settlement," *New Times*, No. 23, 1976, p. 9.

13. *Pravda*, July 16, 1976, p. 3.

14. Galia Golan, *Soviet Policies in the Middle East Since World War II*, London: Cambridge University Press, 1990, p. 152.

15. Saudi-sponsored negotiations during the month of October 1989 produced a new national charter for Lebanon that could distribute political power more equally among the Moslem and Christian communities. The Syrian military victory in Lebanon in 1990 will protect the interests of the Moslems, and could lead to redeployment of Syrian troops from Beirut to central Lebanon, the Bekaa valley, and a highway that links Beirut with the Syrian capital. Syria reportedly has agreed to discuss withdrawal in a joint Syria-Lebanese military committee after the formation of a new Lebanese government. (*Washington Post*, October 23, 1989, p. 1, "Lebanese Agreement Approved," by Nora Boustany.) If the accord survives and actually leads to some Syrian withdrawal, it would mean that in a twelve-month period, Soviet forces had withdrawn from Afghanistan and such Soviet clients as Cuba, Syria, and Vietnam had withdrawn or agreed to withdraw forces from Angola, Lebanon, and Cambodia, respectively. (See Chapter 5 for a discussion of Soviet policies toward Asia, Africa, and the Middle East.)

16. Captain V. Yaremenko, "Stormclouds over the Persian Gulf," *Kommunist Vooruzhennykh Sil*, No. 24, 1987, pp. 73–77.

17. *Vestnik Ministerstba Inostrannykh Sel SSSR* (Moscow), Number 15, August 1988, pp. 27–46, FBIS, September 22, 1988, p. 6.

18. Anwar Sadat, *In Search of Identity: An Autobiography*, New York: Harper and Row, 1978, pp. 286–287. Mohamed Heikal, *Road to Ramadan*, New York: Quadrangle Books, 1975, p. 171.

19. *The New York Times*, April 30, 1987, p. 16.

20. Alvin Z. Rubinstein, *Red Star over the Nile*, Princeton: Princeton University Press, 1977, p. xv.

21. Jaime Suchlicki, *Cuba: From Columbus to Castro*, Washington, D.C.: Pergamon-Bassey, 1986, pp. 155–212.

22. Jorge Dominquez, *Cuba: Order and Revolution*, Cambridge, MA: Harvard University Press, 1978.

23. Edward Gonzalez, *Cuba under Castro: The Limits of Charisma*, Boston: Houghton Mifflin, 1972.

24. Papp, *Soviet Policies*, pp. 120–131.

25. Suchlicki, *Cuba*, pp. 155–212.

26. Gonzalez, *Cuba under Castro*.

27. *Soviet Military Power*, Washington, DC: U.S. Government Printing Office, 1985, p. 120.

28. Raymond Duncan, *The Soviet Union and Cuba: Interests and Influence*, New York: Praeger, 1985, pp. 51–52.

29. Robert Pastor, "Cuba and the Soviet Union: Does Cuba Act Alone?" in Barry W. Levine, ed., *The New Cuban Presence in the Caribbean*, Boulder, CO: Westview Press, 1983, pp. 191–209.

30. Raymond Duncan, "Soviet Interests in Latin America," *Journal of Inter-American Studies and World Affairs*, May 1984, pp. 168–175.

31. Raymond Duncan, "Castro and Gorbachev: Politics of Accommodation," *Problems of Communism*, Vol. 30, March–April 1986, pp. 45–57.

32. *The New York Times*, April 7, 1989, p. 3.

33. *The New York Times*, November 14, 1989, p. 17. "For Castro, More Isolation and Economic Trouble," by Larry Rohter.

34. *The Pentagon Papers: The Defense Department History of United States Decision Making on Vietnam*, Boston: Beacon Press, 1971, Volume 3, p. 365. During a similar period, the Soviets were placing nearly 20,000 advisers and technicians in Egypt, flying defensive patrols on behalf of the Egyptian air force, and generally introducing air defense systems to Egypt before similar systems arrived in Vietnam.

35. It has always been the view of this author that President Sadat's decision to expel Soviet advisors and technicians from Egypt and Kim Il-Sung's decision to improve relations with China were direct reactions to the USSR's failure to defend the interests of an important client state—Vietnam—at a time of peril.

36. *The Christian Science Monitor*, December 23, 1986, p. 3. "Moscow Pleased Vietnamese Reformers Got Boost in Shuffle," by Paul Quinn-Judge.

37. *The Washington Post*, October 17, 1988, p. 23. "Soviet-Vietnamese Ties Showing Signs of Strain," by Murray Hiebert.

38. TASS, August 31, 1987; TASS, October 17, 1987.

39. *Pravda*, May 27, 1988, p. 5.

40. TASS, July 20, 1988; TASS January 7, 1989.

41. The willingness of the two Yemens to enter into a form of political unification in the spring of 1990 was probably encouraged by Moscow's retreat from the Third World and the prospect of less Soviet military and economic assistance.

42. The coup d'état in South Yemen confronted Gorbachev with his first "crisis" in the Third World. Apparently caught by surprise, Gorbachev waited for the dust to settle and maintained a safe distance from the rival party and tribal factions of the ruling Yemen Socialist Party (YSP) until Ali Salem al-Bidh, the new general secretary of the YSP, and Prime Minister Haider abu Bakr al-Attas

established control in Aden. The Soviets were far more interested in protecting their access to naval and air facilities in Aden than trying to determine the outcome of the coup.

43. Mohammed Heikal, *The Sphinx and the Commissar*, New York: Harper and Row, 1978, pp. 275–289.

44. On the rising costs the Soviets face in Third World countries, see Jerry Hough, *The Struggle for the Third World: Soviet Debates and American Options*, Washington, DC: Brookings Institution, 1986.

45. Joseph Whelan, *The Soviet Union in the Third World, 1980–1982: An Imperial Burden or Political Asset*, Washington, DC: U.S. Government Printing Office, 1984, pp. 295–296.

46. Vladimir Lee and Georgi Mirski, "Socialist Orientation and New Political Thinking," *Asia and Africa Today* (English edition), No. 4, 1988, pp. 65–66.

47. *Pravda*, April 25, 1987, p. 2.

48. G. Mirsky, "K voprosu o vybore puti i orientatsii razvivayushchikhsya stran'," *MEMO*, No. 5, 1987, p. 76.

49. R. Avakov, "Novoe myshlenie i problema izucheniya razvivayiushchikhsya stran'," *MEMO*, No. 11, 1987, p. 53.

50. *Kommunist*, January 1988, pp. 42–50.

51. *Pravda*, July 10, 1987, p. 5.

52. *The Washington Post*, May 29, 1987, p. 34.

5

The Regional Implications of Gorbachev's "New Political Thinking"

The USSR's Third World policy since the mid-1950s reflects both its national interests and ability to capitalize on international developments. Although ideology has shaped Moscow's view, it has not been a major factor in determining Soviet interests or behavior. And though policy in the Third World has been keyed to ambitions vis-à-vis the United States, Moscow until recently has not allowed such concern to deter it from pursuing its global interests.[1]

In the decade following the Second World World the Soviets failed to capitalize on the collapse of Western imperial systems in Africa, Asia, and the Middle East, growth of radical nationalism, and new responsiveness of "revolutionary democrats" in the Third World. Stalin carried out a European policy, and carefully avoided Third World conflicts, restricting support to communist regimes contiguous to the USSR.

At the Twentieth Congress of the Communist Party of the Soviet Union in 1956, the Soviets codified a new approach toward the Third World when Khrushchev described the "disintegration of the imperialist colonial system" as a "postwar development of historical significance." He and his successors, but not Gorbachev, viewed the Third World as the appropriate area for competing with the West and supporting national liberation movements without the risk of confrontation. Moscow's initial, and still most effective, approach has been military assistance. The pattern of arms deliveries in the 1950s and 1960s clearly revealed the new policy—emphasis on emerging "bourgeois" regimes. Most exports went to noncommunist countries; arms were shipped to Egypt and Syria before the Suez War in 1956, Yemen before the border clashes with Aden in 1957 and 1958, Algeria during its brief border struggle with Morocco in 1963, and Indonesia during internal conflicts from 1958 to 1965. The scale of military assistance was modest, but the political and military importance of Moscow's shift has proved considerable. Military assistance has provided an entrée for courtship of Third World states; and it has earned a substantial bonus—hard currency that eases the burdens of involvement.[2]

SUCCESSES IN THE 1970s

During the 1970s, the period of greatest success in the Third World, the Soviets appeared to believe that the larger setting of international relationships had become more favorable. New governments emerged in Afghanistan, Ethiopia, Indochina, Nicaragua, South Yemen, and in the former Portuguese colonies of Angola and Mozambique; all of these regimes chose a socialist orientation. Third World revolutions prompted the Soviet Union to emphasize relations with radical governments and stress revolutionary vanguard parties on a Marxist-Leninist basis.

In addition to improvement in their own military position, the Soviets beheld other favorable trends:

- Capitalist society was in crisis— possibly deeper and more long-lasting—with resulting erosion of the West's common purpose.
- The United States, in particular, had suffered international reverses in the wake of the defeat in Vietnam and was experiencing domestic difficulties and, as a result, had lost prestige.
- The Soviet position, in contrast, appeared strong in Eastern Europe and had been strengthened by a European security agreement that in effect confirmed the division of Europe.
- The USSR's growing strategic forces and improved capability for conventional warfare had increased its stature.

During this period, Vietnam's military success in Indochina, the consolidation of the Angolan government, Ethiopia's defeat of Somalia, and Cuba's assertive military policy in Africa were attributed to Soviet assistance. Moscow took no part in the emergence of leftist, Marxist, anti-American regimes in Ethiopia, Grenada, Mozambique, Nicaragua, and Zimbabwe, but gained from the international triumphs of Soviet-style regimes. Collapse of the Shah in Iran and Ferdinand Marcos in the Philippines contributed to a perception of U.S. failure, after the embarrassing withdrawal from Indochina. Soviet alignments with such national liberation movements as the ANC,

SWAPO, and the PLO revealed a Soviet Union on the "side of the angels."

As a result of these developments, the chief of the Central Committee's International Department, Ponomarev, was able to write in 1980 that world politics in the 1970s had changed in the direction of Moscow. He claimed that:

- the correlation of forces in the international arena had improved in favor of socialism and national liberation;
- détente had major successes, such as seriously restricting the "freedom of maneuver" of the most aggressive imperialist forces;
- and the anti-imperialist struggle had broadened, drawing in all of the national liberation struggle.[3]

SETBACKS IN THE 1980s

By the time of Gorbachev's accession to power, these trends had changed and prospects for radical regimes and national liberation movements in the Third World had become bleak. Third World states with so-called vanguard parties (Afghanistan, Angola, Ethiopia, Mozambique, Nicaragua, and South Yemen) were having political and economic difficulties, and facing insurgent or tribal military threats. The Soviets were becoming a counterinsurgency power, a role for which they were not trained and were having little success. Moscow's involvement on behalf of radical regimes, not one of them strategically significant, was compromising relations with the United States and China.

Gorbachev had inherited a series of economic and social problems that had exposed weaknesses in the Soviet system and threatened to undermine the communist government. The Soviet consumer was facing shortages in every foodstuff except vodka, and Gorbachev mistakenly was trying to limit that. Productivity was plummeting and the most important source of growth, technology, was failing. The era of cheap and abundant raw materials had come to an end in the USSR as new sources of minerals and energy were becoming more expensive and difficult to extract. Primitive transportation and communications systems had resulted in bottlenecks for the economy and obstacles in investment.[4] Indeed, the Soviet infrastructure was more typical of a Third World state than an advanced industrial power.

Gorbachev's response was nonideological and immediate as he called for virtual renunciation of Moscow's hegemony over Eastern Europe, elimination of confrontation with the United States and China, comprehensive arms control and confidence-building measures, and an entirely new approach toward the Third World.[5] At the twenty-seventh Soviet party congress in 1986 he left no doubt that Moscow was far less interested in the Third World and that the "bleeding sore" in Afghanistan had to be cured. Later he delivered an indictment of Brezhnev's foreign policy to a meeting at the foreign ministry, and Shevardnadze called for "restructuring" the work of the foreign ministry.

Shevardnadze's restructuring has led to changes throughout the Third World. The beginning of a diplomatic dialogue with Israel was a harbinger toward the Middle East, and a speech by Gorbachev at Vladivostok in 1986 outlined a policy toward Asia that included unilateral troop withdrawals from Mongolia and the Sino-Soviet border. Willingness to include SS-20 medium-range ballistic missiles deployed in Soviet Central Asia in the INF treaty with the United States was completely unexpected and convinced the leadership in Beijing and Washington that Gorbachev was serious about ending the obstacles to rapprochement with China.

In 1988 there were indications that the Soviets wanted to reduce the stake in Angola and favored a Cuban troop withdrawal if the South African threat to the government in Luanda could end. The Cubans had begun their retreat from Ethiopia, and the Soviets were beginning to reduce aid to Mozambique. Gorbachev had signaled that in former colonial areas important to the USSR during the Brezhnev era—Africa, Asia, the Middle East—the leadership in the Kremlin was engaged in new thinking (*novoe myshlenie*) that would alter the Soviet position.

"NEW POLITICAL THINKING" IN THE THIRD WORLD

The new expression of Soviet interests in the Third World was described in a series of authoritative articles that outlined failures of the Brezhnev era and revealed limits of policy under Gorbachev. The benchmark article was by an advocate of Gorbachev's reforms, Vyacheslav Dashichev of the Institute of the Economics of World Socialist System, who favored a link between improved relations with the United States and regional settlement in the Third World.[6] He argued that the USSR had incorrectly "assessed the global situation" and "disregarded" the effect of Moscow's behavior in the Third World on "détente between the USSR and the West."[7] In a warning to radical Third World states, he stated that Soviet interests "lay by no means in chasing petty and essentially formal gains associated with leadership coups in certain countries." Several weeks earlier a foreign ministry official argued on Moscow radio that the Brezhnev regime had become so enmeshed in "complexities of specific situations" that it had lost its bearings, and that "certain fundamental processes," including the emergence of newly industrialized countries, "somehow escaped our attention."[8]

Officials have been critical of the spread of the East-West confrontation to the Third World. In *International Affairs*, the journal of the foreign ministry, Andrei Kozyrev and Andrei Shumikhin stated that

> direct and indirect Soviet support for some forces and regimes in the Third World prone to use force to settle international problems prompted propagandistic accusations that the Soviet Union was bent on expansion and intended to use the lessening of tensions in Europe to gain an edge on the West in the Third World.[9]

Like Dashichev, they were critical of policy mistakes, particularly waste of economic resources, and defended Gorbachev's "new political thinking," which questions support for radical movements in the Third World.

Third World leaders were being confronted with statements that questioned the applicability of the Soviet model and economic assistance to such radical states as Cuba and Nicaragua. Kozyrev and Shumikhin argued that Brezhnev had ignored the "fundamental Leninist idea that the Third World states were awakening to independent life" and "simplistically viewed these countries as objects of our influence which had to follow our example."[10] Georgi Mirski, a senior Third World specialist at the Institute for World Economics and International Relations, recorded that Third World radical states suffered from "economic mismanagement...low labor productivity...excessive growth of managerial staff and shortages of consumer goods for the population," and implicitly questioned continued Soviet economic assistance.[11]

Soviet Third World scholars conceded that the USSR could not guarantee movement to new societal means of production "because of its own economic-technological backwardness and serious deformities in social order."[12] Another reform advocate, Nikolai Shmelyov, told the Congress of People's Deputies in 1989 that the Soviet Union, facing economic collapse within the next few years, should cut aid to the Third World, citing the annual $6 billion in largesse to Cuba and Nicaragua as a source of funds for "maintaining the balance of the consumer market" in the Soviet Union."[13] The State Department and the Central Intelligence Agency believe that military and economic aid to Afghanistan, Angola, Cuba, Ethiopia, Nicaragua, and Vietnam is worth more than $15 billion annually, which is more than three times the amount of hard currency Moscow earns from weapons sales to energy-rich states in the Middle East.[14] The Soviets are continuing to receive hard currency from Libya, but Syria is falling deeper into debt for military assistance. The Iraqi invasion of Kuwait in August 1990 ended arms sales, of course, to both countries; both had been paying hard currency for Soviet weaponry.

GORBACHEV'S "NEW THINKING" IN THE MIDDLE EAST

Since the Soviet Union embarked on a Third World policy in the 1950s, the Middle East has been the area of greatest interest. Such clients as Cuba, India, and Vietnam are essential to Moscow's geostrategic position as well as its posture in the Third World—and receive the bulk of aid. The Middle East, however, is the most important region for several reasons: geographic proximity to the USSR, strategic location and resources, and opportunities it has provided as a consequence of Arab-Israeli tensions. Of additional importance are gains by the Soviets in terms of political ties, hard currency, and access to air and naval facilities.

Over the past decades, the Soviets have been the supplier of military equipment to many Arab states, earning currency and establishing a sizable presence. With exception of energy exports, particularly oil and natural gas, arms sales to Third World countries represent the largest earner of hard currency—more than 15 percent of total earnings. Arms, in turn, have contributed to Syria's ability to threaten Israel as well as Jordan and the Palestinians, enabling it to act as spoiler of Arab-Israeli negotiations that do not take Syrian interests into account. Arms enabled Iraq to wage a ground and air war aginst Iran for ten years and bolstered Muammar Qadhafi's confidence to pursue regional ambitions.

In the Middle East the Soviets have concluded treaties with Egypt (since abrogated), Iraq, Syria, North Yemen, and South Yemen. They believe these treaties have helped legitimize their role. At one time or another, they have had naval and naval air access to most of these states as well as Libya.[15] The Iraqi and Yemeni treaties will have to be renegotiated.

Despite this record, Gorbachev inherited a Middle East policy that had made no major gains since the early 1970s and appeared to be losing to U.S. influence. The turning point occurred in 1972 when Anwar Sadat, the new president of Egypt, ordered the Soviets to remove twenty thousand advisers from Egypt, transfer military installations to Egyptian control, and either sell all Soviet-controlled military equipment to Egypt or remove it. At the end of withdrawal, only a few hundred Soviet military personnel remained and most equipment had been withdrawn, including Soviet-piloted MiG-25 interceptors and TU-16 reconnaissance aircraft used to monitor the U.S. Sixth Fleet.[16] Sadat's rejection culminated in 1976 with his abrogation of the Soviet-Egyptian treaty of friendship and downgrading of diplomatic representation.

Egypt's turn toward the West had significant consequences for Moscow's position in the Middle East—all negative. First, the Soviets had lost a significant military presence in the region—one they have never regained.[17] Second, the Soviets were to be excluded from the Arab-Israeli peace process started by Secretary of State Kissinger after the 1973 war and culminating in President Carter's Camp David agreements in 1978. Third, the absence of a geopolitical position in Egypt—the key Arab actor in the region—weakened efforts to counter Arab disunity and forge a pro-Soviet, anti-U.S. Arab position with respect to the Arab-Israeli conflict. Finally, as part of the cul-de-sac Gorbachev inherited, the Soviets found themselves isolated with the radical states in the region—Syria, Libya, and South Yemen—and discovered they had virtually no control over their sometimes unpredictable actions.

To strengthen policy in the Middle East, Gorbachev made a series of moves to improve Moscow's political position, gain a place at the Arab-Israeli bargaining table, and enhance the Soviet Union's image as a responsible superpower intent on solutions to disputes. His initiatives in the Middle East have not been as sweeping as his arms control proposals or as comprehensive as the approach toward Asia outlined in speeches at Vladivostok in 1986 or Krasnoyarsk in 1988. They appear to be based on a similar perception that the USSR's strong military position had not translated into political gains.

Gorbachev has pursued increasingly flexible policies with respect to a variety of Middle East issues, including relations with Israel and the moderate Arab states (including conservative Gulf states), and diplomatic solutions to conflicts between the Arabs and Israelis as well as between Iran and Iraq. These steps have been accompanied by the airing of differences with Arab clients such as Libya and Syria over terrorism, military parity, and relations with Israel. In 1986, Gorbachev lectured visiting Libyan official Abd al-Salam Jallud about the need for "restraint" and avoidance of any pretext for imperialist attacks, "above all terrorism in all its forms."[18] Qadhafi has been showing restraint since this time, although the U.S. bombing of Libya military facilities and the command and control center and administrative buildings of El-Azziziya Barracks in Tripoli in the previous month was the principal factor. In 1987, Gorbachev urged President Assad to seek a political solution to the Arab-Israeli impasse and indicated Moscow would no longer support efforts to attain military parity with Israel.[19] The Soviets pressed the PLO in 1988 to enter a dialogue with the United States and have made no attempt to complicate U.S.–brokered talks between Egypt, Israel, and the Palestinians.

"NEW DIRECTIONS" TOWARD ISRAEL

As Galia Golan of the Hebrew University in Jerusalem noted in *Foreign Affairs* in 1987, Moscow's moves toward an opening to Israel represents a "new direction" in Soviet policy and an effort by Gorbachev to broaden Soviet options in the Middle East.[20] Gorbachev is the first general secretary to pursue ties with Tel Aviv and offer concessions to Israel to enhance Moscow's regional flexibility and international credibility. Moscow had broken relations with Israel during the Six-Day War in response to Arab pressure and to bolster its credibility, lost during Israel's lightning success against Soviet-supplied Arab opponents. The move put it at a disadvantage vis-à-vis the United States in terms of mediating the conflict and contributed to the stagnation of the Soviet position in the Middle East.

Gorbachev in 1985 had moved to expand the dialogue with Israel, sanctioning meetings in Paris and Washington between the Soviet and Israeli ambassadors and allowing Poland and Hungary to arrange the establishment of interests sections in Israel.[21] The Polish Interests Section opened in 1986, and the Hungarian Interests Section in 1988. By 1990, Poland, Hungary, and Czechoslovakia had established full diplomatic relations with Israel. (Later in this chapter it will be noted that Poland and Hungary have been the first Warsaw Pact states to establish relations with South Korea.)

The first official meeting between Soviet and Israeli representatives in nearly twenty years took place in Helsinki in 1986 and Foreign Minister Shevardnadze and then Israeli prime minister Shimon Peres met at the United Nations in the highest-level discussions between Soviet and Israeli officials since 1967. Neither meeting accomplished much, but reflected the interest of both sides in pursuing a dialogue and were followed by more contacts.

In a gesture to both Israeli and Western sensibilities, Gorbachev allowed huge increases in Jewish emigration. Over eight thousand Soviet Jews left in 1987 compared with under one thousand the year before, and nearly twenty thousand Jews left in 1988. More than seventy thousand Jews left the USSR in 1989, marking the highest level of emigration since creation of the State of Israel. Around 200,000 Soviet Jews arrived in Israel in 1990, and one million could arrive before the mid-1990s, a number that will change Israeli domestic politics. Although this shift was probably aimed to help relations with the United States, it had resonance in Israel where officials regarded it both as a response to their appeal for a more forthcoming Soviet position and as "proof" of a dialogue with the Soviets.[22] The Soviet embassy in Washington held a news conference in November 1989 to announce that the Supreme Soviet would revise emigration laws to permit freer emigration and, in return, asked that the United States lift trade barriers against Soviet exports.[23]

Since more emigrants from the USSR arrived in Israel, it appeared that Moscow had become far less concerned with Arab opposition to Jewish emigration. In December, moreover, the official airlines of the Soviet Union and Israel agreed to direct flights for Soviet Jews emigrating to Israel but this arrangement was cancelled several months later when Israeli officials began to boast about the increase in emigration and Arab states became concerned about settlement of Soviet emigrants on the West Bank and in East Jerusalem. The Israelis subsequently placed a media ban on discussion of direct flights but the Soviets appeared leery about the effect of Aeroflot flights into Tel Aviv and El Al into Moscow.

The Soviet Union and Israel exchanged their first delegations in 1987 and 1988, a Soviet consular delegation to Tel Aviv, which marked the first Soviet delegation to visit Israel since 1967, and an Israeli delegation in Moscow to inspect its interests section at the Dutch embassy. Arrival of the Soviet delegation in 1987 was a victory of sorts for Gorbachev's policy as Israel had linked such a visit to one by an Israeli delegation or resumption of full relations. The Israelis agreed to the Soviet visit, and an Israeli delegation did not arrive in Moscow until 1988. Nevertheless, Soviet willingness to approve the Israeli request was striking given Israel's brutal handling of Palestinian demonstrations in the occupied territories.

In recent steps to lay the ground for restoration of diplomatic relations with Israel, the Soviets raised the status of the Israeli delegation to "consular" status and decided to abstain rather than vote to expel in the annual Arab exercise to drive Israel from the United Nations. The latter step marked a Soviet effort to move from reflexive alignment with the radical Arab states, particularly Libya and Syria, and presumably ended Moscow's efforts to delegitimize Israel within international organizations, particularly UNESCO and the International Telecommunications Union. Most of the Soviet bloc joined Moscow in abstaining on expulsion, but Hungary and Romania actually voted in favor of Israel's membership. Third World countries that have the most to fear from Moscow's more moderate position— Afghanistan, Angola, Cuba, and Nicaragua—voted with the Arabs.

During the Persian Gulf Crisis, moreover, Moscow asked the Security Council to postpone a vote on a resolution critical of Israel, a task usually performed solely by the United States. To balance support for Israel at the United Nations, the Soviets upgraded to embassy status the mission of the Palestine Liberation Organization in Moscow.

The Soviets are easing conditions for restoration of diplomatic relations. In an interview with *Izvestia*, First Deputy Foreign Minister Yuli Vorontsov indicated that to reopen diplomatic ties Israel merely had to "agree to move toward a settlement" or "take steps toward convening an international conference."[24] Moscow previously insisted on negotiations before relations could be resumed. Shevardnadze hinted in 1990 that Israeli guarantees not to settle Soviet immigrants in occupied territory could lead to recognition.

In September 1990, following discussions between Shevardnadze and Foreign Minister David Levi, the two sides announced the establishment of full consular relations and consultations at the level of Foreign Minister. Soviet officials like Vorontsov are emphasizing that contacts with the Israelis will continue regardless of developments in the Middle East and restoration of diplomatic relations can be expected to take place soon.

IMPROVED TIES WITH ARAB MODERATES

As upgrading the dialogue with Israel serves Moscow's broader strategic and regional goals, so does expanding contacts with moderate Arab regimes. Shortly after coming to power, Gorbachev signaled eagerness to move these relations forward. The target of this approach was Egypt, whose gradual move back into the Arab fold during this period was consistent with Moscow's efforts to encourage a more united Arab approach to conflict with Israel. The Soviets have established diplomatic relations with Bahrein, Oman, the United Arab Emirates, Qatar, and Saudi Arabia since Gorbachev's accession.

Under President Hosni Mubarak, there was until 1987 only glacial improvement in Soviet-Egyptian relations. Mubarak permitted the Soviet ambassador to return to Cairo in 1985, but allowed little other progress. An obstacle to improved relations was disagreement over repayment for Egypt's military debt to the USSR. Since 1977, Egypt had refused to make payments, and Moscow had made such payments a condition to delivery of spare parts and for improved commercial relations.[25]

Soviet overtures to improve relations with Egypt began in 1985 and during the next year there were exchanges of visits and messages of goodwill. Appointment of a high-level trade official (G.K. Zhuravlev, formerly first deputy minister of foreign trade) as ambassador in 1986 gave impetus to the search for solution to the debt. In 1987, Moscow agreed in principle to Egypt's terms for repayment including a six-year grace period and generous terms for the subsequent nineteen years of repayment.[26] Soon after, the two sides signed bilateral economic agreements and renewed discussions of military supply.[27] Later Egypt allowed the Soviets to reopen their consulates in Alexandria and Port Said.[28]

In 1988, Cairo endorsed Moscow's calls for an international conference on the Middle East and stated that the USSR should play a leading role in such a conference.[29] Later, Egyptian Foreign Minister Ismat Abd al-Majid made the first foreign ministerial visit to the Soviet Union in thirteen years and emphasized the USSR's role in a Middle East settlement. Even this modest improvement in relations with Egypt has strengthened Moscow's mediating role in the Arab-Israeli conflict.

The Soviets moved to improve state-to-state ties with Jordan. They gave red-carpet treatment to King Hussein in 1987 during his first visit to Moscow since 1981, and press reports indicated they offered to sell Amman the advanced MiG-29 fighter aircraft, which only Cuba, India, Iran, Syria, and Iraq currently possess.[30] For a brief period Moscow appeared more supportive of Jordan's position in the peace process while its commitment to the PLO's role became ambiguous.[31] Soviet spokesmen indicated that the PLO need not be represented directly at a peace conference but could be included in a united Arab delegation or in a joint Jordanian-Palestinian delegation.[32] This appeared to mark a shift from Moscow's opposition to the Hussein-Arafat accord of 1985–1986, which was designed to produce a joint Jordanian-Palestinian delegation to negotiate with Israel. This ambiguity was intended to convey the impression that Moscow was open to any constructive approach to an international conference and was willing to compromise on participation by a joint Jordanian-Palestinian delegation. Soviet flexibility on these issues came to an end in 1988, however, with worsening of the Palestinian uprising on the West Bank and Hussein's renunciation of a Jordanian role in the West Bank.

GORBACHEV'S "NEW THINKING" IN ASIA

Until Gorbachev, the Soviets had rarely displayed flexibility or political acumen in dealing with Asian neighbors. Often highhanded with Chinese and Japanese, the Soviets found themselves at a disadvantage in Asia as China normalized relations with the United States and Japan, and Japan benefitted from a new political and economic activism. The USSR, for the most part, was excluded from the diplomatic activity and burgeoning economic development of the region, perceived by Asian states as a European power with threatening military assets in the Pacific.

The USSR's Eurasian plain stretches from the Urals to Mongolia, and the Soviet Far East is isolated from industrial and population centers of the Soviet Union. These distances have had a negative effect on economic development of the Soviet Far East, and Moscow's ability to deploy men and equipment, provide reinforcements, and resupply. As compensation, the Soviets deploy their largest fleet in the Pacific, nearly one third of their combat forces in the Soviet Far East, and two thousand combat aircraft in north Asia. This heavy concentration has added to Moscow's problems.

As Gorbachev examined the Soviet position in Asia in 1985, he could have concluded that Moscow's policy had been a failure. Nowhere was the gap between the military strength and political position more apparent. The Sino-Soviet dispute prevented any Asian state from favoring an increased Soviet presence for fear of antagonizing the Chinese. Soviet occupation of the Northern Territories, the four islands north of Japan, since the end of the Second World War, and inclusion of these islands in the Soviet security belt was an obstacle to improvement in Soviet-Japanese relations. Moreover, the military buildup under Brezhnev from 1964 to 1982 had led to increased cooperation between the United States, China, and Japan on security, leading to an informal anti-Soviet coalition between these states, South Korea, and the Association of Southeast Asian Nations (ASEAN).[33] The Vietnamese invasion of Cambodia in 1978 and the invasion of Afghanistan added to Moscow's regional problems.

Gorbachev probably has made his most dramatic attempt to alter the political environment and shift perceptions in Moscow's favor in Asia. As in the Middle East, the components of Moscow's "new thinking" are less on military instruments, stress on peaceful resolution of disputes, an end to ideology, and emphasis on traditional diplomacy. This approach was articulated in speeches in the Soviet Far East (at Vladivostok in 1986 and Krasnoyarsk in 1988) that appealed to China for an end to the Sino-Soviet dispute, announced an initial withdrawal of forces from Afghanistan in 1986, recognized the navigational channel of the Amur-Ussuri River as the border between the USSR and China, and urged negotiation to reduce fleets in the Pacific.[34] Gorbachev made an unconditional offer to limit nuclear weapons in the Asia-Pacific region and in the winter of 1989–1990 withdrew most Soviet forces from Cam Ranh Bay. The Soviets have supported calls for nuclear-free zones by the states of ASEAN and the south Pacific.

SOVIET RAPPROCHEMENT WITH CHINA

Gorbachev's major success in Asia has been a rapprochement with China that rivals his success in institutionalizing relations with the United States and sponsoring a comprehensive position on a variety of arms control measures. From the outset he emphasized improving relations with China and, since his speech at Vladivostok in 1986, border tensions have diminished and trade increased tenfold over 1982 levels, to reach more than $3 billion annually.[35] Soviet experts and technicians are renovating nearly twenty Chinese factories and constructing seven new ones; scientific and cultural exchanges have increased dramatically. Polemics have been muted, particularly since Gorbachev's decision in 1987 to shut down Moscow's clandestine Ba Yi radio station, which for decades had broadcast disinformation to foment uncertainty within the Chinese People's Liberation Army.

The symbolic and substantive highlight of rapprochment was, of course, Gorbachev's visit to China in May 1989, particularly his meetings with senior leader Deng Xiaoping and Premier Li Peng. These meetings officially ended the Sino-Soviet dispute after thirty years of hostility and marked the first Sino-Soviet summit since Khrushchev visited China in 1959. The joint communiqué referred favorably to Gorbachev's "new political thinking" and, for the first time, Chinese media acknowledged similarity between Gorbachev's thinking and Deng's concept of a new international order.[36] The communiqué stressed determination to reduce military confrontation, endorsing measures to reduce forces along the border to a "minimum level."

The communiqué noted progress on border issues and indicated that negotiations on eastern and western sectors of the border would be merged and held at the foreign ministerial level rather than that of deputy foreign minister. Talks took place in October 1989 and, for the first time, both sides acknowledged "some progress" that could lead to a foreign ministers meeting to resolve the most contentious issues.[37] It is noteworthy that the Chinese anniversary greetings to the Soviet leadership, only one week after the end of border talks, were sent in the name of the Chinese communist party's Central Committee, for the first time since 1967, and included an optimistic assessment of prospects in Sino-Soviet relations.[38]

Presumably this progress could not have taken place without Gorbachev's willingness to move on all of the three conditions (or "obstacles") that Beijing had established for reconciliation: withdrawal from Afghanistan, Vietnamese withdrawal from Cambodia, and unilateral Soviet reductions on the Sino-Soviet border. In January 1987, Moscow announced its decision to withdraw a division (10,000 to 12,000) from Mongolia and, in his speech to the United

Nations in 1988, Gorbachev announced a substantial reduction along the Sino-Soviet border. During his visit to Beijing in February 1989, Shevardnadze stated that the USSR would remove two hundred thousand troops from the border as well as three fourths of its troops in Mongolia by 1991. Soviet withdrawal from Afghanistan was completed in February 1989 and later in the year the Vietnamese completed withdrawal from Cambodia.

The Soviets and the Chinese held their first round of talks in November 1989 on reducing forces on the Sino-Soviet border, with the sides agreeing that "mutual reductions . . . would be of significance."[39] Moscow began unilateral reductions in the Soviet Far East and has withdrawn nearly twenty-five thousand troops from Mongolia.[40] The Soviets plan to withdraw most of their forces from Mongolia by the end of 1990, and Gorbachev told Chinese leaders in 1989 that Moscow plans to withdraw all forces from Mongolia. An accord reducing forces along the border was announced in April 1990 when Li Peng became the first Chinese government leader to travel to Moscow since 1964, and high-level military discussions took place in June to deal with conversion of defense industries to the civilian economy. Defense Minister Yazov's visit to Beijing in March 1991 could lead to the resumption of arms sales to China.

JAPAN: LIMITS TO SOVIET PROGRESS IN ASIA

The empty place in the pattern of improved Soviet relations in Asia has been Japan, a key country for Moscow because of its location, close ties to the United States, and burgeoning strength and influence. The Soviets have wanted to slow the emergence of a U.S.–Chinese–Japanese entente and erode U.S.–Japanese security ties, but the issue blocking improved relations is the continuing Japanese claim to the "northern territories," the four islands occupied by the USSR since the end of the Second World War.

Gorbachev has made tentative efforts to improve the climate of relations, trying pressure and persuasion to establish a dialogue. He has accused the Japanese of taking a "lopsided attitude" on the territorial issue and warned against making "ultimatums" in international affairs.[41] Before Shevardnadze's trip to Tokyo in December 1988, Soviet media took a tough stance on return of the islands. But Gorbachev also has been optimistic about relations, citing Japan's "flexibility" on Soviet-Japanese differences (i.e., the northern territories) and agreed to schedule a long-awaited visit to Japan for April 1991.[42] The agreement on Gorbachev's visit was announced following a meeting between the Soviet and Japanese foreign ministers at the United Nations in September 1989.

The Soviets hinted that Soviet-Japanese relations were being reviewed at the highest level and that the Kremlin might consider "joint administration" of the islands. During a visit to Tokyo in November 1989 as head of a Supreme Soviet delegation, then Politburo member Aleksandr Yakovlev stated that Moscow would pursue a "new initiative" to improve relations and that the northern territories could be on the negotiating table.[43] The Japanese are now hinting that they are willing to discuss economic assistance and investment in Siberia as long as Moscow is willing to resolve the territorial issue before the Gorbachev visit.[44]

Yevgeniy Primakov, a close adviser to Gorbachev, has claimed that Moscow would match any flexibility shown by Tokyo.[45] The Soviets, however, appear to fear any concession on territorial issues before resolving border issues with China, and would not want to yield the larger, northernmost islands because of their role in protecting Soviet strategic submarines in the Sea of Okhotsk, which Soviet military writings describe as a "bastion area," or sanctuary. A compromise on the territories, moreover, would undermine Moscow's case for holding the Baltic states of Estonia, Latvia, and Lithuania.

"NEW THINKING" ON THE KOREAN PENINSULA

Gorbachev is responsible for a Soviet approach toward the two Koreas to get withdrawal of the U.S. military presence in the South and, more important, be part of any broader political discussion of the Korean question. Efforts have been made to improve geopolitical and military relations with Pyongyang and initiate a dialogue with Seoul. North Korea has been receiving MiG-23 fighter aircraft from the USSR and North Korean naval units and fighter aircraft have visited the Soviet Union.[46] Trade relations between the Soviets and South Korea are increasing and diplomatic relations have been established. Two members of the Warsaw Pact (Poland and Hungary) have established diplomatic relations with Seoul. The Soviets are dropping hints about a two-state solution to the Korean problem, a prospect they formerly dismissed.

Moscow's balancing act toward the two Koreas (as well as the USSR's ostensibly neutral attitude toward political turmoil in Eastern Europe) has led Pyongyang to improve relations with China and show displeasure with the Soviet Union. President Kim Il-Sung visited Beijing in November 1989 for the first time in more than two years and Pyongyang downgraded its representation to the USSR's October Revolution anniversary. Shevardnadze's endorsement of relations between the Soviet Union and South Korea did not improve the situation with Kim.[47] Gorbachev's meeting with the South Korean president in 1990 led to the establishment of Soviet-South Korean relations later in the year and some improvement in the South Korean dialogue with the North as well. South Korean President Roh Tae Woo visited Moscow in December 1990; Gorbachev used the talks to call for a nuclear-free zone on the Korean peninsula.

MOSCOW SEEKS IMPROVED TIES TO ASEAN

Gorbachev has embarked on a campaign to improve relations with noncommunist states of Southeast Asia, to burnish Moscow's image, increase economic participation in the region's rapid growth, integrate Vietnam in the region, and improve the environment for the USSR's broader strategic objectives. Shevardnadze has visited such ASEAN (Association for Southeast Asian Nations) states as Indonesia, Thailand, and the Philippines, and Deputy Foreign Minister Igor Rogachev, on tours of ASEAN states in 1988 and 1990, endorsed the region's call for a zone of peace and neutrality.

Thailand has been the focus of Gorbachev's attention to the ASEAN states because of growing military relations with China and strong opposition to Vietnamese presence in Cambodia. Thai Prime Minister Prem Tinsulanon's visit to Moscow in 1988 and visits between Soviet and Thai commanders-in-chief in 1987 were unprecedented.

The Soviets have had success in convincing the Manila government that Moscow has not been helping the local communist party or the New People's Army.[48] Rogachev visited Manila in 1988 and met with President Cory Aquino, and Shevardnadze made the first visit by a Soviet foreign minister in December 1988 to arrange Aquino's visit to the USSR. Philippine Foreign Minister Raul Manglapus visited Moscow in 1989 and also made the first high-level visit to Vietnam by any Philippine official since the invasion of Cambodia in 1978. For the past several years, Gorbachev has been encouraging reconciliation between Vietnam and the ASEAN community, particularly Indonesia, Thailand, and the Philippines.

Gorbachev has provided a direction to policy in Asia that had not been present since the end of the Second World War. By moving "beyond containment" with regard to China, the Soviets are convincing Asian states that Moscow's policies do not threaten their interests. And by deideologizing and demilitarizing Soviet policies in the region, they have improved relations with key states of East and Southeast Asia. In remarks that would have been ideological heresy in the past, Gorbachev told Deng in 1989 that neither Marx nor Lenin had answers to today's problems for the USSR and China. Two years earlier, in his speech at the 70th anniversary of the Bolshevik Revolution aimed at China and non-Soviet members of the Warsaw Pact,

Gorbachev stressed diversity among socialist states and criticized "arrogance of omniscience."[49]

In addition to improving relations with China, the Soviets have developed entrée to the ASEAN states and improved relations with both Koreas. The USSR is no longer "odd man out" in the Asian quadrilateral, and Gorbachev's arms control and confidence-building measures could lead to improved relations with the states of the South Pacific as well. Moscow's economic problems will be a constraint on Soviet influence and presence in Asia, but stabilization between the USSR and China should have favorable implications throughout the region. The improvement of Soviet–U.S. ties could open the way for dialogue with Japan as reduction of Soviet–U.S. tensions makes Moscow more attractive as a negotiating partner.

GORBACHEV'S "NEW THINKING" IN AFRICA

Gorbachev inherited a policy in Africa that included success in Ethiopia in rebuffing a Somali invasion in the 1970s and consolidation of a regime in Angola when the Portuguese cut bait and ran in the mid-1970s. Unfortunately for Soviet interests, the regimes that Moscow has supported over the past fifteen years have never controlled the whole of their national territories. A Soviet-led Cuban military force enabled Ethiopia to deal with Somalia, but the Mengistu regime had no success in turning back internal challenges from Eritreans and Tigreans. The Dos Santos regime is holding on in Luanda but Jonas Savimbi's UNITA forces in southern Angola became more powerful in the 1980s with military support from South Africa and then the Reagan administration. Mozambique faces a wretched situation against a guerrilla group (Mozambique National Resistance or Renamo) that practices urban terrorism and banditry throughout the country.

All these so-called Marxist states (Ethiopia, Angola, and Mozambique) have received bad economic advice and less economic assistance from the Soviet Union. Ethiopia may be the poorest country in the world, with some of the worst weather, worst agricultural policies, and most dramatic starvation. Angola is potentially wealthy, with oil, gold, and diamonds, but most of these assets remain unattended. Mozambique's situation may be the most wretched of all, with mercenaries required to protect farms and lines of communication. The Soviets now want these states to attract Western assistance, and the Africans are following Soviet counsel in this regard. Ethiopia has reestablished relations with Israel and wants a U.S. ambassador; Angola no longer has a communist government; Mozambique no longer calls itself Marxist. All three states are shopping for Western financial assistance.

Gorbachev appears to have decided that Africa is peripheral to Soviet security and that too much attention had been devoted to undermining Western influence in the region and promoting pro-Soviet and leftist governments. Air and naval access always had been modest in Africa and, in many cases, Soviet forces made very little use of facilities that were offered. Soviet exclusion from most of the diplomatic negotiations in the region did nothing to enhance Moscow's credentials and failure of the Soviet ideological blueprint has not impressed African regimes.

Until the December 1988 agreement regarding Angola and Namibia, the Soviets had been excluded from diplomatic discussions that dealt with Angola, Mozambique, Namibia, and Zimbabwe. Moscow played no role at the Lancaster House talks in the United Kingdom that led to creation of Zimbabwe, and the Nkomati and Lusaka accords in 1984 appeared to catch the Kremlin off guard despite Soviet military assistance on behalf of Mozambique and Angola.

The Lusaka Accord, signed in Zambia on 1984, called for withdrawal of South African forces from southern Angola in return for Luanda's commitment to prevent forces of the South West People's Organization of Namibia (SWAPO) from entering. A joint monitoring commission was established to police the area of disengagement and prevent infiltration of northern Namibia by SWAPO guerrillas.

The Nkomati Accord, signed in the Mozambican border town of Nkomati in 1984, called for nonaggression between Mozambique and South Africa. It stipulated that neither side would allow its territory to be used to prepare violence against the other. Equally important to Maputo were subsequent agreements on economic and financial assistance, trade, and tourism, and on joint operations of the crucial Cabora Bassa hydroelectric project.[50]

Gorbachev has taken advantage of every opportunity to arrange a role in any discussions in Africa to reduce Moscow's involvement in conflicts in the region and reduce tension with the United States. The turning point took place in 1988, when the Soviets took a behind-the-scenes part in ending the thirteen-year presence of Cuban expeditionary forces in Angola, the South African presence in Angola, and South African administration of Namibia. The United States, which does not have diplomatic relations with Angola or Cuba, could not have mediated the agreement, signed in 1988, at the United Nations, without Soviet pressure on both Luanda and Havana. The Angolan issue, a symbol of collapse of détente in 1975, became the focal point of Soviet–U.S. cooperation in resolving regional disputes in the Third World. According to Charles W. Freeman, Jr., Deputy Assistant

Secretary of State for African Affairs from 1986 to 1989, the Soviets held their own discussions with both Angolans and Cubans in support of U.S. efforts and apprised the U.S. delegation.[51] By the summer of 1988, Deputy Foreign Minister Anatoly Adamishin and the foreign ministry's African Director Vladillen Vasev had become partners in an agreement that traded Cuban and South African withdrawal from the region as well as an end to South African assistance to UNITA and withdrawal of the African National Congress (ANC) from military bases in Angola.

Since signing the agreement, the Soviets have thrown support to negotiated settlements of the prolonged civil wars between the Luanda regime and UNITA, the Ethiopian government and Eritreans, and Mozambique and Renamo. Adamishin has met with Angolan, U.S., and Zairian officials, and Soviet spokesman have supported a role for UNITA in the Angolan government.[52] Adamishin has maintained pressure on Addis Ababa by meeting with leaders of the Eritrean People's Liberation Front (EPLF) in London and approving efforts of former president Jimmy Carter to mediate.

The Soviets are signaling to their clients in Africa that they are stepping back from confrontations that have required large amounts of military and economic assistance and created problems with the United States. And following Soviet-American persuasion, the Luanda regime and UNITA are expected to achieve a ceasefire and a date for free elections in 1990. Soviet–U.S. pressure also led to an Ethiopian-Eritrean agreement in 1990 to reopen the Red Sea port of Massawa and permit food deliveries to millions of refugees.

In another indication of Moscow's less rigid approach toward South Africa since Gorbachev's accession and in a gesture toward the new government in Pretoria, Shevardnadze praised South Africa for its stance on the Namibia issue and raised the prospect of continuing improvement of relations. In an interview broadcast to South Africa, the foreign minister conceded it was "not easy" for Pretoria to consent to Namibian independence and called the move an "important first step" that could return South Africa to the "international community."[53] The Soviets have used the ceasefire in Angola to justify contacts with South Africa, including visits of foreign ministry officials. Moscow signaled a shift in its position toward Pretoria in 1988, when Soviet media became less polemical and acknowledged diplomatic contacts with Pretoria during negotiations on the Angolan ceasefire.

Shevardnadze made his first trip to southern Africa in March 1990, when he traveled to independence celebrations in Namibia as well as Angola, Mozambique, Zambia, and Zimbabwe. The foreign minister stressed national reconciliation in Angola and Mozambique, and reform in South Africa. On the eve of departure for Africa, he reaffirmed Moscow's desire to end ideological competition with the West in the Third World and fashion a more pragmatic approach to relations in the Third World.[54] At the end of the trip, he acknowledged that the "intensive quality" of Moscow's relations with African states had declined and defended the higher priority assigned to ending the arms race and resolving regional conflict.[55]

OUTLOOK FOR SOVIETS IN THE KEY THIRD WORLD REGIONS

The Soviets are anticipating that withdrawal from Afghanistan in addition to Vietnamese withdrawal from Cambodia and Cuban withdrawal from Angola will pay dividends throughout Southwest and Southeast Asia, the Middle East and Africa. Bilateral relations with Iran have improved and prospects for improvement in Soviet-Pakistani relations are good. Soviet–Saudi Arabian diplomatic relations have been reestablished and Moscow has improved relations with other members of the Gulf Cooperation Council (GCC), established after the invasion of Afghanistan. GCC states have loaned the Soviets more than $3 billion in return for Moscow's support against Iraq. No Muslim state was ever comfortable with Soviet military presence in Afghanistan and no noncommunist Asian state supportive of the Soviet role in Cambodia in support of Vietnam. These military retreats reduce the chance for Soviet–U.S. and Sino-Soviet rivalries in areas of vulnerability and are particularly welcome to India, Thailand, Iran, and Pakistan, which have their own regional aspirations. Finally, both the United States and China linked improvement in bilateral relations with the Soviet Union to military withdrawal from Afghanistan.

Improved Sino-Soviet relations since the 1988 announcement of withdrawal from Afghanistan are having resonance in terms of better relations with Asian and Pacific states. Vietnamese withdrawal from Cambodia is leading to improved ties for both Vietnam and the USSR with members of the Association of the Southeast Asian Nations (ASEAN). In only two years Gorbachev has managed to reverse many of the unsatisfactory trends following the invasion of Cambodia by Vietnam in 1978. Gorbachev appeared to recognize that Moscow's generally crude handling of Asian sensibilities strengthened an anti-Soviet consensus in the Pacific and encouraged a resurgence of U.S. military power and political prestige.

Gorbachev, unlike any of his predecessors, has been willing to acknowledge the role of the United States in these areas in defense of its own interests. In his account of perestroika, written in 1987, he stated he did not want any settlement in the Middle East to "infringe upon the interests of the United States and the West. We are not bent on elbowing the U.S. out of the Middle East—this is simply unrealistic," but warned that the United States "should not commit itself to unrealistic goals either."[56] He has been supportive of a U.S. role in the Pacific, and in an unusual acknowledgement of U.S. interests an aide to Gorbachev commented that Moscow "understood" U.S. military support for President Aquino during the coup attempt in December 1989.[57] The aide, who was accompanying Gorbachev during the general secretary's meeting with Pope John Paul II, explained that "democratically elected" governments had to be "maintained as well as defended."

In Africa, Gorbachev has been responsible for a shift in policy that will probably lead to more normal relations with both African states and South Africa. The shift in 1988 toward a peaceful settlement of the Angolan crisis is part of a larger effort to resolve regional problems in Ethiopia and Mozambique as well as a way to reduce Moscow's presence and support throughout the continent. Gorbachev has lowered the geopolitical importance of Africa and appears prepared to ignore the increased volatility of a region that faces systemic economic and environmental problems. Moscow's disillusionment with the so-called vanguard parties, the "socialist orientation" of such states as Angola and Ethiopia, and military regimes in the region has led it to turn from competition with the United States and the West in Africa and emphasize cooperation in economic ties with African states. States that were ignored because of their capitalist orientation (Kenya, the Sudan, Tunisia, Zaire) are now objects of increased attention. States governed by populist military elements (Burkina Faso, Ghana, Liberia) are being ignored. Mozambique and Benin have renounced Marxism.

In addition to arranging the Angola-Namibia settlement with South Africa, the Soviets are now favoring political settlement throughout southern Africa and dissociating themselves from military objectives of the African National Congress and the South West Africa People's Organization. A deputy foreign minister remarked in 1989 that these groups were not going to "build socialism in this part of the world."[58] Anatoly Gromyko, son of the late president and foreign minister and head of the USSR's leading African institute, favors a political solution to the problems in South Africa even if it required "sitting down for negotiations for two, three, or however many years."[59]

PROBLEMS OF PROLIFERATION

Soviet efforts over the next several years will probably be devoted to reducing the chances for military confrontation with the United States in all of these regions and to defusing regional conflict, particularly in the Middle East and South Asia due to the proliferation of chemical weapons and ballistic missiles. In the past year, India has fired its first medium-range ballistic missile, thus enabling India to join the United States, the USSR, China, Britain, France, and Israel as states with the capacity to produce surface-to-surface ballistic missiles.[60] India has now established self-reliance in nearly all of its major weapons systems—ballistic missiles, fighter aircraft, and tanks—which means a loss of leverage for the Soviet Union. Pakistan has acknowledged concern over Indian weapons programs and, at the same time, has held its own widely publicized tests of tactical missiles with ranges short of 200 miles.

India and Pakistan have joined several Middle Eastern states with a capability to deploy or develop medium-range ballistic missiles. Israel launched a satellite vehicle in September 1988, which means that it is capable of extending the range of its Jericho medium-range missile, and in April 1990 launched Ofek-2, which marked another step toward an independent satellite photography capability. The latter liftoff proved that Israel had missiles capable of carrying a warhead 1,500 miles, well within range of Baghdad.

Iraq also has reported tests of a rocket capable of carrying satellites into space.[61] Iraq fired Scud missiles in its war with Iran in the 1980s and has been working with Argentina to develop a more accurate missile. Egypt had been working on the Condor missile program with Iraq and Argentina, but recently announced that it had cut its links with the program.[62] Iraqi firing of Scuds against Irsrael and Saudi Arabia in 1991 presumably will lead to a Soviet-U.S. dialogue on the problems of proliferation.

Saudi Arabia purchased Chinese CSS-2 medium-range ballistic missiles in 1988, and both Iran and Syria have Soviet-built Scud short-range missiles. There were rumors in the summer of 1989 that the Syrians were planning to purchase an unspecified number of Chinese M-9 surface-to-surface missles (with a range of 300 miles) but, on the eve of General Brent Scowcroft's arrival in Beijing in December 1989, China announced that it planned no additional sales of missile systems to countries in the Middle East.[63] In addition to Scud missiles (with a range of 175 miles), the Syrians possess Soviet-supplied SS-21 (75 miles) and Frog-7 (45 miles) surface-to-surface missiles. The Soviets have thus far refused to supply the Syrians with SS-23 missiles (375 miles) which could reach Tel Aviv.

Even before most of this activity, the United States, Japan, and the key states of Western Europe had formed the Missile Technology

Control Regime (MTCR) in 1987 to stop the transfer of ballistic missile technology to Third World states. The MTCR is not a formal treaty or a binding agreement, but it is the only Western multilateral effort to curb missile proliferation other than the regime established by the Nonproliferation Treaty. The Soviets have thus far pursued parallel steps to stop the flow of Soviet missiles with ranges of more than 300 miles to the Third World, but have been unwilling to join the MTCR. In any event, the MTCR has failed to prevent the successful test launches of indigenously developed, short-range ballistic missiles by India and Pakistan as well as recent West German and Chinese efforts to assist India and Pakistan, respectively.

Presumably the Soviets realize that it will be easier to limit the proliferation of these systems in South Asia than the Middle East because India and Pakistan have a better understanding of the limits of an arms race in the area of ballistic missiles and, since their war in 1971, of the impact of war in the region. In 1990, India and Pakistan agreed not to attack each other's nuclear facilities. Conversely, there is the risk that Indian and Pakistani expertise and technology will be shared with the states of the Persian Gulf and Southwest Asia. Limits will be difficult to establish in the Middle East because of the bitter political animosities between Israel and the Arab states as well as between Syria and Iran, on the one hand, and Iraq, on the other.

Baghdad, moreover, is responsible for the most provacative rhetoric in the region as President Saddam Hussein has threatened to use chemical weapons to "eat half of Israel if it tries to wage anything against Iraq."[64] Egypt, Iran, Israel, Libya, and Syria also have chemical weapons and the means to deliver them to enemy targets by missiles or aircraft. Suddenly, Israel's long-presumed nuclear capability remains a monopoly but not necessarily an effective deterrent.

The Soviets, as a result, now appear more willing to engage in multilateral efforts to deal with at least the problem of nuclear proliferation in the Third World. During his meeting with Secretary Baker in December 1990, then Foreign Minister Shevardnadze proposed the establishment of a "nuclear-free and chemical-free zone" in the Middle East that would include Iraq and Israel.[65] Moscow appears less concerned with actually being targeted by any of these systems in South Asia or the Middle East than with the problem of dealing with a major regional confrontation that could lead to the use of ballistic missiles or chemical weapons against one of its clients.

Moscow's experience in previous regional confrontations has been that its clients have pressured the Soviets for direct combat support that the USSR has been thus far unwilling to provide. Crisis management in these regions could become more difficult and time urgent as states acquire more sophisticated and lethal weaponry. (See Chapter

6 for a discussion of Soviet crisis management in the Third World.) It is particularly ironic that the key states in these regions are acquiring intermediate-range ballistic missiles just as the United States and the Soviet Union have agreed in their own INF treaty to eliminate such weapons from Europe and to move toward abolishing stocks of chemical weapons.

In order to limit the need for a Soviet military presence in various regions of the Third World and reduce the risk of Soviet–U.S. confrontation, Moscow will support and endorse a variety of confidence-building measures, including the establishment of nuclear-free zones and naval arms limitations. Gorbachev's speeches at Vladivostok in 1986 and Krasnoyarsk in 1988 called for the "renunciation of foreign bases in Asia and the Pacific Ocean" and the reduction of "activity of naval fleets—primarily ships equipped with nuclear arms—in the Pacific Ocean."[66] Gorbachev has already expressed support for Indian and Pacific Ocean nuclear-free zones and, to back these proposals, has withdrawn nuclear-capable ships from these oceans. On the eve of the summit in Malta with President Bush, Gorbachev ordered a reduction of the naval presence in the Mediterranean which could be a harbinger of Soviet proposals on naval limitations in the Middle East. The reduction of Soviet military assistance and Moscow's advisory presence in Africa points to a Soviet emphasis on conflict resolution in that region as well.

Soviet regional policy under Gorbachev is likely to continue to move more actively and deliberately toward finding peaceful solutions to regional conflicts, particularly in the Middle East, and to establish full diplomatic relations with such non-Marxist Third World states as Israel and South Africa. Moscow is making a special effort to play a major role in any settlement of the Arab-Israeli conflict and the Iraqi-Iranian dispute, and has placed special emphasis on working with the United States to find diplomatic solutions to those long-term crises. The presence of Foreign Minister Shevardnadze and Secretary of State Baker in Namibia in March 1990 for independence ceremonies was not only a symbol of peaceful transition in southern Africa but, from the Soviet point of view, a paradigm for Soviet–U.S. cooperation in Third World peacekeeping. The Soviets appear to want to disengage themselves from all protracted conflicts in the Third World in order to put their own domestic house in order and reduce the cost and risk of their presence around the world.

In order to focus on the importance of Soviet–U.S. cooperation on regional issues, the Soviets already have significantly reduced this presence. Gorbachev has ended military assistance to Nicaragua and reduced assistance to some of the more radical states in the Third World, particularly Syria and Vietnam. Soviet military advisers are being withdrawn from Angola, Ethiopia, Mozambique, and Syria. Assad, Castro, Mengistu, and Qadhafi are being exposed to the limits of Soviet support, and Third World leaders presumably realize that Moscow's determination to pursue a strategic dialogue with the United States has become far more important than the transitory nature of involvement in the Third World. The Soviets are clearly signalling that, in an age of nuclear parity and minimal deterrence, continued Soviet–U.S. cooperation is essential to further progress in the Third World and that, in any event, such areas as the Middle East, Southwest Asia, and South Asia have lost much of their strategic significance. Soviet–U.S. cooperation in the Persian Gulf could deter other Third World leaders from use of military force to resolve political differences.

NOTES

1. See Robert Donaldson, ed., *The Soviet Union in the Third World: Successes and Failures*, Boulder, CO: Westview Press, 1981; Carol Saivetz and Syliva Woodby, *Soviet–Third World Relations*, Boulder, CO: Westview Press, 1985; W. Raymond Duncan and Carolyn McGiffert Ekedahl, *Moscow and the Third World Under Gorbachev*, Boulder, CO: Westview Press, 1990.

2. See Roger Kanet, ed., *The Soviet Union and Developing Countries*, Baltimore: Johns Hopkins University Press, 1975.

3. B. Ponamarev, "The Joint Struggle of the Working Class and the National Liberation Movement against Imperialism and for Social Progress," *Kommunist*, No. 16, November 1980, p. 32.

4. Holland Hunter and Deborah Kaple, "Transport in Trouble," in *Soviet Economy in the 1980s: Problems and Prospects*, Part I. Selected papers submitted to the U.S. Congress Joint Economic Committee, Washington, DC: Government Printing Office, 1983, pp. 239–240.

5. Mikhail Gorbachev, *Perestroika: New Thinking for Our Country and the World*, New York: Harper and Row, 1987, pp. 171–189.

6. Dashichev, head of a department in the Academy of Sciences Institute of the Economics of the World Socialist System, condemned Stalin's economic system as hopelessly inefficient and a "serious threat" to the Soviet Union in an article in *Moskovskaya Pravda* in July 1987 and Moscow's international economic isolation in a roundtable discussion that was reported in *Izvestia* in October 1987. In an article in *Izvestia* in April 1988, Dashichev compared Stalin to Hitler for trying to destroy independent and creative thought and expression in the USSR. The director of Dashichev's institute, Oleg Bogomolov, also has criticized Soviet foreign policy, particularly the decision to intervene in Afghanistan, which he contended his institute had criticized in a memorandum to the "relevant authorities." (See Chapter 2 for a discussion of Soviet decision making in the Third World.)

7. Vyacheslav Dashichev, "East-West: Quest for New Relations," *Literaturnaya Gazeta*, May 18, 1988, p. 14, in Foreign Broadcast Information Service, *Soviet Union Daily Report* (hereafter FBIS), May 20, 1988, pp. 7–8.

8. TASS, April 25, 1988.

9. Andrei Kozyrev and Andrei Shumikhin, "East and West in the Third World," *International Affairs* (Moscow), No. 3, 1989, p. 68.

10. Ibid., p. 66.

11. Vladimir Lee and Georgi Mirski, "Socialist Orientation and New Political Thinking," *Asia and Africa Today*, No. 4, 1988, pp. 68–69.

12. I. Zevelev and A. Kara-Murza, "The Fate of Socialism and Afro-Asian Peace," *Aziya i Afrika Segodnia* (Asia and Africa Today), No. 1, 1989, p. 43.

13. *The New York Times*, June 9, 1989, p. 3. "Radical Plans to Save Soviet Economy," by Bill Keller.

14. *The New York Times*, December 7, 1989, p. 42, "U.S. Offers Moscow a Few Ideas on How to Improve Its Economy," by Michael R. Gordon.

15. The sole exception is North Yemen.

16. Jon Glassman, *Arms for the Arabs*, Baltimore: Johns Hopkins University Press, 1975, p. 96.

17. The Soviets had aircraft operating from seven Egyptian airfields as well as repair and supply facilities at the Egyptian ports of Alexandria, Port Said, Mersa Matruh, and Sollom. See Karen Dawisha, "The Soviet Union in the Middle East: Great Power in Search of a Leading Role," in *The Soviet Union in the Third World*, ed. by E.J. Feuchtwanger and Peter Nailor, New York: St. Martin's Press, 1981, p. 122.

18. TASS, May 27, 1986.

19. *Pravda*, April 25, 1987, p. 5.

20. Galia Golan, "Gorbachev's Middle East Strategy," *Foreign Affairs*, Vol. 66, No. 1, Fall 1987, p. 41.

21. *Davar*, (Israel), February 14, 1987.

22. The Soviets have taken a number of other steps designed to improve relations with Israel—and, more importantly, with the United States. They have permitted prominent *refuseniks* to leave, allowed Soviet emigrants to return on visits, clarified emigration procedures, and made modest gestures to improve conditions for Jews who remain in the USSR. Jews are currently leaving the Soviet Union in greater numbers than the United States can absorb them.

23. *The New York Times*, November 17, 1989, p. 1. "Soviets to Liberalize Emigration, Hoping to Gain U.S. Trade Deal," by Robert Pear. A 1974 law, known as the Jackson-Vanik Amendment, states that Communist countries may not receive favorable tariff treatment or credits from the United States unless they permit free emigration by their citizens. The law appeared to have more to do with slowing down Secretary of State Henry Kissinger's policy of détente with the Soviet Union than with slowing down Soviet imports to the United States, which have never been significant in Soviet or U.S. trade statistics. (President George Bush announced at the Malta summit with Gorbachev on December 2, 1989 that the Jackson-Vanik restrictions would be lifted when the Soviets implemented their new emigration policy.)

24. *Izvestia*, September 23, 1989, p. 5.

25. Karen Dawisha, "The Soviet Union in the Middle East: Great Power in Search of a Leading Role," *The Soviet Union in the Third World*, ed. by E.J. Feuchtwanger and Peter Nailor, New York: St. Martin's Press, 1981, p. 126.

26. Middle East News Agency (MENA), Cairo, March 23, 1987.

27. Ibid., April 7, 1987.

28. TASS, October 26, 1987.

29. *Izvestia*, March 19, 1988, p. 5.

30. *Al-Qabas* (Kuwait), December 27, 1987, p. 5.

31. In a November 1987 article in *New Times*, Aleksandr Zotov, then a member of the Central Committee's International Department and currently Soviet ambassador to Syria, outlined some flexible approaches to the Palestinian issue. He suggested that, if they were given the right to create their own sovereign government, the Palestinians might in fact opt for a federation or confederation with Jordan. See, Zotov, "Palestinians: 40 Tragic Years," *New Times*, (Moscow), November 27, 1987, No. 48, p. 18.

32. Nirmin Murad, report of a press conference by Soviet ambassador to Jordan, Aleksandr Zinchuk, *Jordan Times*, May 23, 1988, p. 1.

33. The members of ASEAN are Indonesia, Thailand, the Philippines, Malaysia, Singapore, and Brunei.

34. *Pravda*, July 29, 1986, p. 4; TASS, September 16, 1988.

35. *Pravda*, March 12, 1985, p. 1. In his speech to the Communist Party plenum that elected him general secretary in March 1985, Gorbachev declared that the USSR favored a "serious improvement in relations with the PRC and considers that, given reciprocity, this is fully possible." Three days later, he gave substance to his words by meeting with Chinese Premier Li Peng, the head of the Chinese delegation to the funeral of former general secretary Chernenko, marking the first meetings between a Soviet general secretary with any Chinese official in more than two decades.

36. *Renmin Ribao*, May 18, 1989. Cited in FBIS, *China Daily*, May 20, 1989, p. 15.

37. TASS, October 31, 1989. The two sides have also conducted a joint survey of the Amur River (1987), agreed on the use of border water resources (1987), and met routinely to discuss river navigation.

38. TASS, November 8, 1989.

39. TASS, November 28, 1989.

40. TASS, November 29, 1989, see FBIS, *Soviet Daily Reports*, November 30, 1989, p. 9.

41. *Pravda*, May 6, 1989, p. 5.

42. TASS, September 28, 1989.

43. KYODO (Japan), November 19, 1989, in FBIS, *Soviet Daily Report*, November 20, 1989, p. 15.

44. *The New York Times*, December 3, 1989, p. 25, "Tokyo Hopes Lure of Closer Ties Will Lead Soviets to Return Tiny Islands," by Steven R. Weisman.

45. TASS, October 27, 1989.

46. Melvin A. Goodman, "The Soviet Union and the Third World: The Military Dimension," *The Soviet Union and the Third World: The Last Three Decades*,

ed. by Andrzej Korbonski and Francis Fukuyama, Ithaca and London: Cornell University Press, 1987, p. 54.

47. TASS, November 18, 1989.

48. There is no convincing evidence to support the contentions of Alvin Z. Rubinstein (*Moscow's Third World Strategy*, p. 118) and Leif Rosenberger ("Philippine Communism and the Soviet Union," *Survey*, Spring 1985, pp. 143–144) that Moscow has been strengthening ties with the New People's Army, the military arm of the Communist Party of the Philippines.

49. *The New York Times*, November 5, 1987, p. 1. In conceding that there was "no model of socialism to be emulated by everyone," Gorbachev essentially removed the ideological rationale for the so-called Brezhnev doctrine and set into motion that events that culminated in the fall of 1989 with new governments in East Germany and Czechoslovakia.

50. See Peter Clement, "Moscow and Southern Africa," *Problems of Communism*, March-April 1985, pp. 35–41. Clement's article is particularly useful as an analytical review of the African situation that Gorbachev inherited in March 1985 upon his accession to power.

51. Charles W. Freeman, Jr., "The Angola/Namibia Accords," *Foreign Affairs*, Vol. 68, No. 3, Summer 1989, p. 135.

52. *Izvestia*, June 27, 1989, p. 5.

53. *Novoye Vremya* (*New Times*), November 26, 1989, p. 18.

54. *Izvestia*, March 18, 1990, p. 5.

55. TASS, March 26, 1990.

56. Mikhail Gorbachev, *Perestroika: New Thinking for Our Country and the World*, New York: Harper and Row, 1987, p. 174.

57. AFP (Paris), December 1, 1989, as reported in FBIS, *Soviet Daily Reports*, December 1, 1989, p. 13.

58. *The Washington Post*, July 17, 1989, p. 23.

59. *The New York Times*, July 27, 1989, p. 19.

60. *The New York Times*, March 24, 1989, p. 2, "Spread of Missiles is Seen as Soviet Worry in Mideast," by Thomas L. Friedman; *The New York Times*, May 23, 1989, p. 9, "India Reports Successful Test of Mid-Range Missile," by Barbara Crossette.

61. *The New York Times*, December 8, 1989, p. 7, "Iraqis Announce Test of a Rocket," by Michael R. Gordon.

62. Ibid.

63. *Inside the Pentagon*, August 18, 1989, p. 1, "Report Says Syria Signed Deal with China to Buy Surface-to-Surface Missiles," by Richard Lardner; *The Washington Post*, December 12, 1989, p. 1.

64. *Time*, April 16, 1990, p. 30, "Stumbling Toward Armageddon?", by Jill Smolowe.

65. *The Washington Post*, December 12, 1990, p. 29, "Shevardnadze Urges Nuclear-Free Zone in Middle East," by David Hoffman.

66. *Pravda*, July 29, 1988, p. 1; *The New York Times*, September 17, 1988, p. 1, "Gorbachev Offers Disputed Radar for Peaceful Exploration of Space," by Philip Taubman.

6

Soviet Power Projection and Crisis Management Under Gorbachev

Three decades ago the Soviet Union was a continental power whose military focus was defense of the homeland and whose military reached regions contiguous to its own. Today Gorbachev commands a global power with worldwide naval deployments and the ability to monitor Western forces; Moscow has gained access to military facilities in strategically located client states and can be a factor in any regional crisis.

Moscow's success in achieving Third World objectives—securing a military position in every region of the globe, challenging the West and China, influencing governments of key regional states—has been accomplished almost entirely through military policy. Through assistance and the use of surrogate forces, the Soviets have served the security needs of Third World countries and received benefits, particularly access to naval and air facilities.[1]

The Soviets have encountered obstacles, but growth of Soviet power has paid dividends. The acquisition of naval access in distant waters serves both operational and political purposes. Foreign facilities contribute to Moscow's ability to sustain worldwide deployment and monitor Western naval forces. Naval forces abroad underscore Moscow's commitment to local regimes and must be taken into account.

Third World vulnerability has enhanced the Soviet Union.[2] The vulnerability of Ethiopia and South Yemen led to military facilities on the Horn of Africa and the Arabian peninsula. Internal instability in Angola and Mozambique improved the Soviet military and political position in southern Africa. The Chinese invasion of northern Vietnam in 1979 produced access to base facilities in Cam Ranh Bay. All of these

Marxist and non-Marxist Third World states have concluded friend-ship treaties with the Soviets, which stress the need for consultation and cooperation.

Expansion of the military role in the Third World strengthened Moscow's global position, gave ability to challenge Western interests, and bolstered the Soviet economic base by hard currency from arms sales. The number of pro-Soviet regimes in the Third World increased dramatically as Moscow used its military assistance to capitalize on anticolonial sentiment, regional conflicts, and the search for assistance by nationalist regimes. The Soviets gained such allies as Cuba, India, Syria, and Vietnam, all in key areas of the world. The Soviets won support in international forums and Gorbachev's diplomacy became a factor in regional disputes.

Every Third World country with Soviet military facilities has received substantial arms aid and political support, and regimes have benefited from naval demonstrations during internal crises.[3] Naval units have moved near territorial waters of Guinea and the Seychelles in response to challenges to the leadership there, and the Soviet Mediterranean Squadron has followed the U.S. Sixth Fleet (at a safe distance) during disturbances in the Middle East. Elements of the international community in South Yemen were evacuated by the Soviet Navy in 1986 during the political and military upheaval in Aden; a similar evacuation from Egypt and Syria in the autumn of 1973 was an indication of Moscow's expectation of the October War.[4]

It is more difficult to assess Moscow's operational planning and advisory role with Third World clients. Soviet involvement was a factor in the 1970s in Ethiopian successes against the Somalis, and in the 1980s in Angolan military successes against National Union for the Independence of Angola (UNITA) and South Africa, and Vietnamese successes in Cambodia. But Soviet operational planning has not helped Arab client regimes against the Israelis, nor has it led to sustained successes for Ethiopian forces against the Eritreans. In-ability to train and discipline the Afghan army was a reason for Moscow's inability to limit the Afghan insurgency, which increased after the Soviet invasion.

Military assistance has led to support in the Third World for Soviet positions in such forums as the United Nations, but has not prevented Syria from policies against Moscow's interest in regard to Israel, Lebanon, or the Palestine Liberation Organization. Libya has pur-chased billions of dollars of Soviet military equipment but ignored Soviet interests with respect to the Iran-Iraq war, terrorism, Chad, and Egypt. Cuba, India, and Vietnam have received billions in aid from the USSR over the past decades but at the same time displayed an extreme independence in pursuit of national interests and domestic policies.

The steady increase in size and capability of Soviet forces operating abroad, as well as quantity and quality of Soviet weapons systems provided Third World states, has enhanced Moscow's military reach. Success in Angola, Ethiopia, South Yemen, and Vietnam does not represent a shift in forces, but—extending its military reach—the USSR has developed a network of communications and intelligence collection sites, gained access to military facilities, managed military and advisory roles of its Eastern European and Cuban allies in Africa, Central America, and the Middle East. The Soviets have not succeeded in eroding the role of the West in Third World states, and expansion of Soviet military power—which has led to a gradual increase of Moscow's role in the former colonial areas of Africa, the Middle East, and Asia—did not secure pro-Soviet Marxist governments in Angola, Ethiopia, and South Yemen.[5]

SOVIET MILITARY SUCCESSES IN THE THIRD WORLD

Several indicators demonstrate that Moscow has acquired the capacity for world military involvement. During the Cuban missile crisis in 1962, the Soviets were forced to capitulate because of shortfalls in both strategic and conventional power, particularly naval and naval aviation forces. Moscow was so ill-prepared that during the crisis Ambassador Anatoly Dobrynin lacked secure telephone or radio communication and had to rely on Western Union. Dobrynin recently explained that General Secretary Nikita Khrushchev's crucial messages during the worst days of the crisis were conveyed simultaneously through the Soviet embassy in Washington and Radio Moscow to make sure his proposals would reach the Kennedy administration as soon as possible.[6] The Soviets were at similar disadvantage during the first years of the Vietnam war and could not transmit sensitive messages from their embassy in Vienna during the Strategic Arms Limitations Talks in the early 1970s.

The Soviets have strengthened their military position in the Third World over the past decades. They have dramatically increased military agreements and arms deliveries, doubled Soviet military personnel outside Warsaw Pact countries, and sharply increased naval deployments through access to naval facilities and ports of call. Moscow has enhanced its command and control systems, particularly in Cuba and Vietnam as well as from ships in all regions of the world.

Soviet forces on occasion have played a combat and combat advisory role in regional confrontations during this period.

- In the late 1960s and early 1970s Soviet air and air defense forces were used in the Middle East. In the civil war in North Yemen in the 1960s, advisers took part in combat operations and fighter pilots flew operations missions. Advisers manned surface-to-air missile sites on the west bank of the Suez Canal during the war of attrition with Israel in the winter of 1969–1970, and in the October War in 1973 the USSR conducted a massive resupply to Egypt during hostilities.
- In the mid-to-late 1970s Soviet logistics forces transported and sustained surrogate Cuban forces for intervention in Angola and Ethiopia. In the Ogaden war in 1977–1978 between Ethiopia and Somalia, high-level commanders were directly involved in planning military operations during the Third World conflict. The leader, V.I. Petrov, was named first deputy defense minister in 1985.
- In 1979, Soviet combat ground and air units invaded Afghanistan, marking the first direct involvement of Soviet ground forces outside the Soviet bloc. The last commander of Soviet forces in Afghanistan, Lt. Gen. Boris Gromov, is now deputy chief of the Interior Ministry.

Moscow's ability to project power has improved over the past decade. Naval reconnaissance aircraft now operate out of Cuba, Vietnam, Angola, Ethiopia, Yemen, Syria, and Libya; years ago only Cuba provided access. Military transport aircraft now have use of Angola, Yemen, Syria, Afghanistan, and Vietnam; only Syria was used years ago. Ground and air defense troops are in Cuba and the Middle East, military technicians and security advisers in the Middle East, Africa, Asia, and Latin America. All of this activity has declined since Gorbachev's accession to power in 1985.

BENEFITS OF EXPANDED ACCESS

Expansion of capabilities has had benefits, enabling the USSR to break out of its traditional realm in the Baltic Sea and the Black Sea. Soviet air and naval power can now project virtually anywhere, Moscow enjoys intelligence-gathering in strategic locations, and Soviet military air transport can deliver tanks, troops, and self-propelled artillery.

The USSR has taken advantage of opportunities in regions to use combined naval exercises. Military and economic support for Vietnam has resulted in a substantial naval buildup in the South China Sea, and Soviet-Vietnamese exercises demonstrate that Soviet interests and capabilities have to be taken into consideration by regional countries, particularly China. Soviet-Cuban exercises contribute to Cuban military capabilities, which far surpass those of other Third World states in the region, while asserting Moscow's right to operate in the Caribbean and Gulf of Mexico. Exercises with allies in the Middle East and Persian Gulf demonstrate commitment and presence. The Soviet military presence in Syria has made Israel more tolerant of Syrian presence in Lebanon. Israeli and South African forces would have to contend with more sophisticated air defense in planning operations against Libya and Angola.

There have been military and political gains in most regions. In the Middle East, one of the USSR's priority areas, the Soviets continue a close relationship with Syria through military weapons transfers. Moscow uses Syrian facilities for reconnaissance flights and has conducted joint naval exercises with the Syrians. Moscow has access rights to naval air facilities in Yemen. Access enhances logistics and reconnaissance in both the Mediterranean and Indian Ocean. The Soviets have a lucrative arms relationship with Libya, and sales to Algeria provide the basis for bilateral ties.

In Southeast Asia a Soviet military force replaced the United States at Cam Ranh Bay, providing Moscow with leverage against Beijing and logistical support for naval operations in the South China Sea and Indian Ocean. Hanoi agreed to a Soviet presence in 1979, after China attacked northern Vietnam. Until the winter of 1989–1990, the Soviets maintained naval aircraft in Vietnam which conduct reconnaissance, intelligence-collection, and antisubmarine warfare missions in the South China Sea. They maintained a squadron of MiG-23 Flogger fighter aircraft; twenty to twenty-five Soviet naval vessels, including several attack and cruise missile submarines, routinely operate from the base.[7] The forces conduct patrols in the South China Sea and are situated to operate against sealanes. Before their withdrawal, Soviet forces at Cam Ranh Bay could augment the Indian Ocean Squadron.

An air unit comprised of naval TU-16 Badger and eight TU-95 Bear aircraft was deployed at Cam Ranh airfield during this period to conduct reconnaissance, intelligence-collection, and antisubmarine warfare missions throughout the South China Sea. The Badger's strike range from Cam Ranh Bay included not only regional states but the Philippines, Guam, and the western portion of Micronesia. In addition to more than two thousand military advisers in Vietnam, including a small naval infantry security detachment, a contingent of AN-12 Cubs operated in Vietnam, Laos, and Cambodia from 1979 to 1989 to deliver supplies to Vietnamese forces in Cambodia.

In Africa the Soviets have access to facilities in Ethiopia, which expand capabilities in the Indian Ocean area. The Soviet presence in Ethiopia is modest because of reluctance to invest large sums in a nation that cannot subdue an insurgency in Eritrea as well as Moscow's memory of being expelled from bases in Egypt and Somalia in the 1970s. As a result, Soviet assets in Ethiopa are for the most part movable or "removable," including floating piers and drydocks, tenders, and repair ships at Dahlak Island off the coast.[8] Guided-missile cruisers and nuclear-powered submarines regularly call at Dahlak for repair and supplies and, due to the vulnerability of Dahlak, the Soviets maintain a naval infantry security detachment that is the primary Soviet unit for amphibious operations.[9] The USSR formerly deployed two IL-38 antisubmarine and maritime reconnaissance aircraft to Asmara Airfield, until destroyed by Eritrean rebels in 1984. The decision not to replace these aircraft was consistent with Soviet caution in Third World countries, where forces have come under attack.[10]

In western Africa the Soviets have the use of Angolan facilities as well as the capability to use naval facilities in Guinea. Guinea stopped TU-95 reconnaissance aircraft from deploying at Conakry airfield, although the Soviets use Conakry as a stopover for military flights to Angola. Luanda is one of the largest and best natural harbors on the west coast of Africa and is the support base for the Soviet Navy's West African Patrol. Other assets include a floating drydock, a communications station, and access for TU-95 Bears, which patrol the South Atlantic sealanes. The patrol's apparent mission is to maintain a presence and provide a show of force with the six or seven ships based in Luanda. Other naval units have called on the Mozambican port of Maputo and on Port Louis in Mauritius.[11] These facilities bolster Moscow's ability to project force in southern Africa, which provides credibility to the Soviet presence in the entire region.

In the Caribbean, Moscow enjoys port and air facilities in Cuba, as well as intelligence capabilities relative to U.S. activities in the Caribbean and North Atlantic. At the Lourdes complex near Havana, the Soviets have three sites dedicated to signals intelligence collection against U.S. commercial satellites.[12] Soviet naval and naval air deployments allow Moscow to project power into international waters near the United States, to threaten shipping lanes, and to apply a kind of countervailing power to offset Soviet perceptions of the U.S. threat closer to Soviet borders. Soviet and Cuban efforts on behalf of the Sandinista regime in Nicaragua and the Popular Movement for the

Liberation of Angola (MPLA) led to opportunities to advance its influence elsewhere.

Combined naval operations with the Soviet Union enhance a Third World navy. The exercises display growing military capability and signal that the country, given strong ties to the Soviet Union, is a power to be reckoned with. Such countries as Cuba, Syria, Libya, and Vietnam probably intend exercises to balance U.S. military operations. Finally, Moscow's Third World clients probably realize that combined naval training helps sharpen skills, particularly in countries with a limited military tradition.

SOVIET MILITARY LIMITATIONS IN THE THIRD WORLD

Although military capabilities in the Third World have improved over the past decades, they have not accomplished all Moscow's objectives or in many cases satisfied expectations of clients. The Soviets refused Arab demands for intervention against Israel in the Six-Day War in 1967 and the October War in 1973. The Soviets did not have the ability to counter the Israeli invasion of Lebanon in 1982, which resulted in an embarrassing defeat for Syria, which lost more than eighty fighter aircraft to the Israelis, without any Israeli losses. And in spite of extensive arms deliveries to Syria and close relations with Damascus, they are unwilling to give the Syrians a commitment—because they have neither the capability nor willingness to confront the Israelis or the United States.

Similarly, they have been reluctant to provide guarantees to Cuba, witness the Soviet-Cuban Friendship Treaty of 1989, which makes no mention of security or military guarantees. Castro's willingness to sign a friendship treaty without a security commitment is a far cry from his earlier interest in joining the Warsaw Pact, which was of course a mutual security arrangement. There are limits to the projection of Soviet power to noncontiguous Third World areas, particularly Africa and South America, far from Soviet borders and with less importance to Moscow.

The unwillingness to extend commitments has led to setbacks. The most dramatic to date was expulsion from Egypt in 1972, shortly after the Soviet–U.S. summit in Moscow. The Soviets had access to facilities in Egypt, as well as a sizable physical presence, and expulsion led to a downturn in Soviet naval presence in the Mediterranean and in deployment of naval aircraft in the Third World. Perhaps most important, the Soviets considered Egypt of importance and thus lost what they saw as a major advantage.

Sadat reportedly told the Soviet ambassador in the summer of 1972 that Moscow's failure to comply with a timetable for the delivery of Soviet weapons systems led to the Egyptian decision:

> Brezhnev lied to me in March 1971; Podgorny lied to me in May 1971; Brezhnev lied to me in October 1971. Do you think I don't know your game? You have agreed with the Americans that there is no war. Let me tell you that you have no tutelage over us.[13]

The Soviets had refused to give the Egyptians such offensive weapons as MiG-23 fighter aircraft and Scud surface-to-surface missiles.

The Soviets were expelled from Somalia and the facilities at Berbera following a Soviet-Ethiopian arms deal in 1977. In this case Moscow had decided that Ethiopia had more potential as a client than Somalia and made the choice—although it may have hoped to retain assets in both states. The loss of naval and naval air facilities in Somalia made the Soviets dependent on less secure facilities in Ethiopia and led to complications for the naval presence in the Indian Ocean. Somalia—as well as Egypt—unilaterally abrogated friendship treaties with the USSR, negotiated earlier in the 1970s.[14] Loss of facilities in Egypt and Somalia has made the Soviets even more dependent on auxiliary ships and anchorages, a military problem for presence in out-of-area waters. The Soviets appear to have abandoned their facilities in Ethiopia as well.

POLITICAL LIMITS OF MILITARY INFLUENCE

Difficulty in translating Soviet military capability into political power to influence developments in the Third World is evidenced in several charateristics of Moscow's presence. Even when dependent on military aid, Third World states have their own goals, capabilities, and independent priorities. When interests coincide, Moscow and Third World states cooperate; when interests differ, friction ensues. Continuing strains with such clients as Cuba, Syria, and Vietnam illustrate the difficulty of translating military power into political influence.

Other factors complicate Moscow's efforts to derive advantage from military capability. Many Third World regimes supported militarily are governing extremely weak states and are threatened by insurgent groups that have transformed the USSR into an often ineffective counterinsurgency power. Assisting counterinsurgency programs in weak states places the USSR in the awkward position of supervising a process that generally weakens economic development. Introduction of Soviet force may create a series of problems for the Soviets—

witness the diplomatic and political problems in the Middle East and Southwest Asia following the invasion of Afghanistan.

MILITARY LIMITS OF MILITARY PRESENCE

There also are constraints on Soviet forces in distant operations. Despite access in some areas such as Cuba and Vietnam, the Soviets lack large-scale foreign bases from which to mount operations and are no match for U.S. forces. In the Indian Ocean and Red Sea, the United States has a base at Diego Garcia, which could accommodate B-52s and a storage and transshipment facility. Airbases in Oman offer prepositioned equipment and an antisubmarine warfare capability; Bahrain houses an important command, control and communications facility; and airbases in Kenya could support transport operations. Soviet access to Ethiopia and Yemen offers no comparable network.

In the western Pacific the Soviet presence at Cam Ranh Bay and Da Nang and the airfield at Bien Hoa was never comparable to U.S. power in the Philippines. Clark Field supports a Tactical Air Command fighter wing and substantial reserve stocks; the navy base at Subic Bay contains ship repair facilities and a command and control center; smaller Philippine facilities provide air defense installations and an electronic warfare range. Soviet military forces in the Pacific will have to be devoted to the China problem regardless of improvement in Sino-Soviet relations.

Lack of aircraft carriers with conventional fighter aircraft and the limited range of Soviet tactical aircraft create problems of tactical air support, aggravated by lack of aerial refueling capability for fighter aircraft and by the political problem of overflight. Soviet naval infantry is small and the amphibious lift capacity of any single fleet of the Soviet Navy is limited, as is naval gunfire support available for operations against well-armed Third World forces.

The Soviets are particularly inferior to U.S. forces in airlift capabilities. Unlike the United States, which has transport aircraft designed for long distances, Moscow is far more concerned with problems along the border, particularly in Eastern Europe. Moscow has problems in aerial refueling, airbase support, and overflight. The United States is superior in jet engine technology and in aircrews per transport aircraft. Soviet problems in this area make the use of Soviet airborne divisions, highly dependent on transport aircraft, unlikely in noncontiguous areas.

These shortcomings have contributed to caution in crisis management in the Middle East, Southeast Asia, and the Caribbean—and, as a result, to a perception in Third World states that the USSR is unreliable. Worsening of relations with both Egypt and North Korea in the early 1970s related directly to Moscow's unwillingness to take risks on its clients' behalf. Sadat reportedly stated in 1972 that he expelled the Soviets because he wanted "complete freedom of maneuver"; he indicated that Moscow was an obstacle in any Egyptian decision to go to war against Israel.[15] Reestablishment of diplomatic relations between Ethiopia and Israel in 1989 and Addis Ababa's interest in increasing ties with the United States presumably reflect Mengistu's disappointment with support from the Soviet Union. Cuba's signal in 1989 to rejoin the Organization of American States acknowledges a sense of isolation in view of Gorbachev's more conciliatory posture in the Third World.

Third World leaders presumably realize that Soviet willingness to use force on its borders never indicated comparable willingness to get involved in noncontiguous areas. Airborne forces have participated in every invasion on Moscow's borders since the Second World War (Hungary in 1956, Czechoslovakia in 1968, Afghanistan in 1979), but have never been deployed in noncontiguous Third World areas. The Soviets have sent air forces into such crisis spots as Egypt in 1970, but fighter deployments would require access to regional bases that are crowded and often inadequate and could encounter overflight problems. Merchant ships have been used in military supply during Arab-Israeli wars, and transport aviation has been used for weapons deliveries in the Third World, but the Soviet Navy has avoided confrontation in out-of-area waters during regional crises.[16]

CRISIS MANAGEMENT AND SOVIET FOREIGN POLICY

There is no indication that any crisis management group or staff exists or that the Soviets are engaged in any effort to correct their deficiencies in force projection.[17] They have no designated forces and, unlike the United States, little historical or military experience with rapid deployment forces or carrier task forces. They have no operating responsibility for overseas bases in the Middle East and Persian Gulf, and continue to deemphasize out-of-area naval deployments in the region.[18] Naval support on behalf of Third World clients has been confined to symbolic uses, such as visible political support for such leaders as President René of the Seychelles or, as in 1973 before the October war, evacuation of military personnel and dependents. The Soviets airlifted assistance to the South Yemeni forces led by Prime Minister Haider abu Bakr al-Attas during the bloody coup of January 1986.

Soviet leaders in time of crisis management have been the general secretary, chairman of the Council of Ministers, and chairman of the Presidium of the Supreme Soviet. The minister of defense, according to former Egyptian president Sadat, apparently played a key role when advice was needed, and in time of crisis before Gorbachev's accession to power in 1985 the foreign minister and chief of the International Department played only peripheral roles, with the foreign ministry secondary to the defense ministry.[19] The chairman of the Committee for State Security (KGB) and the Politburo member responsible for ideology and propaganda also have participated in talks with Third World leaders during times of crisis.

In crisis situations the Politburo has played the key role, with Moscow-based members of the Politburo being the most important actors. The general secretary has had to proceed cautiously and even slowly because of the collective nature of decisions, but the same collectivity has provided bureaucratic protection when Politburo decisions have been criticized. In the wake of the Six-Day War in 1967, Moscow party boss Nikolai Yegorychev reportedly attacked Brezhnev for failing to provide greater support to Egypt and Syria,[20] and several months later lost his post as party first secretary. Ukrainian party chief Petr. Y. Shelest lost his Politburo post after criticizing Brezhnev's decision to proceed with a summit meeting with President Richard M. Nixon after the increased bombing of North Vietnam.

Sadat was critical of Moscow's restraint in the early 1970s. According to memoirs of one of his closest confidants, the Soviets refused to supply such weapons systems as the MiG-25 fighter aircraft, previously promised Egypt, and would not discuss the possibility of a joint Soviet-Egyptian strategy against Israel.[21] Sadat believed Moscow wanted to "see our hands tied, so that we were unable to make a decision."[22]

GORBACHEV AND CRISIS PREVENTION

Since Gorbachev has not been tested in a crisis in foreign policy, it is difficult to determine his effect on decisions. Nevertheless, his efforts since 1985 to demilitarize the political ethos of the Soviet state indicate that he is more concerned with crisis prevention than management and, in any event, is trying to avoid use of Soviet military power in noncontiguous areas. Over the past five years, there has been a decline in the status of the military in the Soviet Union, a reduced military role in decisions, a reduction in defense spending and modernization of strategic weapons. The top echelons of the military have been reshuffled, including the defense minister, first deputy defense minister, commanders of Soviet theater-level forces, chiefs of military districts, and chief of the Main Political Directorate of the Army and Navy. The latter position is particularly important because it is within the defense ministry but subordinate to the Central Committee of the Party.

In addition to cutbacks in modernization of Soviet strategic forces, including the USSR's principal nuclear submarine class, the Typhoon; the most threatening intercontinental missiles, the SS-18 and the mobile SS-24; and the most sophisticated strategic bomber, the Black-jack; there has been a decline in operational tempo and presence of Soviet naval and naval aviation forces in the Third World.[23] In the most important indication of declining Soviet interest in power in the Third World, the Soviets have delayed construction of their first large air-craft carrier and halted construction of their large nuclear-powered cruisers. Naval exercises have been cut and joint exercises with Third World navies have become more infrequent as Moscow clearly is trying to economize on fuel and protect aging elements of the fleet.

It is apparent that the Soviet leader has made an effort to end the military's monopoly on military expertise in the area of national security. Creation of the International Commission under Aleksandr Yakovlev pointed to a greater role for the Central Committee's International Department in areas previously dominated by the general staff or the defense ministry. Research institutes are becoming more active in study of military issues, and the defense ministry can no longer protect details of policy in secrecy.

Gorbachev has encouraged Soviet specialists and journalists to become more critical of national security decisions and appears to favor the Supreme Soviet to serve as an oversight instrument in foreign policy. At least two committees of the Supreme Soviet will be examining sensitive military matters, including the defense budget and arms control. Civilian officials and academics have been encouraged to get more involved in military matters. Oversight will require greater resources for the committees as well as a measure of political independence, and it is not yet certain that even Gorbachev is willing to make such a commitment.

Shevardnadze's criticism of decision making under Brezhnev, particularly decisions involving use of the military, suggests that the Gorbachev leadership favors greater political control and a lesser role for the military. The former foreign minister was critical of the decision to invade Afghanistan, introduction of SS-20 missiles, "bulk production of chemical weapons" for almost two decades after the United States stopped producing such weapons in 1969, and construction of a radar tracking station at Krasnoyarsk in violation of the Anti-Ballistic Missile Treaty.[24] Shevardnadze's criticism indicates there will be more oversight in national security and a greater civilian role in military policy. Civilian members of the Defense Council presumably will play an even more important part, particularly with the naming in November 1989 of Lev Zaikov, the civilian leader of the USSR's military-industrial complex, as the first deputy chairman of the defense council.[25] Gorbachev told the Supreme Soviet in 1989 that a closed session of the legislature would define the composition and function of the council.[26]

POWER PROJECTION AND SOVIET FOREIGN POLICY

The most significant aspect of Soviet naval operating patterns since Gorbachev's accession to power in 1985 has been the reduction in naval activity beyond Soviet home waters. According to the Defense Intelligence Agency, the presence of such deployed forces, and their capability to respond quickly to developing crises, has dropped approximately 15 percent from the levels of 1980 to 1985.[27] In marked contrast to the U.S. Navy, the Soviet Navy historically has not maintained significant numbers of ships in distant waters and even Soviet naval forces at home operate at a much lower activity level than their U.S. counterparts. Currently, the Soviets seem much more concerned with protecting their sea-based strategic strike submarines and defending against sea-based attack along the maritime approaches to the Soviet Union than with operations in out-of-area waters. These trends cannot be reassuring to Soviet Third World clients such as Vietnam and Cuba who in the past have looked for a Soviet naval show of force as a counter to U.S. operations.

Despite the advances in Moscow's ability to project power into the international arena over the past two decades, the USSR never maintained more than a limited capability for global operations. The USSR traditionally has emphasized the importance of global reach through military aid missions, acquisition of access, and small-scale naval deployments. A comparison of the U.S. and Soviet navies reflects this difference, with the United States emphasizing out-of-area deployment with widespread rights of access and the USSR being far more dependent on sheltered anchorages and naval auxiliaries. Although the Soviet Navy has increased its capability to interdict Western shipping in the event of East-West hostilities, it is more likely that initial Soviet naval operations would involve defensive measures to protect Soviet submarines carrying strategic nuclear missiles and to keep U.S. aircraft carriers away from Soviet territory.

Third World security concerns will remain secondary to Moscow and, even with improvements to Soviet forces, the USSR will be inferior to Western forces abroad in the Mediterranean, the western Pacific, and the Indian Ocean. Moscow almost certainly will try to achieve favorable military balances in the regions close to Soviet borders, but not in noncontiguous areas. Even in the Mediterranean, the Soviets have been reducing their naval presence; on the eve of the Malta Summit with President George Bush, Gorbachev cut the Soviet presence by more than 50 percent.[28] Then Foreign Minister Shevardnadze hinted that Moscow no longer required access to Cam Ranh Bay in the South China Sea.

The current delay in the construction of Moscow's first 65,000–ton attack aircraft carrier, moreover, is another indication of Gorbachev's caution regarding power projection in the Third World and his unwillingness to orient scarce investment resources toward operations in noncontiguous areas. This decision also prolongs the uncertainty over whether this new platform will continue to rely on helicopters and vertical short takeoff and landing aircraft or will introduce higher-performance aircraft that require stronger performance characteristics to withstand carrier landings, pilots trained in the art of carrier landings and perfected catapults to launch planes and arresting gear to stop them at high speeds.

Although it will take several years after launch and fitting-out and training with an operational air wing to develop a credible operational effectiveness, the new Soviet carrier would enable the Soviets to extend their operations beyond the umbrella currently provided by land-based aviation. The Soviet Navy thus will be able to extend its influence, but the United States—which currently has fourteen deployable carriers—will be able to send more carriers than the Soviets to global trouble spots for the foreseeable future. The reduction in Soviet military spending that has taken place since 1988 strongly suggests that Gorbachev is not interested in new systems with high risk, particularly in the area of power projection. The political debate in both Moscow and Washington indicates that both sides are looking for "lower-cost, lower-risk" ways to project power into the Third World.

The USSR could, nevertheless, opt for more substantial forward deployment that would include more attack submarines and strike aircraft and could expand the power projection capabilities of its overseas facilities to accommodate greater forward deployment and expanded integrated operations. Another indicator in the direction of increased power projection to noncontiguous areas would be the development of a more viable forward strike posture, which would include construction of air and naval missile storage and handling facilities in the key Third World regions, increased production of long-range aircraft and nuclear-powered submarines, the organization of rapid deployment force headquarters with supporting communications units, and the construction of large fuel storage capacities at airfields likely to be used to support Soviet airlifts. Gorbachev does not appear willing to engage in these costly and risky activities at this time.

None of these developments, in any event, would ease significantly the vulnerability of Soviet forces abroad; such forces, moreover, would remain susceptible to the decisions of host governments in the Third World which may be unwilling to risk becoming involved as belligerents, particularly in potential Soviet–U.S. confrontations. Military facilities in the Third World are particularly vulnerable and Soviet forward deployments would be at risk in wartime. (In peacetime, such deployment patterns would contribute marginally to regional perceptions of a stronger Soviet presence in the Third World.)

In the past Soviet deployment activities in the Third World have been curtailed in Egypt, Guinea, and Somalia and have encountered resistance in Algeria, Iraq, and India. Algeria and India have never been willing to allow the Soviets access to military facilities; most Soviet forces abroad are co-stationed with indigenous forces and therefore lack security and privileged access. Except for Mersa Matruh in Egypt and Berbera in Somalia, which were lost to the Soviets in the 1970s, Moscow never actually acquired a military base in the Third World for its exclusive use in the proper sense of the word. Soviet military resources, over the near term, appear to be inadequate for priority missions abroad, and the costs of substantial increases in forward-deployed forces may not be justified by the potential benefits or gains in the Third World.

GORBACHEV'S IMPACT ON SOVIET FORCES IN THE THIRD WORLD

Until recently, the past three decades have seen a concerted Soviet effort to improve the USSR's military position in all areas. Total Soviet military manpower increased by about one-third to its present size of about five million. Weapons production capacity expanded by nearly 60 percent, and research and development facilities nearly doubled. The number of deployed intercontinental nuclear delivery vehicles increased nearly sixfold, and battlefield nuclear forces more than tripled in size. The Soviet navy evolved from a coastal defense force with limited capabilities for operation on the high seas to a force that now demonstrates the global reach of Soviet military power and counters the previously unconstrained Western use of the seas.

Gorbachev's accession to power has seen a reversal in most of these trends as the Soviet leader has moved to cut Soviet military manpower, the defense budget, Soviet divisions in East Europe, and even Soviet central strategic systems. The apparent decision to reduce the prominence of the Soviet military in the decision-making process suggests a lesser military role in the Third World and decreased investment in forces for power projection. The Soviets have conceded that their model of socialist development has failed in the Third World, that they have less treasure to invest in underdeveloped countries, and that the ideological optimism of the past cannot be revived. Soviet Foreign Minister Shevardnadze told a high-level gathering of his ministry in 1987 that Moscow had "promoted, and sometimes provoked, enormous material investments in hopeless external political projects...which to this day are costing our people dearly."[29]

Gorbachev has ordered the first serious reduction in Soviet military manpower in more than thirty years, a signficant reduction in the defense budget over the next several years, and a decline in military procurement. At the twenty-seventh party congress in 1986, he signaled that Moscow's military role in the Third World would be less important and that his leadership would concentrate on economic issues and improving relations with the United States. Moscow's operational involvement in the Third World, including out-of-area naval deployments and naval air reconnaissance, has declined as a result, and represent the Third World equivalent of Moscow's willingness to withdraw SS-20 and SS-23 missiles from Eastern Europe and Central Asia. Soviet arms transfers to the Third World are down, and references to the liberating mission of the Soviet armed forces have virtually disappeared from Soviet military writings. All of these trends are consistent with the notion of some disillusionment with the globalism of the Brezhnev era.

Gorbachev's efforts to reduce the Soviet military role in the Third World is part of a larger effort to reduce the political role of the military in general. Over the past several years, the Soviet general secretary has reshuffled the top military leadership and, in addition to the withdrawal from Afghanistan, Gorbachev has reduced the Soviet presence in Eastern Europe and Mongolia and along the Sino-Soviet border. He has ignored criticism from the military for his unilateral troop reductions as well as his unilateral test moratorium in 1985–1986. Military advisers have been withdrawn from Ethiopia and Mozambique and the withdrawal of Cuban and Vietnamese forces from Angola and Cambodia, respectively, presumably will lead to a smaller Soviet advisory presence there as well.

Indeed, Soviet behavior in the Third World since 1985 suggests that Gorbachev does not believe that the so-called successes in such countries as Angola, Ethiopia, Nicaragua, and Yemen have offset the failures in Egypt, Mozambique, Somalia, and the Sudan and that, in any event, the impact of the Soviet role in the Third World on the more important East-West relationship has been strongly negative. The Soviet general secretary has every reason to believe that Soviet preoccupation with "geopolitical momentum" in the Third World over the past three decades has not only failed but that, during the same period, the United States has managed to strengthen its relations with the key states of Western Europe and East Asia at the expense of Soviet interests.

In terms of power projection and crisis management in noncontiguous Third World areas, therefore, Gorbachev is likely to be even more cautious than his predecessors who were unwilling for the most part to commit Soviet combat forces to hostile regional confrontations. Soviet naval forces have established or augmented a presence in regions of conflict in the Third World but have not engaged in conflict. Airborne units have been placed on alert during times of conflict in the Third World, particularly in the Middle East, but have not been introduced into noncontiguous areas. Soviet combat ground forces have not appeared in confrontations in noncontiguous areas, and Soviet pilots have not operated outside friendly territory. In view of the limitations on Moscow's ability to project power into the Third World and Gorbachev's cautious stance toward regional conflict, the Soviets will probably continue to exercise considerable constraint in the near term in committing their own forces to regional crisis.

NOTES

1. See Uri Ra'anan, Robert Pfaltzgraff, and Geoffrey Kemp, *Power Projection*, Hamden, CT, Archon, 1982.

2. Alvin Z. Rubinstein, *Moscow's Third World Strategy*, Princeton, NJ: Princeton University Press, 1988, p. 207.

3. So argues Bruce Porter, *The USSR in Third World Conflicts*, Cambridge: Cambridge University Press, 1984.

4. See Jon D. Glassman, *Arms for the Arabs: The Soviet Union and War in the Middle East*, Baltimore: Johns Hopkins University Press, 1975, p. 123. Since the Egyptian message to the Syrians warning of the attack was not sent until September 30, it is unlikely that the Soviets had warning much before the beginning of the evacuation on October 3.

5. See Alex P. Schmid, *Soviet Military Interventions since 1945*, New Brunswick, NJ: Transaction, 1985.

6. *The Washington Post*, November 16, 1989, p. 17, "1962 Missile Crisis via Western Union," by Don Oberdorfer.

7. Melvin A. Goodman, "The Soviet Union and the Third World: The Military Dimension," *The Soviet Union and the Third World: The Last Three Decades*, ed. by Andrzej Korbonski and Francis Fukuyama, Ithaca and London: Cornell University Press, p. 52; *The Washington Post*, August 1, 1986, from an interview with Admiral Ronald Hays, former Commander-in-Chief of U.S. Pacific Command.

8. *Soviet Military Power, 1985*, Washington, DC: U.S. Government Printing Office, 1985, p. 123.

9. Because of limited force strength, insufficient assault lift capabilities, and the absence of a Soviet sea-based airpower capability to support an amphibious landing against significant opposition, Soviet naval infantry forces are not capable of being employed as a major distant power-projection combat force. See *Soviet Military Power: Prospects for Change 1989*, Washington, DC: U.S. Government Printing Office, 1989.

10. On July 30, 1970, the Israelis baited Soviet-piloted fighter aircraft into action, ambushed them, and downed four MiG-21s with Soviet pilots near the Suez Canal. The Soviets never reported the incident in their media and abruptly ended fighter patrols over the Canal on behalf of Egyptian forces. (See *The New York Times*, August 12, 1970, p. 1.)

11. *Soviet Military Power*, Washington, DC: U.S. Government Printing Office, 1986, pp. 131–132.

12. *Soviet Military Power, 1985*, Washington, DC: U.S. Government Printing Office, 1985, p. 120.

13. Mohamed Heikal, *Road to Ramadan*, London: Collins, 1975, pp. 116–117.

14. Friendship treaties negotiated since 1971 do not require the USSR to defend its Third World partner, but most of them do require that both sides enter into consultations to eliminate a threat to the Third World country concerned. The obligations of these treaties are described in only vague terms, although the contracting parties usually agree not to permit their territory to be used for purposes detrimental to the security of the other. The only friendship treaty negotiated by Gorbachev with a Third World state, the 1989 Soviet-Cuban Friendship Treaty, contains no clause calling for such consultations.

15. The Insight Team of the London Sunday Times, *The Yom Kippur War*, New York: Doubleday and Co., 1974, p. 58.

16. The Soviet Navy has been extremely cautious in responding to the presence of the U.S. Navy during the Libya attack in 1986 and the increase of U.S. naval forces in the Persian Gulf in 1987.

17. Goodman, "The Soviet Union and the Third World: The Military Dimension," pp. 46–66.

18. The former U.S. chairman of the Joint Chiefs of Staff, Admiral Wiliam J. Crowe, remarked that "there is no question that we have seen less forward naval deployments," which seems to reflect a pattern in Soviet naval deployment since 1984. The Soviets did not send a naval task force to the Caribbean for the first

time in nearly ten years and have reduced the number of naval reconnaissance aircraft flights to Cuba and Angola. See *The New York Times,* July 17, 1988, p. 1.

19. *The Road to Ramadan,* pp. 165–184, and *The Sphinx and the Commissar,* New York, Harper and Row, 1978, p. 11.

20. Jon D. Glassman, *Arms for the Arabs: The Soviet Union and War in the Middle East,* Baltimore: Johns Hopkins University Press, 1975, p. 59.

21. *Road to Ramadan,* pp. 116–117.

22. Anwar Sadat, *In Search of Identity: An Autobiography,* New York: Harper and Row, 1978, pp. 220–221.

23. *The New York Times,* November 14, 1989, p. 14. "Military Spending by Soviets Slows," by Thomas L. Friedman.

24. *Pravda,* October 24, 1989, pp. 2–4. (Shevardnadze speech to the USSR Supreme Soviet in Moscow titled "Foreign Policy and Perestroika.")

25. The decision to invade Afghanistan in 1979 probably was made exclusively by the political leadership. In the first authoritative account of the high- level military debate surrounding the decision, General of the Army Valentin I. Varrenikov, a deputy defense minister, stated in an interview with the weekly magazine *Ogonyok* that the General Staff was opposed to the invasion but was overruled by Defense Minister Dmitri F. Ustinov. Varrenikov was the senior defense ministry official in Afghanistan for the last four years of the war and, after the Soviets completed the withdrawal of forces, was named commander of ground forces. Varrenikov added that Marshal Nikolai Ogarkov, then chief of the general staff, and Marshal Sergei F. Akhromeyev, who later became chief of the general staff, also opposed the intervention. See *The New York Times,* March 19, 1989, p. 27 and *The Washington Post,* March 20, 1989, p. 23. In an interview with *Red Star* on March 4, 1989, former Deputy Defense Minister Kulikov suggested that the decision to invade Afghanistan was presented to the military as a *fait accompli.*

26. *The Washington Post,* November 22, 1989, p. 17, "Prominent Hard-Liner Loses Moscow Party Post," by Michael Dobbs.

27. *Soviet Military Power, 1989,* p. 78.

28. *The Washington Post,* December 1, 1989, p. 21. "U.S., Soviet Competition Has Run 20 Years," by Don Oberdorfer. The U.S. Sixth Fleet in the Mediterranean usually totals 24 ships—17 combat ships, including an aircraft carrier, and seven support vessels. The Soviet presence in the Mediterranean over the past several years has usually totaled 31 to 45 ships, mostly merchant tankers and support ships. The recent Soviet withdrawals brought the Soviet presence down to 27 ships, including 19 merchant tankers and auxiliaries. Instead of 5 to 7 Soviet submarines in the Mediterranean, there currently are two.

29. *Far Eastern Economic Review,* March 3, 1988, p. 16. A RAND Corporation study concluded that the total costs of the Soviet involvement in the Third World in the early 1980s represented more than 7 percent of Soviet GNP or more than $40 billion.

7

Soviet Military and Economic Aid

Military and economic assistance has been a significant aspect of Soviet policy toward the Third World since 1954 when Moscow extended its first economic credits to its Asian neighbors and provided small arms to Guatemala.[1] The USSR has used assistance to contest Western influence in the Middle East and Latin America, and to expand trade with less developed countries, gain access to strategic raw materials, and increase hard currency. Next to earnings from exports of petroleum and natural gas, the sale of weapons—particularly to the Middle East—represents the largest earner of hard currency and nearly a fifth of all earnings.[2]

Economic assistance has not had the importance of military assistance; it has been smaller and more difficult to deal with. During the Khrushchev years, when Third World states were unwilling to accept a Soviet military presence, economic and military pledges were about the same. The gap widened under Brezhnev, when the Soviets benefited from international developments that opened opportunities. Dissolution of the French and British empires in the 1950s and 1960s as well as the breakup of the Portuguese empire in the 1970s created opportunities in Algeria, Angola, Mozambique, and South Yemen. Other developments, particularly Arab-Israeli and Indo-Pakistani wars, produced opportunities as did revolutions in Cuba and Ethiopia and conflict in Southeast Asia.

Under Gorbachev, the Soviets have professed interest in political solutions to military crises in the Third World and there has been a decline in military and economic assistance. Fidel Castro remarked in 1989 that he could no longer guarantee that Soviet assistance would "continue to arrive with the usual clocklike punctuality and as previously guaranteed."[3] In Gorbachev's first year, the Soviets signed aid agreements with only fourteen countries, compared with twenty in the previous year, and many of these pledges required no long-term commitment of resources.

Like his predecessors, Gorbachev presumably realizes military and economic aid has made possible a more assertive policy, competition with the United States in Asia, Africa, and the Middle East, and increased influence in Cuba, Syria, and Vietnam. Arms sales have increased rapidly since agreements with Guatemala in 1954, Egypt in 1955, Syria and Indonesia in 1956, and Guinea in 1959.[4] Military advisers have quadrupled since the beginning of the Brezhnev era and military involvement in Third World conflicts has evolved.

In the late 1960s Soviet air and air defense forces appeared in the Middle East; in the mid-1970s, logistics forces transported and sustained Cuban forces for intervention in Angola and Ethiopia; combat and air units invaded Afghanistan in 1979—the first direct involvement of ground forces outside the Warsaw Pact. The Soviets have leveraged military and economic assistance to create an infrastructure of naval and naval air facilities, which allows pursuit of a global foreign policy.

The Soviets were in a position to pursue these policies because of the expansion of military production facilities and transport capabilities during the Brezhnev years. An expanding airlift capability enabled the Soviets to dispatch arms to Egypt and Syria during the 1973 war and to forces of the Popular Movement for the Liberation of Angola (MPLA) in 1975 and 1976. During a crucial stage in the conflict over the Ogaden in Ethiopia, the Soviets used long-range aircraft— which comprise nearly 15 percent of the Soviet military transport fleet—to ferry supplies that helped to turn the tide against Somalia.[5] The navy and merchant fleet also have played a part in ferrying arms to clients in the Middle East and Southeast Asia.

SOVIET MILITARY ASSISTANCE TO THE THIRD WORLD

For the past three decades, military assistance to the Third World has been the primary instrument for the increased Soviet presence in developing countries and expanded influence in countries of "socialist orientation." There is no agreement on which Third World countries are socialist, but such Marxist clients as Angola, Ethiopia, and Mozambique are invariably included.[6] Recently Maputo dropped all reference to Marxism from its constitution and other state documents, and Benin renounced Marxism in 1990.[7] Such states as the

Congo, which express fealty to Marxism, are referred to as countries of socialist orientation, but so are such non-Marxist states as Algeria, Guinea, Libya, and Syria. Some Soviet specialists list countries that espouse an independent brand of socialism, such as Tanzania; others do not. In any event, the Soviets have supplied military weaponry to all these countries.

The two most widely used sources on arms deliveries (publications of the United States Arms Control and Disarmament Agency [ACDA] and the Stockholm International Peace Research Institute [SIPRI]) agree that the United States and the Soviet Union are by far the largest exporters of military hardware and that four-fifths of weapons transferred are for Third World consumers.[8] NATO states have a larger share of the market than the Warsaw Pact, and nearly half of all arms transfers slated for Third World states are delivered to the Middle East and North Africa. The Soviet Union was the leading exporter to the Third World from 1978 to 1982, but the United States was the largest from 1982 to 1985.

The USSR is the principal supplier to the Middle East, which continues to be the major market. Over the past decade, states of the Middle East have received more than a third of the arms import market, although there has been some decline in recent years due to decrease in petroleum prices and end of the Iran-Iraq war. Of the top ten importing countries in the 1980s, six were in the Middle East. Iraq and Saudi Arabia represent the two largest markets in the world and Egypt, Israel, Libya, and Syria have received billions of dollars in assistance during this period. Egypt, Iraq, Libya, and Syria have purchased short-range ballistic missiles from the Soviets, but Moscow has rejected Iraqi and Syrian requests for longer range and more accurate missiles.

The Iran-Iraq war not only proved a bonanza for Soviet sales to the Middle East, but allowed China to export more weapons in the mid-1980s than in the previous twenty-five years. China sold arms to both belligerents and has supplanted North Korea as Iran's principal supplier.[9] Chinese production of older Soviet-style weaponry has enabled Beijing to establish relations with such states as Egypt, which formerly relied on the USSR for military assistance and continue to require spare parts and replacement systems.

Since the early 1970s the Soviets have received vast amounts of hard currency from sales to the Middle East, particularly from Algeria, Iraq, Libya, and Syria. Moscow began to demand hard currency in return for military assistance after the embarrassment surrounding the Soviet expulsion from Egypt in the summer of 1972, and Arab states—because of the steep increase in oil prices after the October War in 1973—had hard currency resources to upgrade arsenals. Exports to

Arab states in the five-year period after the October War were five times greater than in the five-year period after the Six-Day War of 1967.[10] These hard currency transfers, in turn, are important to Moscow for purchase of agricultural products and high-technology industrial equipment from the United States and Western Europe.

Weapons transfers help to foster diplomatic and military dependence on the USSR and ties with the armed forces of recipient countries. Military training on behalf of these countries has had mixed results, but the Soviets have acquired access to Arab and Africa military elites, who often move to important and sometimes sensitive political positions. The Military Assistance Group in Cuba includes 2,800 Soviet military advisers attached to military schools and to units with such equipment as MiG fighter aircraft and surface-to-air missiles; 2,000 personnel attached to a signals intelligence facility; and 2,600 personnel in a motorized rifle brigade.[11]

AID TO THE MIDDLE EAST

Before the Egyptians ended the Soviet advisory presence in 1972, the USSR had more than twenty thousand advisers and technicians in Egypt. The largest Soviet military presence in the Middle East is currently in Syria, where there are approximately twenty-five hundred advisers.[12] There are more than one thousand ground force advisers, eight hundred assigned to the Syrian air force, and one hundred to the navy. Advisers are headquartered in Damascus subordinate to the Soviet General Staff, and in communication with Moscow. Smaller missions are in Algeria, Libya, and South Yemen where the Soviets are assigned to combat units and equipment repair installations. Transfer to the Middle East of sophisticated military equipment, especially air defense systems, fighter aircraft, fighter bombers, and assault helicopters, has usually meant increase in the Soviet advisory presence.

Third World vulnerability opened the way to Soviet arms sales in the 1950s to the Arab states of the Middle East as well as Cuba and Vietnam. These states must cope with military potential of a more powerful regional neighbor and want to pursue an activist foreign policy. Third World clients believe they can use military and economic assistance without compromising independence, adhering to Soviet political demands, or altering policies. Indeed, the Soviet political leadership has discovered that dependent clients in the Third World, unlike their counterparts in the Warsaw Pact until recently, prove independent actors in their decision-making arenas.

Billions of dollars of Soviet military assistance have been transferred to Algeria, India, Iraq, Libya, and Syria over the past ten years, but there is no indication the Soviets have been able to manipulate these states.[13] There has never been a correlation between assistance and influence. Syria has received large amounts of military hardware, but has pursued independent policies. Libya is dependent on arms, but has embarrassed Moscow with policy toward Chad, Iran, the Sudan, and Tunisia. Algeria has been a Soviet client for two decades, but refused access to excellent naval facilities on the Mediterranean. India and Iraq have been stubborn about allowing the Soviets access to facilities. Algeria and India have never been willing to allow more than a modest number of advisers.[14] Cuba and Vietnam certainly pursue their own interests regardless of assistance.

Soviet threats to terminate or delay weapons to such states as Syria and Egypt have not led to changes in policy. Soviet opposition to Sadat's desire to go to war in 1971 and 1972 and restraint on arms transfers led to Cairo's decision to expel advisers. On a visit to the Kremlin in 1971, Sadat failed to arrange a joint military and political strategy with the USSR and gain support for parity with Israel.[15] Moscow refused to supply MiG-25s with air-to-surface missiles and was dragging its heels on resupplying Egypt with surface-to-air missile batteries lost in the war of attrition of 1969–1970.

The Soviets, of course, were ultimately unsuccessful in their efforts to get the Egyptians and Syrians not to go to war against Israel in 1973. Moscow was concerned that another round of hostilities in the Middle East could upset détente with the United States and even draw in the superpowers.[16] Several years later the Soviets delayed deliveries of equipment to Syria in response to Hafez al-Assad's decision to deploy four thousand troops and 250 tanks in Lebanon against the Palestine Liberation Organization.[17]

AID TO CUBA

In recent years, three recipients of military assistance (Cuba, Syria, and Vietnam) have provided access to facilities throughout the Caribbean, the Middle East, and Southeast Asia. Moscow has provided Havana with nearly $10 billion in equipment at little cost, with large deliveries from 1981 to 1985. Items delivered included MiG-21 and MiG-23 aircraft, SA-3 surface-to-air missiles, ZSU-23-4 self-propelled anti-aircraft guns, T-62 medium tanks, and Bm-21 multiple rocket launchers for modernization and expansion.[18]

Modernization allowed Havana to provide older equipment to Nicaragua—T-55 tanks, BTR-50 armored personnel carriers, SA-7 surface-to-air missiles.[19] Gorbachev's willingness to reduce shipments of weapons systems, which he announced in a letter to President Bush in 1989 presumably was made with the understanding that Nicaragua's requirements would be met by Havana and other communist states.[20] Soviet equipment and training has allowed Havana to conduct its first integrated amphibious exercises using Soviet landing ships and Cuban naval infantry. In the early 1980s the Cubans provided Grenada with Soviet equipment, including rifles, machine guns, rocket launchers, and anti-aircraft guns.

Although Gorbachev is willing to consider limits on Cuba's ability to transfer Soviet weaponry to allies, he is proceeding apace with modernization of Cuban forces, particularly air defense. As recently as the autumn of 1989, the Soviets delivered high-performance MiG-29 fighter aircraft, which confirmed rumors that had been circulating in Washington since 1986.[21] MiG-29s are neither in violation of the Soviet pledge in 1962 not to introduce offensive weapons into Cuba nor the 1978 tacit assurance not to provide nuclear-capable varients of combat aircraft. The MiG-29 is primarily an air defense fighter against low-flying targets and no match for the U.S. F-16, delivered to Venezuela several years ago. Several hundred of these aircraft are now in Third World inventories, some selling for as much as $30 million each.

AID TO VIETNAM

Over the past years, Soviet military assistance to Vietnam has reached nearly $10 billion, which allows Hanoi to pursue an assertive policy in Southeast Asia and provides the Soviets with military and intelligence facilities.[22] The Soviets and Vietnamese concluded a friendship treaty in 1978 (one month before the Vietnamese invasion of Cambodia) and in 1982 the Soviets encouraged the Vietnamese to sign the Nonproliferation Treaty, ratified by the United States and USSR in 1968. To present Vietnam as a threat to China's southern flank, the Soviets have provided the Vietnamese with vast amounts of equipment including SU-22 swing-wing fighters, MI-24 attack helicopters, missile attack boats, tanks, and a variety of surface-to-air missiles.[23]

Over twenty-five hundred Soviet military advisers are in Vietnam to support Moscow's assistance program, which enables Vietnam to field the world's third largest army—over 1.2 million troops—and maintain at one point nearly 200,000 troops in Cambodia. Soviet presence in Vietnam includes use of seven piers, expanded and protected petroleum and ordnance storage facilities, high-frequency-direction finding sites, an electronic intelligence collection complex, and—until January 1990—a command post ashore at Cam Ranh Bay.[24]

From 1979 through 1989, TU-95 maritime reconnaissance aircraft and TU-16 bombers staged routine flights from Cam Ranh as part of the Soviet counter to Chinese pressure on the Vietnam border.

AID TO SYRIA

The Syrian buildup in the 1980s is an impressive measure of close relations between Damascus and the USSR. Damascus has received some of the most sophisticated military equipment in the Soviet inventory: MiG-29 fighters, T-72 tanks, and the SS-21 surface-to-surface missile capable of reaching many of Israel's population centers and reportedly equipped with chemical warheads. There are unconfirmed rumors that Moscow will be delivering advanced SU-24 attack bombers, although a system of this type would give the Syrians offensive capability against Israel.[25]

Following the Israeli invasion of Lebanon in 1982, the Soviets significantly upgraded Syria's air defense capabilities by installing two operational SA-5 surface-to-air missile complexes—the first operational SA-5s outside the Soviet Union. In addition to long-range SA-5s, the Soviets provided short-range SA-6s, SA-8s, and SA-11s, and linked Syrian command, control, and communications networks to Soviet systems in the Caucasus. The Soviets have provided TU-126 Moss reconnaissance and early-warning aircraft. There are now more Soviet advisers in Syria than any other Third World country.[26]

Gorbachev has stressed that Moscow will not support Syria's efforts to reach parity with Israel and encouraged Damascus to achieve "reasonable sufficiency" that will allow the Syrians to deter an attack. The new Soviet ambassador, Alexander Zotov, who is a specialist on Arab-Israeli affairs, commented in November 1989 that Soviet deliveries will be based on the "limits of our capabilities" to provide sophisticated equipment as well as Syrian "ability to pay".[27] Syria holds a $20 billion foreign debt and much of it is a military debt to the Soviet bloc. Zotov stressed reasonable sufficiency, defined as the "capability to inflict unacceptable losses" on Israel after an attack on Syria.[28]

AID TO INDIA

India has purchased billions of dollars of Soviet military hardware over the past two decades, but placed limits on military presence. Both India and Vietnam share with the Soviets a deep distrust of China, find that their policy positions are similar to those of the Soviets, and rely on Soviet weapons systems. Unlike Vietnam, the Indians have never provided access to military facilities.

India has cleverly used the threat of arms diversification to cajole unprecedented coproduction schemes from the Soviets and avoid payment for weaponry in hard currency. In the wake of an Indian arrangement to purchase Anglo-French Jaguar fighter aircraft, the Soviets offered a $1.6 billion loan and extended coproduction contracts for MiG-23 fighter aircraft and the T-72 tank. Indian negotiations with the French for purchase of Mirage 2000 aircraft led to Soviet willingness to allow coproduction for the MiG-29 and the T-80 tank before either system had become part of the Soviet operational inventory.[29] Other deliveries of Soviet equipment include submarines, transport aircraft, and surface-to-surface missiles.[30]

Gorbachev's first trip to a Third World state was to India in 1986, and Dobrynin, then chief of the Central Committee's International Department, completed a weeklong visit in 1987.[31] Although total Soviet military assistance to Third World countries has declined, there is no indication of reduction in deliveries to India. India could become the first Third World state to receive the MiG-31 foxhound, which is a high-altitude, long range interceptor, designed to counter cruise missiles.

AID TO IRAQ

The USSR's inability to stabilize bilateral relations with Iran and deterioration of the Iraqi military position in the Iran-Iraq War led to the decision to renew military deliveries to Baghdad. As a result, Iraq became the largest third-world export market for Soviet arms, paying Moscow more than $1.5 billion in oil and $300 million in hard currency annually. In 1983 and 1984, Iraq received large shipments of MiG-25s and T-72 tanks, making Iraq the largest Third World recipient of Soviet military assistance at that time. In 1985 and 1986, Moscow sold Baghdad more than $3 billion of arms and equipment. Iraq has received the MiG-29, the most advanced fighter now in the Soviet arsenal, as well as the medium-range TU-22 Blinder bomber and SU-25 ground-attack aircraft.

Even before the Soviet arms embargo of 1990, the Iraqi-Soviet relationship was hampered by Soviet cultivation of Iran, arms sales to Syria, Iraq's major Arab rival, and independence of the Saddam Hussein regime. The Soviets also enforced an arms embargo against Iraq for nearly two years, after the Iraq invasion of Iran. The Soviets probably will resume military shipments after the Persian Gulf crisis is resolved, but Moscow may limit high-technology systems in order to protect its improved relations with Iran.

ARMS SALES AND GORBACHEV

Under Gorbachev, Soviet foreign policy took on a more open and vigorous style that initially included increases in military assistance to Soviet clients. In 1985 and 1986, Angola, Iraq, and Nicaragua received substantial military aid. Hundreds of transport flights to Angola took place in 1986, moving heavy arms and war materials— reportedly including ground-to-air missiles—from the capital in Luanda to Huambo in south-central Angola for an offensive against South Africa–backed rebels fighting the Marxist government.[32] The regime's counterinsurgency strategy against the National Union for the Total Independence of Angola (UNITA) has been marked by the same flexibility characteristic of the Soviet struggle against the mujahideen in Afghanistan.

In 1986 the Soviets provided Angola with MiG-23 fighter aircraft, MI-8 combat helicopters, SA-3 and SA-8 surface-to-air missiles, and tanks, artillery pieces, and BMP armed vehicles, which allowed Angolan and Cuban forces to pursue more aggressive tactics.[33] Soviet and Cuban advisers had some success in developing the Angolan armed forces into an organization effective enough to permit withdrawal of some Cuban forces. The arms buildup in Angola presumably was responsible in part for success against South African forces in 1988, which led to Pretoria's acceptance of a ceasefire in Angola and withdrawal of South African forces from southern Angola, which was linked to Cuban withdrawal.

Gorbachev's first year as general secretary was marked by an increase in military deliveries to Nicaragua with Warsaw Pact states providing 23,000 tons of military and military-related equipment worth $115 million. Deliveries in 1986 included six MI-24 helicopter gunships, twenty-four MI-8 combat helicopters, transport aircraft and patrol boats, and 1,200 vehicles for probable military use.[34] The MI-24 assault helicopter and MI-17 general purpose military helicopter are equipped with air-to-ground rockets, and some models carry machine guns.

Helicopters were first delivered in late 1984 and early 1985 and became an essential part of the Sandinista battle plan, moving combat units to confront insurgents whenever sighted.[35] The use of the helicopters was demonstrated during a Contra attack in 1986, when a helicopter force counterattacked a Contra village near the Honduras border and inflicted dozens of casualties and forced withdrawal. Helicopter missions were presumably assisted by a Soviet-supplied AN-30 reconnaissance aircraft in use since 1986. Nicaraguan air forces now appear to have twelve MI-24s and thirty-five MI-17s as well. In all, according to James P. Wooten of the Congressional Research Service, they made the task of the Contras "very, very difficult."[36]

Although the USSR has been the largest seller of arms to nearly every region of the Third World since 1985, the Soviet share of total arms deliveries to the Third World has dropped from half of the total in 1987 to one-third in 1988.[37] In 1988, military sales to the Third World declined and U.S. sales nearly equaled the Soviet level: $9.9 billion for the USSR and $9.2 billion for the United States.[38] U.S. sales jumped to $20 billion in 1989–1990 due to sales to South Korea of F-18 fighter aircraft, Saudi Arabia of armored vehicles, and Egypt of tanks and helicopters.[39] Ironically, any conventional arms agreement between the United States and the Soviet Union could allow transfers of military equipment to Third World countries.

Economic and political factors have marked the recent decline in Soviet arms deliveries to the Middle East and Africa. The ceasefire between Iran and Iraq, Libyan military setbacks, and Syria's need to invest in its economy have reduced opportunities in the Middle East. It is unlikely that deliveries to Iraq in the near term could match the $10 billion in transfers between 1984 and 1987.[40]

In addition to the drop in revenues for oil producers in the Middle East, which should contribute to reduced purchases from the Soviets, economic problems of Angola and Ethiopia should reduce Soviet arms transfers to Africa. Deliveries to Vietnam in 1988 were down, and Vietnamese withdrawal from Cambodia as well as Vietnam's economic morass should contribute to continued decline. There was a decrease in military deliveries to Nicaragua in 1987 and 1988, and Gorbachev ended direct supplies of lethal equipment to the Sandinista regime in 1989.[41] Electoral defeat of the Sandinistas in 1990 and South African withdrawal from Angola in 1988 also explains the recent decline in deliveries.

SOVIET ECONOMIC ASSISTANCE TO THE THIRD WORLD

In the decade following the Second World War, the Soviets failed to capitalize on collapse of Western imperial systems in Africa and Asia, growth of radical nationalism, and new responsiveness of "revolutionary democrats" in the Third World. Stalin had a European policy, and Moscow not only carefully avoided Third World conflicts, but restricted support to new communist regimes contiguous to the USSR. In addition to making no effort to develop political or economic ties with such countries as India or Indonesia, he alienated leaders by supporting revolutionary activities. On the eve of the twentieth Soviet party congress in 1956, the USSR was virtually isolated from colonial and newly independent areas of the Third World.

This situation was dramatically reversed at the congress, when Khrushchev described "disintegration of the imperialist colonial system" as a "postwar development of historical significance." He and his successors viewed the Third World as the arena for supporting national liberation movements without risk of superpower confrontation. Khrushchev's optimism about the trends of Third World politics and expansion of Soviet economic aid links to many of these states gave way to Brezhnev's more pragmatic approach and Moscow's realism concerning political and economic development in most Third World countries.

Brezhnev realized that prospects for socialism in the Third World were bleak and instability of many societies meant that leaders disposed toward the Soviet Union might be overthrown by "reactionary elements"—witness the fate of Ben Bella in Algeria, Kwame Kkrumah in Ghana, and Modibo Keita in Mali. Confidence in Soviet-type socialist systems and emphasis on economic "show projects" were replaced by efforts to establish relations with Third World countries that would provide "bases of operations" for expanding contacts and increasing activities.

Soviet leaders became more pessimistic in the 1970s when observers began to notice two developments that undermined the goals formulated in the 1950s and 1960s. First, the colonial era ended with collapse of the Portuguese empire in the mid-1970s, and Soviet commentators began to discuss completion of the "first stage" of the national liberation movement. Soviet setbacks in Egypt, Guinea, and Somalia contributed to the debate on the role of economic assistance.[42] Second, deterioration of East-West relations in the late 1970s affected thinking about the Third World as Soviet leaders and commentators began to frame their discussion of issues in the context of heightened East-West tension and renewed U.S. determination to meet the Soviet challenge. This not only affected thinking on political and military involvement but meant that requests for increased economic assistance had to compete for limited resources with a Soviet military establishment trying to match the Western buildup.[43]

ECONOMIC AID UNDER GORBACHEV

More recently the Soviets have been concerned with their inability to influence the economic plans of such states as Cuba, Nicaragua, and Vietnam that annually receive billions of rubles from the USSR. This is distressing in view of Gorbachev's inability to reverse the slowdown in the Soviet economy.[44] Escalating costs of aid to Third World economies as well as large foreign debts have caused the Soviets to become increasingly impatient with poor economic performance.

The Rand Corporation has concluded that socialist states of the Third World were becoming increasingly burdensome.[45] Costs included trade credits and subsidies, balance-of-payments surpluses, and military operations. By the early 1980s, costs had grown to $44 billion or more than 7 percent of Soviet GNP. The Soviets have become increasingly critical of Third World leaders for expecting socialist states to finance dubious efforts to "force" socioeconomic change through rapid industrialization.[46]

At the same time, the Soviet economy slowed in 1987 and 1988, particularly in machine-building—key to Gorbachev's modernization plan.[47] Agricultural output is down following records set in 1986, and producers of such basic materials as metals and chemicals failed to meet their goals. The Soviet economy continues to suffer from low worker productivity, poor machinery, and a society ill-prepared for economic reforms. The Soviet promise of a 14.2 percent cut in defense spending over the next two years suggests that there will be cuts in assistance to the Third World as a result. The decline in production of oil means that Moscow has less oil to sell on world markets and less hard currency for economic assistance in the Third World. The Soviets have reduced oil deliveries to Eastern Europe and such Third World clients as Cuba and Vietnam. Trade agreements with Cuba and Vietnam in 1991 called for pegging prices of goods at world market levels and conducting trade in convertible currency.

In addition to Soviet criticism of economic management of some of Moscow's closest Third World clients, Soviet commentators have acknowledged shortcomings in assistance programs to the Third World. Few Soviet clients have the infrastructure to absorb Moscow's large mineral and metals processing plants or massive hydropower installations, and Soviet agricultural and industrial technology is not easily transferred to tropical countries with small-scale industry. Moscow's insistence on tying purchase of Soviet goods and services to Soviet projects represents a disincentive to Third World countries in addition to demands for hard currency support for Soviet technicians on aid projects. The USSR's credit terms are no longer as favorable as Western terms (Soviet credit terms are based on 17 years to repay; Western countries allow an average of 30) and only a small percentage of Soviet programs are established as grant aid.[48] (More than half of Soviet aid programs are in ten countries; Western countries extend aid to more than 150.)

As a result, trade with the Third World is still a small part of Soviet trade, and Moscow's economic involvement (trade and aid) is a fraction of that of Western states or even of the United States. In 1985, Soviet trade with Third World states reached nearly $23 billion; Organization for Economic Cooperation and Development (OECD) trade with the Third World was nearly $600 billion; and the United States recorded almost $200 billion. Similarly, Soviet aid to Third World states in that year was less than $2 billion; OECD aid was $25 billion; and the United States recorded more than $6 billion. The USSR's record on agricultural assistance was appalling in view of difficulties of many clients, particularly in Africa where the Soviets provided $15 million in food aid compared to Western deliveries of $1 billion.

Afghanistan has received almost all the USSR's emergency assistance, while less than $5 million annually in Soviet food aid in the 1980s went to the other 145 noncommunist LDCs.[49] Moscow is at a disadvantage because the USSR has been unable to meet its own food requirements in the past twenty years without large purchases from the West; provision of free grain and other food to the Third World requires an expenditure of scarce hard currency, which the Soviet Union does only as a last resort. Farm production in the USSR fell by an estimated 2 percent in 1988, including a grain harvest 8 percent less than in 1987, the worst potato crop since 1951, and stagnating vegetable and fruit production. Increased strikes in the USSR over food suggest that the USSR will be in no position to send food overseas.

Generally, the preference of most developing countries for technically superior Western equipment and consumer goods puts the USSR at a disadvantage in economic aid and trade. The Soviet market pales in comparison to the West's ability to absorb Third World exports, manufactured and traditional. Moscow's hard currency trade balance suffered as exports could not keep pace with surging imports, particularly due to grain purchases. The dollar value of Soviet hard currency exports increased in part due to arms sales to the Third World. Moscow increased imports of oil, largely in payment for arms sales, for resale, particularly in Europe.

Economic aid has probably created the greatest trouble in Soviet relations with both Cuba and Vietnam. The Soviets are disenchanted with the level of aid to both states and believe that much economic assistance is wasted by local inefficiency. The Soviets have become extremely critical of Castro's management of the Cuban economy and, in an article that was banned in Cuba, have reported the appearance of "dissident groups" in Havana that support the "policy of perestroika in the USSR and freedom of religion in Cuba."[50] Moscow is demanding more controls over the use of its aid, and Cuba and Vietnam are becoming increasingly resentful of Soviet highhandedness.

SOVIET ECONOMIC PROBLEMS

Current constraints in the Soviet domestic economy are bringing additional pressures on the USSR to harden the terms of aid and promote projects that promise mutual benefits. Even before the Sandinista electoral defeat in 1990, Nicaragua, which has been almost exclusively dependent on Soviet petroleum since the winter of 1984–1985, learned that the USSR was willing to provide only 40 percent of Managua's crude oil needs instead of the 80 percent that had been provided on highly concessionary terms.[51] A major cutback in Soviet deliveries would put pressure on the hemisphere's only major oil exporters, Mexico and Venezuela, to resume oil shipments to Nicaragua which were ended in 1984 due to the latter's inability to pay for hard currency imports. Following the Sandinistas' electoral defeat, Castro announced the end of military and economic assistance to Nicaragua, which not only serves as a sanction against the new Nicaraguan government but reflects his difficulties in trade ties with the USSR and Eastern Europe.

Castro and Haile Meriam Mengistu have complained publicly about the cutbacks in Soviet economic assistance over the past year. Such African countries as Guinea and Mali have begun to reorient their economies toward the West because of previous experiences with Soviet inability to accommodate special needs of impoverished African states.

The Soviets have been candid about acknowledging their difficulty in providing economic assistance due to the dramatic decline in growth rates of economic production and national income in Council for Mutual Economic Assistance (CEMA) countries in the 1970s, which probably accounted for the sharp decline in Soviet economic aid in the 1980s. Writing in *Voprosy Filosofii* (*Problems of Philosophy*) in 1988, Yuri Novopashin, a sector chief at the Institute of Economics of the World Socialist System (IEMSS), asserted that furthering socialist revolution depended not only on direct assistance to leftist client regimes, but also on the "demonstrative effect" of successes in the communist world. As a result, Novopashin concluded, the Soviet bloc had to be more selective in choosing client states and suggested that the CEMA countries pool their resources in order to compete with efforts of Western countries to step up their "economic expansion" in the Third World.[52]

Although the Soviets recognized the fundamental change in the conditions which shaped policy toward the Third World and became more pessimistic about their prospects, Soviet economic interests and stakes grew throughout this period. Arms sales to the Third World became the largest hard currency earners for the USSR after oil and gas sales to Western Europe. Joint fishing ventures in the Third World accounted for a significant part of Soviet protein needs, although several key West African states have begun to cancel their fishing treaties with the USSR. Moscow invested heavily in such projects as Mali's mining industry, Morocco's phosphate industry, and Guinea's bauxite extraction. The Soviets exploited grain markets as an alternative to the United States and, as a result, Soviet purchases of grain from Argentina helped produce a $1.6 billion Soviet trade deficit with South America in 1984.[53]

These economic ties are complemented by the introduction of Soviet technical services to the Third World as well as thousands of Soviet technical advisers to administer them. In oil-producing states, for example, the Soviets reportedly earn more than $150 million annually in hard currency by providing development services not necesarily related to aid projects.[54] Moscow has been able to exercise some influence over economic decision making by placing advisers at high levels within Third World economic establishments.

The largest number of technicians serve in those countries (Angola, Ethiopia, Iraq, Libya, Syria, Yemen) that are most closely linked to the Soviets in either military assistance or military access. Many of these same states currently enroll approximately one hundred thousand students in Soviet bloc-universities. It is believed that the Warsaw Pact's educational programs have been the most broadly based and generous of all its efforts on behalf of the Third World. The Soviets thus receive access to potential leaders among thousands of students from Third World states with a Soviet military presence (Angola, Ethiopia, Mozambique, Iraq, Yemen, and Syria). Additional students are from those states with whom the Soviets are competing with the West for political and diplomatic influence (Greece, Jordan, Morocco, and Nigeria).[55]

Over the past ten years, the Soviets have been making even greater efforts to tie their economic assistance programs to states that also receive Soviet military assistance. In Asia and Africa, for example, the major beneficiaries of Soviet economic aid are the same states or clients that receive large amounts of military assistance, with special attention directed to states that allow basing facilities or access rights for Moscow's naval and aviation forces. The three major economic aid recipients in sub-Saharan Africa (Angola, Ethiopia, and Mozambique) provide military facilities to the Soviets; the three largest recipients in the Middle East (Iraq, Yemen, and Syria) do so as well; Vietnam also is high on the list of Soviet economic assistance and Soviet military presence. The only major exceptions to this pattern in the Third World are Algeria and India, which have been reluctant to extend military access, despite Soviet pressure.

In the final analysis, Soviet economic assistance efforts are extremely modest in comparison with those of Western states, but the Soviet concentration on a relatively small number of states has given the USSR's aid program more attention and influence than it would otherwise deserve. The Soviets, moreover, have recently expanded the number of intergovernmental commissions on economic and trade cooperation in order to institutionalize ties with key Third World states. In 1985, two new commissions were formed with Nicaragua and Tunisia, and additional commission meetings were held with Algeria, Angola, India, and Mozambique.[56] Angola and India, moreover, were awarded new economic aid packages in recent years worth more than $2 billion and $1 billion, respectively. Notwithstanding the controversy over the effectiveness of Soviet economic assistance arrangements, there is no indication that Moscow will abandon its policy of targeting a select number of key states in order to increase presence and influence.

OUTLOOK FOR SOVIET AID TO THE THIRD WORLD IN THE GORBACHEV ERA

There has been some tightening in the Soviet economic assistance program under Gorbachev. Fewer aid agreements have been signed in recent years, and Soviet projects in the Third World have been avoiding long-term commitment of resources.[57] Soviet pledges in 1986 would have been down in value from the previous year, except for a questionable 18 percent rise in the value of the ruble against the dollar. Aid to Marxist states fell to its lowest level in five years and, for the first time, the USSR is providing substantial local currency to finance projects in Third World states.[58] The 1991 Soviet budget calls for significant cuts in aid, with most assistance going to Afghanistan.

Soviet statements over the past two years indicate that economic assistance will probably decline because of the difficult economic situation in the USSR and official doubts about the efficacy of these assistance efforts. With all the political and ethnic problems that have occupied Gorbachev's agenda, none is considered as critical as the economic issue. A Soviet economist, Nikolai Shmelyov, told the Supreme Soviet in October 1989 that there were no longer "sufficient grounds for spending 10 billion rubles on aid to Third World countries" and several months later an official from Kazakhstan told a meeting of the Central Committee that Moscow should stop "fattening up foreign countries."[59] Even such defenders of economic assistance as Aleksey Vailyev, deputy director of the USSR Academy of Sciences Africa Institute, stressed the need for a more rigorous approach to aid and warned that "every revolutionary, authoritarian dictator" should not expect "our unconditional...support simply because he utters a dozen Marxist-Leninist slogans or pays lipservice to anti-imperialism."[60] Of course, the dissolution of the Soviet bloc in 1989–1990 has led to fewer Third World countries willing to pay tribute to the Soviet model of development.

There also has been a steady decline in the willingness and capability of various Third World states to import sophisticated military weapons systems due, in part, to strong economic pressures and the need to invest greater amounts of capital in civil and social projects. The United States and the Soviet Union, which supply more than two-thirds of all arms exports to global markets, have encountered Third World clients that must choose between increases in expenditures on armaments and increases in investment in economic infrastructure as the "dark cloud of Third World debt...hangs over the world's economic future."[61] Paradoxically, some of these same debt-ridden Third World states are becoming leading suppliers in the competition for global arms sales, particularly Brazil, Egypt, and Argentina. The decline of oil revenues as well as other economic factors have played a key role in the recent decline in arms deliveries to the Middle East, which is now the location of seven of the ten leading Third World arms importers.[62] Arms sales to the Middle East by all suppliers totaled $95.3 billion from 1985 to 1988, as against a total of $113 billion in the previous four years.[63] As long as such Soviet clients as Angola, Nicaragua, and Vietnam remain involved in conflicts that are winding down or in remission then smaller amounts of military assistance will be required in the near term.

Although the Soviet Union earns a considerable amount of hard currency through weapons sales to the Middle East, the Gorbachev regime appears to be acknowledging the economic cost—and Moscow's low position in the international economic hierarchy—of the strategic competition between East and West, particularly the military competition between the USSR and the United States. Gorbachev's speech to the twenty-seventh Soviet party congress and the new Soviet party program indicate that Moscow's role in the Third World was less important than addressing domestic economic concerns and improving relations with the United States. Gorbachev virtually ignored the Third World and, other than Afghanistan, made only passing reference to various regional conflicts that will continue to be potential problems for Soviet-American relations. By ignoring such important issues as the Middle East, Soviet-Indian relations, and Central America, Gorbachev acknowledged that he saw little value in highlighting the more revolutionary and international aspects of Soviet foreign policy at this particular juncture.

Gorbachev's current tactics reflect his sense of priorities. His references to the Third World paled next to Brezhnev's various references in 1971, 1976, and 1981 party congress speeches to numerous examples of Soviet aid, including military assistance, to Third World countries. Ambassador Anatoly F. Dobrynin's appointment to the Secretariat and the retirement of the chief of the International Department, Boris N. Ponomarev, a veteran of the Comintern who had headed the International Department for twenty-five years, also signaled renewed emphasis on the strategic relations with the United States and the possibility of less attention to Third World matters.

More recently, the Soviets have publicized the outstanding debt of various Third World countries as an implicit threat to reduce assistance because of unpaid transfers of military equipment (e.g., Angola, Cuba, Mozambique, Nicaragua, and Syria) or the relative success of their economies (e.g., Algeria, Egypt, and India). Several other Third World countries, including Iraq, North Korea, Yemen, and Vietnam, owe the Soviets more than one billion rubles.[64]

The Soviets clearly have begun reassessing their military aid commitments, leaning on Syria to repay its $15 billion debt and use hard currency for future deliveries.[65] Aid to Cuba, Syria, and Vietnam is declining and the USSR is in a position to apply some pressure on these clients for debt repayment because they lack alternative sources for assistance. Such states as Libya and Yemen, which have become less important to the Soviets, also will confront greater pressure for repayment. Iraq and Kuwait are no longer making hard currency transfers to the Soviet Union.

As a result, many Third World leaders have expressed concern that Moscow may back away from its international obligations. They may also believe that any effort by Gorbachev to address U.S. concerns over East-West competition in the Third World could weaken the Soviet commitment to the countries of "socialist orientation." Castro has reminded Gorbachev that "blood has been spilled" in the Third World, and Mengistu urged the Soviets not to give the issue of regional conflict a lower priority than nuclear matters.

Since Gorbachev's speech to the party congress in 1986, in fact, there has been a decline in both Soviet economic and military assistance to the Third World. Soviet military sales began to decline in 1987 and Soviet sales in 1988 fell by 47 percent from the previous year. Last year's sharp reduction may be no more than a short-term decline in demand from major Third World clients, but it is noteworthy that such key states as India, Iraq, Libya, and Syria are facing reduced military shipments from the USSR. In April 1987, Gorbachev used a dinner speech for Syrian President Assad to encourage resolution of regional conflicts and suggest that there were limits on the qualitative level of Soviet assistance.

Cuban and Ethiopian leaders have begun to complain publicly that the Soviets are reducing economic assistance and, following a visit by a high-level Soviet military delegation to Maputo in May 1989, the government in Mozambique announced that the Soviet Union would be withdrawing its military advisers by the end of 1990.[66] The withdrawal decision was presented as a mutual one by Mozambique President Joaquim Chissano and Defense Minister General Alberto Chipande, but the Soviet move is a reflection of Gorbachev's interest in reducing military commitments in the Third World and promoting political and diplomatic solutions to Third World conflicts. The Soviet decision to withdraw advisers from Ethiopia could not be mutual in view of the military setbacks to the regime in Addis Ababa from the Eritrean and Tigrean resistance forces.

More recently, Soviet officials have begun to criticize the advisability and effectiveness of Soviet economic assistance efforts in the Third World. At a Central Committee plenum in February 1990, a party official from Kazakhstan argued in favor of ending all foreign aid and specifically questioned aid efforts on behalf of Angola, Ethiopia, Nicaragua, Vietnam, and Cuba.[67] An official from the USA and Canada Institute described the foreign assistance effort as an "extravagence" and noted that military asisstance to the Third World represented "unbuilt apartments...unlaid highways...and nonexistent hospitals, schools, and libraries."[68] Other officials have criticized the excessive secrecy that surrounds these aid programs and called for a greater role by the Supreme Soviet in extending and monitoring assistance to the Third World.

More recently, Soviet officials and economists have begun to challenge the entire fabric of assistance to the Third World. An article in a leading economic journal raised doubts about whether the "world socialist economic system" was worth the price, criticizing inflated prices for Cuban sugar and Vietnamese cement.[69] Soviet commentary has been particularly critical of services and subsidies to Cuba which cost the Soviets several billion dollars annually.[70] These articles presumably represent the interests of Russian nationalists who no longer want to support the backward economies of both East Europe and the Third World.

The current Soviet leadership appears to recognize that Soviet assistance has had a role to play in consolidating the political power of such clients as Angola, Ethiopia, and Nicaragua, but that such aid has not led to any shift in the balance of power or the correlation of forces in the Third World. Soviet investments, for the most part, have been to some of the poorest and most beleaguered regimes, particularly

Afghanistan, Angola, Ethiopia, Yemen, and Vietnam, which have not contributed significantly to any weakening of Western influence in Africa, Asia, or the Middle East. The Soviets will continue to play an active role in the Third World and avail themselves of opportunities to compete with the United States, but they appear to be more aware of the accompanying burdens and hazards associated with regional conflicts as well as potential dangers and costs of becoming primary provider of poor, distant states of dubious socialist orientation.[71]

Third World leaders, for their part, realize that the internal changes that have been sweeping all states of the Warsaw Pact will lead to lesser amounts of military and economic assistance. Poland and Czechoslovakia have announced that they will be less involved in military aid programs in the Third World as both states switch from military to civilian production. In the 1980s, Czechoslovakia ranked seventh in the world in earnings from foreign arms sales, particularly from self-propelled artillery, amphibious vehicles, and armored personnel carriers to such states as Iran that Moscow was trying to hold at arm's length. The Eastern European states were also important military suppliers to Nicaragua and the PLO for equipment, training, and logistical assistance.

Arab and African leaders particularly fear that Western investment and developmental capital will now be attracted to opportunities in Eastern Europe and the Soviet Union as the lessening of East-West tensions brings less competition between the superpowers and their allies in the Third World. The dominant sentiment in the region was summarized by a former Kuwaiti official who said that "suddenly we find ourselves alone on a stage from which we should have exited some time ago."[72] A Kenya foreign ministry official remarked that "Eastern Europe is the most sexy beautiful girl, and we are an old tattered lady."[73] The nonaligned movement, after all, got much of its political clout by taking advantage of Soviet–U.S. rivalry and the lessening of global bipolarity lessens the strategic value of real estate in the Third World as well. Soviet clients will have to lobby harder for assistance in the near term.

NOTES

1. The term "Third World" (or "developing world" or "less developed countries"), as used in this book, refers to all countries in Africa except South Africa, all countries in South and East Asia except Japan, all countries in Latin America, and all countries in the Middle East. The term "arms transfers" refers to the provision of weapons, spare parts, support equipment, advisers, training, and information. Arms transfers normally occur in two phases: agreements or

contractual promises to provide military equipment and services, and the actual delivery of goods and services.

2. The largest amounts of weapons sales for hard currency are in the Middle East, where transfers to Syria, Iraq, and Libya exceed those to such communist states as Vietnam and Cuba in the value of military equipment received from the USSR.

3. *The New York Times,* July 28, 1989, p. 2, "Castro Begins to Talk of Decline in Crucial Aid From Soviet Union," by Joseph B. Treaster.

4. Gordon H. McCormick, "Proxies, Small Wars, and Soviet Foreign Policy," in John H. Maurer and Richard H. Porth, eds., *Military Intervention in the Third World: Threats, Constraints, and Options,* New York: Praeger Publishers, 1984, pp. 50–51.

5. Mark N. Kramer, "Soviet Arms Transfers to the Third World," *Problems of Communism,* September–October 1987, pp. 52–68.

6. See Thomas J. Zamostny, "Moscow and the Third World: Recent Trends in Soviet Thinking," *Soviet Studies,* Vol. XXXVI, No. 2 (April 1984), pp. 223–235. For comments on the imprecision of Soviet theoretical categories, see *Narody Azii i Afriki,* No. 6, 1979, pp. 195–199. On the evolution of Soviet thinking on the Third World, see Elizabeth Valkenier, "Trends in Soviet Research on the Developing Countries," in W. Raymond Duncan, *Soviet Policy in Developing Countries,* Waltham, MA: Ginn-Baisdell, 1970, pp. 199–224.

7. *The Washington Post,* July 29, 1989, p. 27.

8. U.S. Arms Control and Disarmament Agency, *World Military Expenditures and Arms Transfers 1972–1982,* Washington, DC: U.S. Government Printing Office, 1984; Stockholm International Peace Research Institute, *World Armaments and Disarmament,* London: Francis and Taylor, 1983.

9. *World Military Expenditures and Arms Transfers 1987,* Washington, DC: Arms Control and Disarmament Agency, 1988, p. 21.

10. See *Communist Aid Activities in Non-Communist Less Developed Countries,* Central Intelligence Agency, Washington, DC: 1979. p. 5.

11. *Soviet Military Power, 1984,* Washington, DC: U.S. Government Printing Office, 1984, p. 120.

12. *Soviet Military Power, 1985,* Washington, DC: U.S. Government Printing Office, 1985, p. 122.

13. See Melvin A. Goodman, "Third World Clients and Third World Dilemmas," in *Limits to Soviet Power,* Waltham, MA: Lexington Press, 1989, pp. 179–203.

14. The largest recipients of Soviet military aid over the past decade have been Algeria, Angola, Cuba, Ethiopia, India, Iraq, Libya, Syria, and Vietnam, which account for three-fourths of all Soviet military transfers. (Except for Algeria and India, all of these littoral or island states permit Soviet access to naval and/or naval facilities.) The U.S. arms program is less concentrated, with the top eight recipients receiving only half of all American arms exports.

15. Mohamed Heikal, *Road to Ramadan,* New York: Quadrangle Books, 1975, pp. 116–117.

16. Rajan Menon, *Soviet Power and the Third World,* New Haven: Yale University Press, 1986, pp. 195–196. Also see Robert O. Freedman, *Soviet Policy Toward the Middle East Since 1970,* New York: Praeger Publishers, 1978, pp. 141–147.

17. See Melvin A. Goodman, "Third World Clients and Third World Dilemmas," in *Limits to Soviet Power*, Waltham, MA: Lexington Press, 1989, pp. 179–203.

18. *Soviet Military Power, 1984*, Washington, pp. 120–122.

19. Ibid., pp. 121–122.

20. *The Washington Post*, May 7, 1989, p. 1.

21. *The Washington Post*, November 16, 1989, p. 8. "Soviets May Have Sent MiG-29 Jets to Cuba," by Don Oberdorfer.

22. Daniel S. Papp, *Soviet Policies Towards the Developing World in the 1980s*, Washington, DC: U.S. Government Printing Office, 1986, pp. 351–352.

23. *Soviet Military Power, 1984*, p. 119.

24. *ASEAN Forecast (Special Supplement)*, "The Cam Ranh Syndrome," June 1984, pp. 101–103; *Soviet Military Power, 1987*, Washington, DC: U.S. Printing Office, 1987, p. 87.

25. *The Washington Post*, November 16, 1989, p. 24. "Syria Urged to Stress Defense," by Caryle Murphy.

26. Papp, *Soviet Policies Towards the Developing World*, p. 248.

27. *The Washington Post*, November 20, 1989, p. 24. "Syria Urged to Stress Defense," by Caryle Murphy.

28. A serious debate is currently taking place in the USSR on the issue of reasonable sufficiency and nuclear deterrence with civilian analysts arguing that Soviet forces were overbuilt during the Brezhnev era, leaving room for substantial unilateral reductions. Military analysts are predictably in disagreement and want future reductions to be based on mutual negotiation. It is not unlikely that a similar debate is taking place with regard to weapons deliveries to Third World states, particularly the efficacy of delivering offensive as opposed to defensive weapons systems.

29. Rajan Menon, *Soviet Power and the Third World*, pp. 201–202.

30. *Soviet Military Power, 1987*, p. 138.

31. *Pravda*, May 27, 1987, p. 3.

32. *The Washington Post*, April 11, 1987, p. 22.

33. *Soviet Military Power, 1987*, p. 135.

34. *Soviet Military Power, 1987*, p. 143.

35. *The New York Times*, July 10, 1986, p. 9.

36. *The New York Times*, October 29, 1986, p. 13.

37. Richard F. Grimmett, *Trends in Conventional Arms Transfers to the Third World by Major Supplier, 1980–1987*, Washington, DC: Congressional Reference Service, 1988, p. 10.

38. Richard F. Grimmett, *Trends in Conventional Arms Transfers to the Third World by Major Supplier, 1980–1987*, Washington, DC: Congressional Reference Service, 1989, pp. 29–31.

39. *The New York Times*, March 25, 1990, p. 18, "Prospect of Arms Pacts Spurring Weapon Sales," by Robert Pear.

40. Richard F. Grimmett, *Trends in Conventional Arms Transfers to the Third World by Major Supplier, 1980–1987*, Washington, DC: Congressional Reference Service, 1988, p. 5.

41. Testimony to the House Armed Services Committee, February 22, 1989, Rear Adm. Thomas A. Brooks.

42. See Elizabeth K. Valkenier, *The Soviet Union and the Third World: An Economic Bind*, New York, Praeger Publishers, 1983, pp. 1–33.

43. See Thomas J. Zamostny, "Moscow and the Third World."

44. On the rising costs the Soviets face in Third World countries, see Jerry Hough, *The Struggle for the Third World: Soviet Debates and American Options*, Washington, DC: Brookings Institution, 1986.

45. See Charles Wolf, Jr., *The Costs and Benefits of the Soviet Empire, 1981– 1983*, Santa Monica, CA: Rand, 1986.

46. Joseph Whelan, *The Soviet Union in the Third World, 1980–1982: An Imperial Burden or Political Asset*, Washington, DC: U.S. Government Printing Office, 1984, pp. 295–296.

47. *Gorbachev's Economic Program: Problems Emerge*, June 1988, paper prepared by the Central Intelligence Agency and the Defense Intelligence Agency for the Subcommittee on Economic Resources, Competitiveness and Security Economics of the Joint Economic Committee, Congress of the United States.

48. U.S. Department of State, *Warsaw Pact Economic Aid to Non-Communist LDCs, 1984*, Washington, DC: Department of State Publication, 1986, p. 4.

49. Ibid., p. 3.

50. *Moscow News*, March 9, 1990, p. 12, "Being True to Principles or Principles Being True," by Vladimir Orlov.

51. *The Washington Post*, June 2, 1987, p. 1.

52. *Voprosy Filosofii*, May 1988, pp. 29–30.

53. *Warsaw Pact Economic Aid to Non-Communist LCDs*, p. 9.

54. Ibid., p. 5.

55. Papp, *Soviet Policies Towards the Developing World*, pp. 112–114.

56. Ibid., pp. 17–18.

57. *Warsaw Pact Economic Aid Programs in Non-Communist LCDs: Holding Their Own in 1986*, Washington, DC: Department of State Publication, August 1988, pp. 1–2.

58. The term "Marxist states" refers to countries that have identified themselves as Marxist-Leninist, many of which rely primarily or entirely on Communist military support to maintain their power, including Afghanistan, Angola, Ethiopia, Nicaragua, and South Yemen prior to unification.

59. *Izvestia*, November 1, 1989, p. 5; *Pravda*, February 8, 1990, p. 6.

60. *Izvestia*, February 6, 1990, p. 5

61. Lester Brown, *State of the World, 1986*, New York: W. W. Norton and Company, 1986, p. 195.

62. Egypt, Syria, Iraq, Libya, Jordan, Saudi Arabia, and Israel. India, in fourth place, was the only country outside the region in the top five.

63. The USSR accounted for 34 percent of all arms sold to the Middle East in the last four years, while the United States accounted for 16 percent. Britain, France, West Germany, and Italy accounted for 21 percent, while other countries accounted for the remainder.

64. *Izvestia*, March 2, 1990, p. 3.

65. Stephanie G. Neuman, "The Arms Market: Who's on Top," *Orbis*, Fall 1989, p. 518.

66. *The Washington Post*, June 1, 1989, p. 1, "Soviet Military Advisers to Leave Mozambique," by Karl Maier.

67. *Pravda*, February 8, 1990, p. 6.

68. *Trud*, February 15, 1990, p. 4.

69. *Ekonomika I Zhizn*, March 1990, p. 27.

70. *Argumenty I Fakty*, March 17, 1990, p. 7.

71. Menon, *Soviet Power and the Third World*, p. 254.

72. *The New York Times*, March 6, 1990, p. 1, "Arabs Fear End; of Cold War Means a Loss of Aid and Allies," by Youssef M. Ibrahim.

73. *The New York Times*, December 27, 1989, p. 17, "Africa Fears Its Needs Will Become Secondary," by Jane Perlez.

8

Soviet Retreat in the 1990s

The prospect in the 1990s for Soviet participation in the Third World is surely less of the same, instead of more. And the reason for this change is in the main economic: Moscow can no longer afford to pay the bill. The Soviet economy is sinking and will not support the cost of regional crises. According to the Central Intelligence Agency, economic problems in the USSR reached "near crisis proportions" in 1989 after a disappointing performance in 1987–1988.[1]

The economy is plagued by unfinished construction projects. Oil production has fallen, for the first time since the end of the Second World War. In this respect it resembles the United States, which once—in the far-off 1920s—dominated world oil markets. Transportation, too, has suffered, with widespread breakdowns interfering with deliveries of raw materials to factories, of finished goods to consumers. Production of consumer goods is one of the sorest points in all of the much-discussed failures of the Soviet economy; it has increased at most—figures are uncertain—by a mere one percent, which hardly equals the rate of population growth. Machinery production— usually the fastest-growing category of industrial output—registered no growth.

The dissatisfaction of Soviet consumers has helped increase such evidence of social tension as strikes and ethnic clashes. Soviet researchers believe that strikes in the USSR rose from two dozen, involving a few thousand workers, in 1987–1988, to more than fifty-five, involving several hundred thousand, in 1989.[2] Erosion of labor discipline and losses in work time due to strikes and ethnic unrest contributed to the economy's poor showing. Ethnic tension in the Caucasus and Central Asia continue to disrupt production and transportation. Price increases and rationing will worsen a situation that already finds 43 million people, or 15 percent of the population, living in poverty, according to former Prime Minister Ryzhkov.

Moscow's international financial position has deteriorated, with the USSR borrowing heavily to finance increased imports. The hard-currency trade balance went from a surplus of $2.6 billion in 1988 to a deficit of $1.8 billion in 1989. Oil exports fell because of a decline in production, labor unrest, and distribution bottlenecks. Increased borrowing raised hard-currency debt to $47 billion in 1989, more than doubling the $22 billion debt in 1984, the last year before Gorbachev's accession. For the first time in decades, in 1990 the Soviets failed to pay for imports on time, and as a result Western bankers have tightened credit to the USSR.

To stabilize the economy the Soviets must cut the deficit, attract Western technology and expertise, break up state monopolies, and create a safety net for their people. Moscow requires membership from such international economic organizations as the World Bank, International Monetary Fund, and General Agreement on Tariffs and Trade, which will not be forthcoming if Moscow pursues an expansionist policy in the Third World. Joint ventures with the United States, Japan, and key states of Western Europe could end should Moscow return to policies of the Brezhnev era. Only stable relations with the United States can provide the international predictability that Moscow requires to concentrate on domestic problems.

Economic confusion has forced Moscow to reduce both defense spending and its position in the Third World. In addition to unilateral cuts in forces in Central Europe and along the Sino-Soviet border, Gorbachev has reduced defense spending, particularly for ground and air forces. The CIA believes there was a 5 percent decline in defense spending in 1989, with procurement expenses dropping sharply, followed by personnel and maintenance costs.[3] Procurement for strategic forces declined by 3 percent in 1989 and larger reductions were taken by ground forces.

Economic problems have helped bring the current malaise within the Red Army, which is showing some of the turmoil afflicting Soviet society. Leon Trotsky had predicted as much when he wrote from exile that the army was a "copy of society and suffers from all its ills, usually at a higher temperature."[4] The declining power of the military has led to ethnic and political dissent, deteriorating living conditions, and separatism. Soldiers in the Caucasus are deserting and joining unofficial "national armies" that resist Soviet security forces. Reservists are not reporting, and protests forced the General Staff to cancel a call for reservists in 1990 during riots in Baku. The introduction of armed forces in the Baltics in January 1991 led to twenty deaths in Lithuania and Latvia.

Draft resistance increased sharply in 1989 and probably will continue to rise because of separatism in the Baltics and Caucasus. When the Soviet Army newspaper (*Krasnaya Zvezda*) published the results of the spring draft in 1990, it showed a lack of response by non-Russians, particularly in Armenia and the Baltics.[5] There have been large drops in republics with heavy populations of Muslims. All this affects any assesment of Soviet military capabilities; the Red Army could reconstitute itself if faced with invasion, but deployment outside Soviet borders, particularly in the Third World, would be difficult.

Gorbachev interrupted his vacation to address a military audience, making the case for an all-volunteer army and nationality-based units.[6] A major step in the direction of a volunteer force took place earlier in the year, when naval seamen were offered contracts as hired employees. In addition, the length of service of navy draftees was reduced from three to two years.

Military and economic crises not only reduce the Soviet threat but add an element of irreversibility to retreat in the Third World. Another Afghan adventure appears remote, and dispatch of large numbers of advisers and technicians to Third World states is unlikely. Naval deployments in out-of-area waters will continue to decline, and the virtual evacuation of Cam Ranh Bay suggests Moscow is losing interest in access to overseas facilities. Military and economic assistance declined in 1989 and 1990, and probably will continue to do so.

MILITARY BALANCE IN THE THIRD WORLD

Unlike Brezhnev, who assigned the highest priority to defense and allocated massive resources to the military, Gorbachev has reduced the role and status of the military, emphasizing domestic economic needs. Brezhnev encouraged the military's monopoly on national security and allowed unlimited secrecy. Gorbachev has reduced the influence of the military on security policy, allowed extensive criticism of the military, and given civilian experts access to sensitive information. Perestroika and glasnost have created a role for public opinion on military issues, for the first time in Soviet history.

Under Brezhnev the Soviets tried to exploit regional conflict, but Gorbachev has stressed cooperation and political resolution. Military policy now supports Moscow's efforts to reform the economy and improve relations with the United States and other powers. Unwillingness to compete with the United States in the Third World means that reducing forces for power projection is just as important as reaching agreement on strategic and conventional forces. Moscow accepted U.S. negotiating positions on INF and a ban on chemical weapons. The Soviet outline for a START agreement resembles that of the United States.

Unlike the United States, the USSR has neither the industrial base to support competition in the Third World nor the doctrine to support spheres of influence in noncontiguous areas. Conventional forces defend Soviet borders and introduce power into contiguous areas, not pressing U.S. interests far from the USSR.[7] Since Gorbachev came to power, there has been a sharp decline in ship days "out-of-area" as well as naval exercises. Gorbachev has encouraged criticism of the deployment of large ships, particularly aircraft carriers, as "status symbols," and decommissioned more ships in the late 1980s than any other time since the end of the Second World War.[8] Soviet critics of the navy are emphasizing that "defensive sufficiency" means restricting combat tasks to defense of the Soviet coast and strategic submarines with long-range missiles. Interdiction of Atlantic and Pacific sea lanes is no longer consonant with a defensive strategy, and searching for and destroying U.S. submarines on the high seas is even more doubtful.

In the Third World, Africa is of no strategic concern to the Soviet Union and South America too far from Soviet borders to be of concern. In event of war the Soviets would concentrate assets closer to the USSR and to actual theaters of combat. The Cape route is not a choke point that could be closed like the Malacca Straits, and a Soviet base in southern Africa is so low in priority that the United States need have little concern.

Unlike Africa and South America, the Middle East and Persian Gulf have significant internal resources that make them important to the United States and the USSR and the balance of power between them. But Moscow lacks the assets available to Washington, and the United States is well positioned in the Persian Gulf and Indian Ocean. The U.S. deployment to the Persian Gulf in 1990 was assisted by air bases in Oman, naval command and control in Bahrain, ASW facilities in Somalia, and airfields in Egypt, Kenya, Morocco, and Turkey.[9] Diego Garcia in the Indian Ocean supports naval operations and could accommodate B-52s operating in Southwest Asia.[10] Modest Soviet facilities at Aden in Yemen and Dahlak Island off the Ethiopian coast are no match for U.S. assets; unification of the Yemens and possible defeat of Mengistu could threaten those bases as well.

In Asia, Moscow's concerns deal with containment of China, protection of ballistic missile submarines in the Sea of Okhotsk, and defense of its border against U.S. and Chinese forces. Bases at Vladivostok and Petropavlovsk in the eastern USSR support these objectives. The United States has facilities in Japan and South Korea, bases at Clark Field and Subic Bay in the Philippines, providing an edge in maritime capabilities, naval long-range strike, and amphibious warfare.[11] Moscow's facilities in the western and southern Pacific were no match for the U.S., even prior to its withdrawal from Cam Ranh Bay and Da Nang in 1990. Gorbachev's speeches at Vladivostok and Krasnoyarsk indicated that Moscow would cut its forces in Asia and pursue arms control to limit U.S. forces.

ECONOMIC SAVINGS IN THE THIRD WORLD

A Soviet party official remarked in May 1990 that Moscow in placing less emphasis on the Third World will undertake a "radical review" of its military assistance.[12] States with the greatest debt to the Soviet Union, such as Cuba, Vietnam, and Syria, are probably most vulnerable to cuts; reductions in 1989–1990 hit the Middle East harder than any other region, with Iraq receiving the largest reductions even before the Soviet arms embargo began in the summer of 1990.[13] Arab officials and intellectuals already believe they have "lost an ally of the kind that stood by them at times of crisis."[14] Afghanistan probably will be protected from cuts in aid until the Soviets reach an understanding with the United States on a new government in Kabul and deliveries of military aid to resistance forces. Similarly, Moscow wants to protect the regime in Cambodia from guerrilla factions supported by the United States and China.

The Soviets are warning Third World clients to expect less. Escalating costs of aid and unpaid debts of Third World states have caused the Soviets to become impatient with poor economic performance. They have criticized Third World leaders for expecting support for "dubious efforts to force" socioeconomic change through rapid industrialization.[15]

For the first time the Soviets have published a list of debtors in the Third World, a warning that assistance will be cut. The list appeared in the government newspaper in March 1990, and reported that the foreign debt to the Soviet Union was more than 85 billion rubles. Cuba and Vietnam were listed as the greatest "socialist" debtors in the Third World, and India and Syria described as leaders among "developing" countries. The article concluded that "effective trade" should replace aid, that generosity had to be curtailed. Third World states were warned to expect less, and Soviet readers were warned "not to count seriously on these debts being repaid soon."[16] The labor newspaper *Trud* reported that the USSR spent $19 billion, or 1.4 percent of its gross national product, on economic aid in 1989.[17]

The Soviets have named Cuba, Nicaragua, and Vietnam as targets for cuts. An economist with ties to Gorbachev, Nikolai P. Shmelyov, told the Congress of People's Deputies in 1989 that it was necessary to cut assistance to these states to balance the Soviet budget.[18] Shmelyov's speech, one of the more radical addresses to the Congress, argued that cutting aid to Latin America would "suffice to improve the consumer market" in the USSR. Following the twenty-eighth party congress in 1990, Gorbachev warned Third World states that Soviet aid wil be reviewed to take into account the "real capabilities of our country."[19]

A message to Cuba, the largest debtor, suggested reductions in assistance in view of the fact that "in certain social indicators" such as life expectancy and infant mortality Cuba is "better off than certain regions of the Soviet Union." This comparison at a time of reform debate in the Supreme Soviet indicates that assistance to Third World states is becoming increasingly controversial. Opponents of foreign assistance are arguing that because of economic problems at home it is no longer possible to extend large amounts of aid. Unless the Soviets are willing to cut assistance to Cuba and Vietnam, which receive more than half of Soviet aid, they will not realize any significant savings in the Third World.

Thus Gorbachev has signaled that commitments are being reduced, assistance will decline. This is particularly true with regard to the Middle East and Africa, where the Soviets have demonstrated they want to work with the United States to end conflicts. The Soviets worked behind-the-scenes with the United States to arrange the Angolan accords of 1988 and have stressed the importance of the ceasefire to Dos Santos. They have focused on a national reconciliation government in Angola that includes Savimbi's UNITA faction. In Ethiopia the Soviets are pressing for negotiations between Mengistu and the EPLF, and in Mozambique reducing aid and advisers to the Chisanno government. On a recent trip to southern Africa, Shevardnadze remarked that Angola and Mozambique have "enough forces" to defend themselves.[20]

The Soviets have cut military deliveries to Arab states that do not pay in hard currency or have debt problems. Arms deliveries to Libya fell 60 percent ($9 billion in 1982–1985 to $3.5 billion in 1986–1989).[21] Deliveries to Syria fell 44 percent, to $5.5 billion from $10 billion. Arms shipments to Iraq declined 35 percent, from $27.5 billion to $18 billion, and the Soviet arms embargo on Iraq could be long lasting. The exception is Afghanistan, where deliveries went from $2.5 billion in 1982–1985 to $9 billion in 1986–1989, but continued Soviet–U.S. dialogue on a political settlement presumably will lead to cuts for Afghanistan as well. Gorbachev's cuts demonstrate resource constraints and the need to limit activities abroad. Reduction of assistance and advisors indicates that he will not allow the Soviet Union to pursue commitments that cannot be sustained. Whereas the historian Paul Kennedy has demonstrated that defense spending stimulated economic growth in Britain in the nineteenth century and Japan in the 1930s, Gorbachev recognizes a negative relationship between defense spending and economic performance.[22]

His "new thinking" is designed to reduce competition and spending in the Third World so that economic resources can be channeled to Moscow's industrial and technological base. This strategy is just one aspect of the effort to gain control over the national security agenda and demilitarize Soviet decision making. Gorbachev believes annual cuts in military aid of $30 billion and in economic aid of $6 billion can produce a "peace dividend," particularly vis-à-vis the largest recipients of assistance—Angola, Afghanistan, Cuba, Ethiopia, and Vietnam.

Gorbachev's willingness to meet with South Korean President Roh Tae Woo in June 1990, during visits of both leaders to the United States, marked the primacy of economic matters in dealing with the two Koreas. Ignoring ties to North Korea, Moscow has established full diplomatic relations with Seoul, exchanging trade missions and consular representatives. Trade between the two countries was less than $600 million in 1989 and could reach $10 billion by the mid-1990s. The meeting with Roh suggests movement toward diplomatic relations, which would represent the largest shift in relations in Northeast Asia since the end of the Second World War. North Korea receives about three-fourths of its military equipment from the USSR, and has threatened that recognition of South Korea will "freeze the division" on the peninsula.[23] Gorbachev presumably believes closer relations with South Korea, as well as the 1990 trade agreement with the United States, will strengthen the Soviet economy and persuade Japan to play a larger economic role in the Soviet Union.

REGIONAL MANAGEMENT IN THE THIRD WORLD

Unlike Brezhnev, who looked for opportunities to expand military presence in the Third World, Gorbachev is reducing the Soviet presence and pursuing solutions to regional confrontation. Brezhnev believed that low-cost, short-term support for Third World regimes in conflict would help secure pro-Soviet regimes; Gorbachev has called for greater activity by the United Nations to settle disputes and combat international terrorism. Brezhnev sanctioned military efforts to protect regimes in Afghanistan, Angola, and Cambodia; Gorbachev has withdrawn forces from Afghanistan and encouraged the Brazzaville Protocol of 1988 to end conflict in Angola. He pressed for withdrawal of Vietnamese forces from Cambodia, completed in 1989, and withdrawal of Cuban from Angola, scheduled to be completed in 1991, and promoted a UN presence to monitor these arrangements.

Moscow and Washington are pressing Luanda's government and Savimbi's rebels to begin talks. During independence ceremonies for Namibia, Shevardnadze and Baker reportedly agreed Angola could provide an opportunity to repeat the collaboration that produced success in Namibia.[24] Zairian President Mobutu Sese Seko, a likely mediator, could repeat the role he played in 1988 in the ceasefire in Angola.

A breakthrough took place at the summit meeting between Gorbachev and Bush in May–June 1990, when the two sides agreed to deliver American food on Soviet AN-24 transports to tribes in Ethiopia isolated by the war with Eritrea.[25] Soviet–U.S. competition contributed to the economic and social problems in the Horn of Africa in the 1980s; cooperation could alleviate them in the 1990s.[26] Moscow and Washington persuaded Mengistu to stop bombing Massawa, a key port held by Eritrean insurgents, to allow food to enter the country. Mengistu agreed to allow a United Nations observer to attend the Ethiopian-Eritrean talks mediated by former president Jimmy Carter in 1989; these talks could lead to an upgrading of U.S. relations with Addis Ababa. Moscow has withdrawn one-third of its advisers from Ethiopia and warned Mengistu not to expect renewal of the four-year, $2 billion arms pact that expires in December 1990. Gorbachev threatened to cut current assistance if Mengistu refused to negotiate with the insurgents.

Gorbachev's flexibility on these African issues is designed in part to establish a Soviet role in the peace process in the Middle East. Over the past years, Soviet diplomats have been paying visits to Arab capitals, and the Kremlin has improved relations with Israel, to increase Moscow's relevance to any negotiating forum. Gorbachev's proposal for a meeting of permanent members of the Security Council, to prepare for an international conference, provides the Soviet Union with a role in the Middle East, particularly in the absence of another viable proposal. Gorbachev's decision to pay Moscow's UN debts and advocate a more effective UN role in the Middle East and Persian Gulf suggests commitment to peaceful resolution of regional conflicts. Efforts to energize the Soviet role in the United Nations and place Moscow at the center of the peace process will put the West on the defensive.[27]

Moscow retains a weak hand in the Middle East because of its nonrecognition of Israel and isolation from negotiations brokered by Washington in the 1970s. Moscow's domestic turmoil and preoccupation with Eastern Europe will keep the Arab-Israeli focus on the United States, and Soviet Jewish emigration will complicate relations with Arab states. But continued stalemate and Israeli intransigence could intensify interest in Moscow's calls for a conference.

Iran and Iraq conditionally accepted Moscow's offer to mediate their dispute even before they reached their own agreement in the summer of 1990. Shevardnadze met with Iranian and Iraqi foreign ministry officials in 1989 and 1990, and both sides agreed to a meeting to "begin practical study of the matter in question."[28] The Soviets were careful not to circumvent UN mediation efforts and willing to press Tehran and Baghdad toward negotiations. Moscow endorsed a return to prewar boundaries based on the 1975 Algiers accord, brokered by Secretary of State Kissinger and previously ridiculed by Soviet leaders, before Iraq proposed such a compromise after its invasion of Kuwait.

Moscow adopted a strong line against Iraqi aggression and in favor of collective security through the United Nations, although the Soviets contended that "this was quite a difficult step."[29] Immediately following the invasion of Kuwait in August 1990, Gorbachev joined the United States in condemning Iraqi actions and suspended arms deliveries to Baghdad. Soviet officials hinted that Moscow would participate in any naval blockade under the auspices of the United Nations. Moscow would benefit from any increase in world prices for oil because of instability in the Persian Gulf, but apparently decided to join the Western campaign against Iraq to buttress the Soviet case for joining such international economic institutions as the International Monetary Fund and the World Bank.[30]

Gorbachev wants Moscow to be perceived as working with the United States to achieve stability in the Gulf. Soviet media trumpeted the "united front" between the United States and the USSR in the wake of the invasion, particularly the "unprecedented step of publishing a joint statement that defined specific practical measures to stop the aggressor."[31] As a result, according to Soviet analysts, the United States and Britain have expanded cooperation with Moscow, particularly on economic matters. A significant long-term U.S. presence in the Persian Gulf, however, should allow the Soviets to improve relations with both Iran and Iraq.

Soviet–U.S. agreement is central to solving the impasse in Afghanistan where casualties are mounting, with the mujahideen no closer to victory. The Soviets have accepted elections supervised by the UN and the Conference of Islamic Countries, and the United States has accepted participation of the ruling People's Democratic Party of Afghanistan (PDPA), but the mujahideen oppose internationally supervised elections. Moscow has proposed that the PDPA and mujahideen administer areas they control, but the United States wants Najibullah to yield before the elections. The USSR and the United States could end the war if both are willing to end military support and involve a wide group of Afghans in a settlement. If they are unable to reach an accord to end the conflict, they could leave the Afghans to work out their rivalries.

The Soviets presumably realize that instability in Southeast and Southwest Asia could lead to greater U.S. military presence and stronger Sino–U.S. ties. Moscow sees no military solution to the war in Cambodia and favors a political settlement along the lines of the Australian initiative of 1988, an enhanced UN presence to enforce a free election. It would involve UN peacekeeping troops and administrators, with a large percentage of the cost borne by Japan. Warring Cambodian factions would be disarmed or relocated, and a UN presence would remain until a new government could handle its security.

The Soviets have been successful in getting the Hun Sen government to agree to Khmer Rouge participation in the Supreme National Council and international oversight of elections. Cambodian factions have agreed that a ceasefire is necessary, but the start of a ceasefire and means of enforcement are uncertain. Soviet acceptance of a UN role in verifying Vietnamese withdrawal in 1989 is an important precedent, but the role of the UN in oversight of an interim government is undecided.

Moscow and Washington agree on supporting the Esquipulas Treaty of 1987, the accord that established a regional peace plan for Central America. They have cooperated in removing Nicaragua from the Soviet–U.S. agenda, with the Soviets ending military aid to the Sandinistas and the U.S. cutting off the Contras. Both supported the election of 1990. As a result, Nicaragua is no longer an irritant in Soviet–U.S. relations, but the insurgency in El Salvador continues, as do differences over the supply of Soviet-made equipment from Cuba to the guerrillas. The Soviets virtually ignored the U.S. invasion of Panama in 1989 and concentrated on improved relations with nearly every Latin American state.

Moscow has not reacted to tensions between India and Pakistan, presumably deferring to New Dehli's preference for resolving the dispute over Kashmir in its own way, without third-party interference. Washington has pressed Pakistan not to provoke India over the Kashmir imbroglio, India to avoid military provocation. Neither the U.S. nor the USSR has the leverage to separate India and Pakistan if tensions continue.

In addition to promoting United Nations peacekeeping the Soviets could become more involved in addressing proliferation in the Middle East and South Asia. Israel is unlikely to give up its nuclear capability, and Arab states are relying on chemical weapons as a counterweight. Israel favors bilateral negotiation on separate nuclear and chemical tracks; Arab states favor multilateral talks that link the weapons. Egypt supports a nuclear-free zone in the Middle East, and the Soviets in 1989 discussed creation of a "risk reduction center" in the region.

Because Iraq must concern itself with Iran, Syria with Iraq, and Egypt with Libya, the Arabs could favor an arms control accord offering *de facto* recognition of Israel as long as it depreciates the Israeli threat. Israel's interest in recognition could lead it to accept multilateral negotiations that provide direct contacts. Thus far Israel continues to dismiss any notion that it subscribe to the Nonproliferation Treaty, and Arab states have not signaled interest in upgrading their observer status in chemical weapons talks at the Geneva-based Conference on Disarmament.

DISSOLUTION OF THE SOVIET BLOC

Radical changes sweeping through the Soviet Union and Eastern Europe are having an effect on Third World states. Moderate African and Arab states fear Western economic resources will be diverted to Eastern Europe; radical states are anticipating further reduction in aid from the Soviets.

Unpopular governments in Iraq, North Korea, and Syria were shaken by the violent overthrow of Romanian dictator Ceausescu in December 1989. Iran was embarrassed because Ceausescu had just returned from a visit to Tehran when he was overthrown. The PLO was upset because of attacks on its diplomatic personnel in Bucharest during the violence, resulting from reports that Arabs had helped Ceausescu's security forces during the fighting. The Libyan government felt it necessary to deny reports its forces had been involved in defending Ceausescu.

New governments in Eastern Europe have changed policy toward the Middle East. All Moscow's Eastern European allies except Romania severed relations with Israel in 1967 as a gesture of solidarity with Moscow and the Arabs, and now all these states except Bulgaria have reestablished relations with Israel. Eastern European arms deliveries to the Middle East declined in 1989 and 1990, as did Soviet, largely because of reduced sales to Iran and Iraq. Czechoslovak armored vehicles and artillery had been sought in the Middle East, but Prague is converting military factories to consumer production. The PLO stands to lose a source of weapons and training, and extremist Palestinian groups will lose facilities in eastern Germany and Poland. Syria lost one thousand Soviet military advisers in 1989, according to the London-based International Institute for Strategic Studies, and is expected to lose more in 1990.[32]

Emigration of Soviet Jews is unsettling to Arab states and the PLO. Increased emigration and U.S. restrictions on immigrants without refugee status has led to ten to twenty thousand Jews emigrating to Israel monthly. The Israeli government is planning for more than one million emigrants by 1994; unlike earlier emigration, the current group is well educated and, according to an Arab journalist, will "enhance Israel's technological superiority in the face of all its Arab neighbors."[33] Emigration will counter population growth among Arabs in Israel and the occupied territories. Direct flights between Warsaw and Tel Aviv in 1990 [and eventually between Moscow and Tel Aviv] point to continued emigration.

The USSR and Eastern European states are cutting economic aid to Cambodia and introducing "pay-as-you-go" exchanges and loans payable in hard currency.[34] Under Brezhnev, the Soviets underwrote the Vietnamese occupation of Cambodia, and Soviet-bloc aid provided the Phnom Penh regime with more than three-fourths of its budget. But the International Monetary Fund has insisted on cutbacks in aid as a condition for membership. Cuts in aid and advisers, an end to subsidies for Soviet oil, and the economic embargo by the noncommunist states and China could imperil a government already dealing with inflation, corruption, and prospect of the Khmer Rouge's return.

Ethiopia is facing a similar prospect. The Soviets are withdrawing aid and advisers while the Eritreans and Tigreans are threatening the regime in Addis Ababa. Moscow's willingness to desert a client of more than fifteen years at a time of national peril is one of the best examples of Gorbachev's retreat. The Soviets are probably prepared to yield their naval facilities on Dahlak Island.

Most Third World states that have a choice are responding to Moscow's radical reforms and retreat from the Third World, distancing themselves from Soviet policy and signaling interest in closer relations with the United States. Huge protests in Benin forced Mathieu Kerekou, President since 1972, to promise elections and disavow Marxism-Leninism. Mozambique has repudiated Marxism and dropped references to "vanguard parties" and "socialist orientation." A shift to competing parties is promised in Socialist Tanzania, nudged by former President Julius Nyerere, who cited the lessons of Eastern Europe. Angola and Ethiopia have become willing to accept UN participation in reconciliation talks with insurgent leaders and exchange diplomatic relations with the United States. Ethiopia has resumed military ties with Israel, broken in 1977, when the Soviet presence expanded in Addis Ababa.

Libyan and Syrian moves to improve relations with Egypt and end isolation in the Middle East were a result of Soviet policy, and unification of North and South Yemen in 1990 reflected Aden's apprehension about continued Soviet support. Elsewhere, Cuban and Vietnamese withdrawals from Angola and Cambodia were in response to Soviet pressure.

Changes in the USSR and Eastern Europe are forcing India to rethink its policy for the first time since independence was achieved in 1947. Foreign Minister Inder Kumar Gujral has stated that New Dehli's non-aligned status is now "irrelevant" and will have to be redefined.[35] India can no longer count on Moscow's generous trade concessions, particularly the ability to pay in rupees for Soviet goods and services. In any event, India is looking to improve relations with both China and Pakistan.

Only North Korea appears "frozen in time," unwilling to protect itself from the reform sweeping the Soviet Union and Eastern Europe. Pyongyang has failed to prevent socialist states from recognizing South Korea, or repair its relations with Eastern European states possessing ties to Seoul. President Roh Tae Woo's meetings with Gorbachev in June and December 1990 were a setback to Kim Il-Sung, who looks to the USSR as his only supplier of modern military technology and his largest trade partner.

An easing of tensions on the Korean peninsula would allow more U.S. troop withdrawals, and encourage Japanese and Chinese economic activity with the USSR. The Gorbachev-Roh summits extended the European détente to Asia, gave Moscow and Seoul a closer connection than Washington and Pyongyang, and further isolated the last Stalinist dictator in the international arena. Pyongyang's careful treatment of the summit indicates that Kim hoped to delay Moscow's recognition of the Seoul government that legitimizes two Koreas.

THE ISLAMIC FACTOR

Moscow's increasing problems with its large Muslim population will be a disadvantage in dealings with Islamic states of the Middle East and Persian Gulf and another factor leading to preoccupation with domestic matters. The surge in ethnic violence in the Central Asian Republic of Kirghizia on the day of Gorbachev's return from his summit meeting in Washington confronted him with another domestic crisis. The violence produced more than four hundred deaths and a thousand injuries, and climaxed another round of confrontations in Central Asia over poverty and allocations of land and water.

Demonstrations by Azeris on the Soviet-Iranian border, such as those in January 1990, could create complications between Moscow and Tehran. About six million Azeris live on each side of the Soviet-Iranian border, and neither Moscow nor Tehran has shown interest in exploiting instability and separatism in the region.[36] The Iranians have signaled they will not take advantage of the USSR's domestic problems and indicated that "extreme nationalism," calling for demolition of borders, would serve neither the USSR nor Iran.[27] Presumably the Soviet decision to put off sending troops to the border until 1990, after two years of nationalist and ethnic discord, reassured Iran.

Faced with violence, the Kremlin has sent forty thousand internal security troops to Azerbaijan, Armenia, Georgia, Uzbekistan, Tajikistan, and Kirghizia. Violence in any of these republics will be criticized in Muslim states, where the Soviet model is already compromised. Turkey is watching Soviet handling of the large Turkish minority in the USSR. Moscow's campaign to prevent a ground war in Kuwait and Iraq in 1991 was part of an effort to prevent a spillover of Islamic fundamentalism into the Soviet Union.

THE SOVIET ROLE IN THE THIRD WORLD

Soviet retreat does not mean that Third World states will lose access to weapons. In a speech to the nineteenth party conference in 1988, Yevgeni Primakov, a senior aide to Gorbachev, recorded that the USSR had "in no way given up its sympathies or its actual support for the forces of progress" and was a "firm opponent of any attempts to export counter-revolution to countries where progressive forces have come to power."[38] The Soviets will continue to use military assets to protect Cuba, Syria, and Vietnam. They have provided airlifts of arms in flashpoint situations and could be expected to do so if there were a confrontation between Syria and Israel or Vietnam and China. Overflight clearances and access to facilities abroad support Moscow's military operations, and naval and air assets in Cuba and Vietnam are used to protect interests abroad, assert rights on the seas, and support Third World states. Nevertheless, the Soviet embargo of Iraq in 1990 will remind such clients as Syria and Vietnam that there is no guarantee that Gorbachev, unlike his predecessors, will provide a shield for Third World states.

Soviet arms transfers will remain a fact of life in the Third World, particularly in the Middle East where exchanges for hard currency to Libya and Iraq previously helped finance Gorbachev's economic modernization. Hard-currency sales of MiG-29 fighters and T-72 tanks to Algeria and Libya will continue. Libya purchased SU-24 fighter bombers in 1989, and Cuba received MiG-29 fighters in 1990. Older Soviet equipment predominates in Third World arsenals, and MiG-21 fighters, T-62 tanks, and artillery pieces will go to India and Syria.

The conventional arms agreement for Europe could release thousands of combat aircraft, attack helicopters, tanks, light armored vehicles, and field artillery pieces for Third World inventories.[39] Arms control and unilateral reductions could lead to lower prices, attracting such Third World debtors as Egypt, Iran, and Vietnam. Iran needs to improve its capabilities against Iraq, and India needs to upgrade armor in the event of hostilities against Pakistan. Conversely, military transfers to such economic basket cases as Ethiopia and Yemen will be scrutinized, as more resources are needed at home to provide a "safety net." An agreement in Europe could lead to availability of U.S. equipment to such clients as Israel, Morocco, and Pakistan.

The Soviets will look for opportunities for military assistance if they can gain access to strategic areas or former clients. Gorbachev has hinted that weapons systems could be available to Egypt and Iran, and it appears likely that Cairo and Tehran will enter into agreements for aid or create the impression of interest to gain access to Western assistance. The Soviets delivered MiG-29 fighter aircraft and surface-to-air missiles in 1990. Soviet sales to Egypt could create demands from Libya and Syria.

There is no indication that Gorbachev is going to remove the USSR from security assistance, as witness continued assistance to Angola and willingness to advise the People's Armed Forces for the Liberation of Angola against the UNITA insurgency. Nevertheless, Gorbachev will presumably devote more attention to the effect of assistance on regional balances and Soviet–U.S. collaboration. He will be more sensitive to proliferation in the Third World, particularly the Middle East and Southwest Asia, where such nonsigners of the nonproliferation treaty as Israel and Pakistan are contributing to an arms race that could complicate the interests of both the United States and the Soviet Union.

Nevertheless, the Soviets believe that a greater military presence in the Third World does not assure greater political security for either the USSR or its clients. In 1987, Gorbachev supported collective efforts to "defuse" conflicts "in all the planet's hot spots" and a greater United Nations role.[40] He announced the decision to withdraw from Afghanistan the following year and since then has cited the Afghan settlement as an "important international landmark."[41] Support for regional settlements through the United Nations, as in Afghanistan, or U.S. mediation as in Angola, has been justified to make sure local conflicts do not "engender confrontation" between the superpowers.[42] The deputy director of the African Institute wrote in 1989 that military assistance has not created allies and regional conflicts have not ended in victories.[43] And at the United Nations on the anniversary of Pearl Harbor, Gorbachev reminded his audience that:

The bell of each regional conflict tolls for all of us. This is particularly true because these conflicts are occurring in the "Third World" which even without this has many troubles and problems on a scale which cannot fail to concern all of us.[44]

He never mentioned "states of socialist orientation," "national liberation movements," or the "world revolutionary process."

OUTLOOK FOR THE 1990s

All indications of change in Soviet security policy suggest demilitarization and a lesser role in the Third World. The military is due for even greater cuts as its proportion of the gross national product declines. Desertion and violence within the military will increase because of ethnic differences. Hazing is a problem in the Soviet military, primarily due to ethnic factors. Theft of weapons and ammunition from bases is becoming a major problem.

The operational tempo of Soviet forces continues to decline, and the Soviet Navy scrapped seventy surface ships and thirty-five diesel submarines in 1990. The rate of space launches declines, and reliance on satellite collection could bring withdrawal from facilities in Cuba and Syria. Disengagement from radical clients is causing shifts in regional relations, and will provide opportunities for U.S. diplomacy.

Soviet preoccupation with domestic crises should continue into the decade. The crackdown in the Baltics in January 1991 points to continued preoccupation with internal matters. Breakdown of food distribution is bringing shortages that resemble wartime. Violence in Central Asia and the Caucasus is not abating, and strikes and lesser agitation are more frequent in the Russian Republic. Separatist activity is likely to continue; more than half the republics have voted to give their own laws precedence over those of the Soviet Union. Finally, Gorbachev's policy of liberalization has already been accompanied by an increase in crime and gangsterism.

As a result, the Soviets will continue to cooperate with the United States to reduce regional confrontation as they have done in Afghanistan, Angola, Cambodia, and Ethiopia. The next stage of their dialogue could include limits on arms transfers to the Third World and procedures for elections that resemble the Nicaraguan model. Having accepted elections in Eastern Europe, the Soviets may be willing to accept political participation for the Khmer Rouge in Cambodia, Savimbi in Angola, and even the mujahideen in Afghanistan. The departure of foreign troops from these states by 1991 should make it easier for the Soviets to accept these "insurgents." Limits on arms transfers would dissociate the Soviets from the conflicts, and international peacekeeping forces from neutral states would allow coalition governments.

Since 1987, Gorbachev has encouraged a role for the United Nations in conflict resolution in the Third World, greater use of UN military observers and peacekeeping forces to separate warring parties and mediate disputes. The Soviets have paid arrears in contributions to the UN and are paying past assessments in peacekeeping. They have cooperated with UN observers in Afghanistan, supported peacekeepers in the Persian Gulf, and sent observers to Namibia. Moscow proposed withdrawal of foreign ships from the Persian Gulf in 1987 and creation of a UN fleet, but this had more to do with the fact that there were several Soviet warships in the Gulf amidst thirty U.S. combatants.[45] In the wake of the Iraqi invasion of Kuwait, Moscow hinted it would participate in a multilateral naval blockade of Iraq and proposed that the Military Staff Committee of the Security Council be given a role in controlling the naval buildup in the Gulf.

Moscow favors permanent members of the Security Council as guarantors of regional security, and in 1989 cosponsored its first UN resolution with the United States to stress the importance of Security Council mandates. Thus far the Soviets have found a consensus at the United Nations for a more active role by the secretary-general in resolving conflicts and cooperating with regional organizations to create an environment for negotiations. Conflict could be contained in this fashion, although ethnic conflict and international terrorism will be more difficult to resolve.

For the first time since the Second World War, the Soviet Union and United States are cooperating in resolving regional conflicts, advancing their own interests as well as those of Third World states. Moscow and Washington have had success in Afghanistan, Angola, and Cambodia, but must resolve problems associated with arms shipments to these states and the formation of coalition governments. In the Persian Gulf, the two sides have entered their first joint crisis-management exercise in the United Nations, pushing through a resolution condemning the invasion and establishing economic sanctions. Gorbachev told Baker during the Gulf crisis, that "we've got to stay together on this."[46]

The Soviets are stressing cooperation over conflict, political interest over class interest, but are not in an economic position to address the domestic causes of turbulence in the Third World. They favor cooperation with the United States to create the impression of involvement and improve relations with noncommunist states. In the wake of Shevardnadze's resignation in December 1990, Soviet officials pledge to continue cooperation with the United States on Third World issues.[47] Since the focus in the Third World will include economic and environmental issues, as well as security and military ones, cooperation would be a positive factor. The choices, in the final analysis, will have to be made by the regional states.

NOTES

1. See "The Soviet Economy Stumbles Badly in 1989," Central Intelligence Agency paper presented to the Technology and National Security Subcommittee of the Joint Economic Committee, Congress of the United States.

2. Ibid., p. 22.

3. Ibid., p. 11.

4. L.D. Trotsky, *The Revolution Betrayed*, London: New Park Publishers, 1967, p. 222 (first published in 1936).

5. *The Washington Post*, August 19, 1990, p. C4, "The Soviet Military's Recruitment Nightmare," by Murray Feshbach.

6. *Pravda*, August 18, 1990, p. 3.

7. Western military writings have tended to exaggerate the importance of power projection to Soviet military planning. See writings of Michael MccGwire, particularly *Military Objectives in Soviet Foreign Policy*, Washington, DC: Brookings Institution, 1987, and John Hines, Phillip Petersen, and Notra Trulock III, particularly their "Soviet Military Theory from 1945–2000: Implications for NATO," *The Washington Quarterly*, Vol. 9, No. 4, Fall 1986, pp. 122–129.

8. *London Times*, April 16, 1990, p. 4, "Russians Likely to Scrap 100 Warships, MoD Says," by Michael Evans.

9. Peter Grier, "Middle East: Laying the Ground Work," *Military Logistics Forum*, September 1987, p. 21.

10. Jeffrey Record, *The Rapid Deployment Force and U.S. Military Intervention in the Persian Gulf*, Cambridge, MA: Institute for Foreign Policy Analysis, 1981, p. 58.

11. *Soviet Military Power: Prospects for Change*, Washington, DC: U.S. Government Printing Office, 1989, pp. 113–117.

12. *The Washington Post*, May 27, 1990, p. 23, "Soviets Plan to Review Military Aid."

13. In March 1990, *Izvestia* published the first detailed breakdown of debts owed to the Soviet Union: Cuba ($24 billion), Vietnam ($15 billion), Mongolia ($15 billion), India ($14 billion), Syria ($10 billion), Iraq ($6 billion), Afghanistan ($5 billion), and Algeria ($4 billion).

14. *The New York Times*, March 6, 1990, p. 1, "Arabs Fear End of Cold War Means a Loss of Aid and Allies," by Youssef M. Ibrahim.

15. Joseph Whelan, *The Soviet Union in the Third World, 1980–1982: An Imperial Burden or Political Asset*, Washington, DC: U.S. Government Printing Office, 1984, pp. 295–296.

16. *Izvestia*, March 2, 1990, p. 3, "Unique Document: Who Owes Us 85.5 Billion Rubles." The article was addressed to Premier N. I. Ryzhkov, Chairman of the USSR Council of Ministers.

17. *The Washington Post*, July 25, 1990, p. 15, "Gorbachev Sets Review of Foreign Aid."

18. *The New York Times*, June 9, 1989, p. 3, "Radical Plan to Balance Soviet Budget," by Bill Keller.

19. Ibid., p. 15.

20. TASS, March 27, 1990, Shevardnadze press conference in Lagos, Nigeria.

21. *The New York Times*, June 21, 1990, p. 17, "Arms Sales to Third World Said to Decline Sharply," by Robert Pear.

22. See Paul Kennedy, *The Rise and Fall of the Great Powers*, New York: Random House, 1987.

23. *The New York Times*, June 2, 1990, p. 3.

24. *The Washington Post*, April 16, 1990, p. 22, "U.S., Soviets Cooperate on Angolan Conflict," by John Goshko.

25. *The New York Times*, June 4, 1990, p. 13, "U.S. and Soviets Will Seek to Prevent Ethiopia Famine," by Clifford Krauss.

26. In the 1950s the U.S. began providing military aid to Haile Selassie in return for naval facilities at Massawa. Moscow responded by supporting Eritrean rebels who have been fighting since 1962 and by helping Ethiopia's hostile neighbors, Somalia and the Sudan. These alliances shifted after Marxist officers ousted the old emperor in 1974. Moscow embraced the new rulers, and Washington supported Somalia and the Sudan. Later, as the superpowers began pulling back, Arab states stepped up aid to Eritrea and Israel renewed its long-broken ties with Ethiopia.

27. The Soviets have followed the same strategy regarding a regional settlement in Cambodia with Moscow advocating a more active role for the United Nations, particularly in the area of peacekeeping forces, despite Vietnam's initial opposition to any UN presence in Cambodia.

28. TASS, January 10, 1990.

29. *Krasnaya Zvezda (Red Star)*, August 10, 1990, p. 3.

30. *The Washington Post*, August 20, 1990, p. 17. The USSR is the leading oil producer in the world, but production has declined somewhat in recent years, falling below 12 million barrels a day for the first time in the past ten years. Moscow is pumping 11.6 million barrels a day and exports 3.3 million of that. (Iraq and Kuwait were pumping about 4.5 million barrels before the invasion, or 9 percent of world production.) A $10 per barrel increase in world prices would bring the Soviets a $30 million daily windfall.

31. *Krasnaya Zvezda (Red Star)*, August 10, 1990, p. 3, "The World Today: Problems and Views," by Manki Ponomarev.

32. *The New York Times*, March 6, 1990, p. 1, "Arabs Fear End of Cold War," by Youssef M. Ibrahim.

33. Ibid.

34. *The Washington Post*, June 8, 1990, p. 23, "East Bloc to Cut Cambodia Aid, Report Says," by Elizabeth Becker.

35. *The New York Times*, March 11, 1990, p. 17, "India Reexamines Its Foreign Policy," by Barbara Crossette.

36. The Cold War can be dated to the Soviet refusal in 1945 to withdraw from Iranian Azerbaijan, where Stalin created two puppet republics along the Soviet and Iraqi borders. President Truman's threat to use force led to Soviet withdrawal, and Iran reneged on its promise of political and economic concessions to the Soviets. This marked the first of Stalin's failures to support liberation struggles in the Third World. See Alvin Z. Rubinstein, *Moscow's Third World Strategy*, Princeton: Princeton University Press, 1988, pp. 82–84.

37. *Tehran Times*, January 8, 1990, p. 3.

38. *Pravda*, July 2, 1988, p. 5.

39. Any agreement will involve older weapons from Warsaw Pact forces, but some modern weapons such as T-72 tanks, BTR armored vehicles, and BM-24 multiple rocket launchers probably will be included.

40. *Pravda*, September 17, 1987, p. 1.

41. TASS, January 18, 1989, Gorbachev speech to the Trilateral Commission; *Krasnaya Zvezda*, February 24, 1989, p. 5.

42. Gorbachev, *Perestroika*, p. 176.

43. *Izvestia*, February 4, 1989.

44. *Pravda*, December 8, 1988, p. 1, Gorbachev speech at the 43rd UN General Assembly.

45. *The New York Times*, December 17, 1987, p. 5, "Soviet Links Iran Embargo to UN Force" by David Shipler.

46. *The New York Times*, November 20, 1990, p. 17.

47. *The New York Times*, December 29, 1990, p. 1.

Bibliographic Essay

There has been a significant amount of writing in recent years on Soviet policy in the Third World. Most books and monographs agree there has been much change in Gorbachev's foreign policy since his accession to power in 1985, but disagree on reasons for change and whether the change is meaningful. One school of thought contends that Gorbachev has modified some aspects of policy but that his approach toward the Third World remains conservative and, in the final analysis, does not differ significantly from his predecessors. The best example of this approach is the writing of Professor Alvin Z. Rubinstein, particularly his well-crafted and well documented *Moscow's Third World Strategy*, Princeton, NJ: Princeton University Press, 1990.

Another conservative school takes a more ideological approach and tends to downplay pragmatic aspects of Soviet behavior in the Third World. Examples of this school are Joseph G. Whelan and Michael J. Dixon, *The Soviet Union in the Third World: Threat to World Peace?*, Washington, DC: Pergamon-Brassey's, 1989, and Walter Laqueur's edited work on *The Pattern of Soviet Conduct in the Third World*, New York: Praeger Publishers, 1983. A final conservative branch of historiography on Soviet policy in the Third World explores so-called cycles or recurrent patterns of Soviet as explained in the writings of Francis Fukuyama in *Moscow's Post-Brezhnev Reassessment of the Third World*, Santa Monica, CA: RAND Corporation, February 1986; "Gorbachev and the Third World," *Foreign Affairs* (Spring 1986); and "Patterns of Soviet Third World Policy," *Problems of Communism* (September–October 1987).

Some scholarship has explored changes in Soviet policy in the Third World and highlights the differences in Gorbachev's policies from those of his predecessors. These works argue that the role of ideology has declined in the execution of Soviet policy and note the importance of economic constraint as a factor in Soviet retrenchment. One of the more timely and balanced studies is W. Raymond Duncan and Carolyn McGiffert Ekedahl, *Moscow and the Third World under Gorbachev*, Boulder, CO: Westview Press, 1990. The decline in ideology is traced in Sylvia Woodby, *Gorbachev and the Decline of Ideology in Soviet Foreign Policy*, Boulder, CO: Westview Press, 1989. One of the best examples of the argument for Soviet retrenchment in the Third World is Jack Snyder, "The Gorbachev Revolution: A Waning of Soviet Expansion?" *International Security* (Winter 1987–1988).

Two of the more interesting and scholarly works in the area of economic constraint are Jerry Hough, *The Struggle for the Third World: Soviet Debates and American Options*, Washington, DC: The Brookings Institution, 1986, and Elizabeth Valkenier, *The Soviet Union and the Third World: An Economic Bind*, New York: Praeger Publishers, 1983. Recent journal articles by Professor Valkenier carry her perceptive argument into the Gorbachev era, particularly "Revolutionary Change in the Third World: Recent Soviet Assessments," *World Politics* (April 1986), and "New Thinking About the Third World," *World Policy Journal* (Fall 1987). Another prescient account is Thomas J. Zamostny, "Moscow and the Third World: Recent Trends in Soviet Thinking," *Soviet Studies* (April 1984).

Little attention has been given to Gorbachev's alteration of the decision-making process, particularly in the Ministry of Foreign Affairs and the Central Committee's International Department. Mathew P. Gallagher's "The Soviet Military Role in Soviet Decisionmaking" (see Michael MccGwire, Ken Booth, and John McDonnell, eds., *Soviet Naval Policy: Objectives and Constraints*, New York: Praeger Publishers, 1975) is still useful but outdated. F. Stephen Larrabbe's "Gorbachev and the Soviet Military," *Foreign Affairs* (Summer 1988), is the best recent monograph on the role of the military in national security decision making.

Jeffrey T. Richelson's *Sword and Shield: The Soviet Intelligence and Security Apparatus*, Cambridge, MA: Ballinger Publishing Co., 1986, discusses the role of the KGB and the decision-making apparatus and Robert W. Kitrinos' "The CPSU Central Committee's International Department," *Problems of Communism* (September–October, 1984) offers a useful description of the party's role in national security policymaking.

For useful anecdotal information on the foreign ministry, see Arkady N. Shevchenko, *Breaking with Moscow*, New York: Alfred A. Knopf, 1985. Vladimir Petrov's "Formulation of Soviet Foreign Policy," *Orbis* (Vol. XVII, No. 3, 1973) is still useful and Carl G.

Jacobsen's "Soviet Think Tanks," *Soviet Armed Forces Review Annual 1* (Fall 1977), remains an important article that deserves to be updated. The same can be said for Richard A. Soll, Arthur A. Zuehlke, Jr., and Richard B. Foster, *The Role of Social Science Research Institutes in Formulation and Execution of Soviet Foreign Policy*, Arlington, VA: SRI International, 1976.

For analyses of Soviet behavior in the international arena, see Hannes J. Adomeit, *Soviet Risk Taking and Crisis Behavior: A Theoretical and Empirical Analysis*, London: Allen and Unwin, 1982, and Alexander L. George, *Managing U.S.–Soviet Rivalry: Problems of Crisis Prevention*, Boulder, CO: Westview Press, 1983. The best treatment of the domestic factors in Soviet foreign policy appear in Seweryn Bialer, *The Domestic Context of Soviet Foreign Policy*, Boulder, CO: Westview Press, 1981 and Morton Schwartz, *The Foreign Policy of the USSR: Domestic Factors*, Encino, CA: Dickenson Press, 1975. *The Conduct of Soviet Foreign Policy*, New York, Aldine Publishing Co., 1980, which was edited by Erik P. Hoffmann and Frederic J. Fleron, is very useful.

Useful studies of Soviet military behavior include Bruce D. Porter, *The USSR in Third World Conflicts: Soviet Arms and Diplomacy in Local Wars, 1945–1980*, Cambridge: Cambridge University Press, 1984; Michael MccGwire, Ken Booth, and John McDonnell, eds., *Soviet Naval Policy: Objectives and Constraints*, New York: Praeger Publishers, 1975; and Jon D. Glassman, *Arms for the Arabs: The Soviet Union and War in the Middle East*, Baltimore: Johns Hopkins University Press, 1975. Mark N. Kramer, "Soviet Arms Transfers to the Third World," *Problems of Communism* (September–October 1987) is a useful analysis of Soviet military aid.

There are several comprehensive accounts on the background to the occupation of Afghanistan and the unsuccessful attempt to impose foreign rule on the fiercely independent Afghans. Henry S. Bradsher, who worked in Afghanistan as an Associated Press correspondent in the 1960s, J. Bruce Amstutz, the U.S. chargé d'affaires in Kabul in the 1970s, and Thomas T. Hammond, a professor of government at the University of Virginia, have written three of the most useful surveys: *Afghanistan and the Soviet Union*, Durham, NC: Duke University Press, 1983; *Afghanistan: The First Five Years of Soviet Occupation*, Washington, DC: National Defense University Press, 1986, and *Red Flag over Afghanistan: The Communist Coup, the Soviet Invasion, and the Consequence*, Boulder, CO: Westview Press, 1984, respectively. Louis Dupree's *Afghanistan*, Princeton, NJ: Princeton University Press, 1980 and Vartan Gregorian's *The Emergence of Modern Afghanistan: Politics of Reform and Modernization, 1880–1946*, Stanford, CA: Stanford University Press, 1969, provide essential background information. The translation efforts of the Foreign Broadcast Information Service for the Soviet Union are essential for an understanding of the view from the Kremlin for Southwest Asia and Afghanistan.

There are numerous studies available to researchers and students on regions other than Southwest Asia. Donald Zagoria, who has written *Vietnam Triangle: Moscow/Peking/Hanoi*, New York: Pegasus Publishers, 1967, and edited *Soviet Policy in East Asia*, New Haven: Yale University Press, 1982, has followed Soviet policy in Asia for more than 30 years. Charles B. MacLane, *Soviet-Asian Relations*, New York: Columbia University Press, 1973, and *Soviet Strategies in Southeast Asia*, Princeton: Princeton University Press, 1966, remain useful. For a recent review of Soviet politics in the region, see Carolyn McGiffert Ekedahl and Melvin A. Goodman, "Gorbachev's 'New Directions' in Asia," *Journal of Northeast Asian Studies* (Fall 1989).

Alvin Z. Rubinstein's *Red Star on the Nile: The Soviet-Egyptian Influence Relationship Since the June War*, Princeton: Princeton University Press, 1977, is arguably the best study ever done on Soviet bilateral relations with a key Third World state. Other useful books on the Middle East are Robert Freedman, *Soviet Policy in the Middle East Since 1970*, New York: Praeger Publishers, 1982, and Mark Kauppi and R. Craig Nation, *The Soviet Union and the Middle East in the 1980s*, Lexington, MA: Lexington Books, 1983. For a comprehensive account of current Soviet policy, see Melvin A. Goodman and Carolyn McGiffert Ekedahl, "Gorbachev's 'New Directions' in the Middle East," *Middle East Journal* (Autumn 1988) and "Trends in Soviet Policy in the Middle East and the Gulf," *International Journal* (Summer 1990).

For Latin America, see Cole Blasier's *The Giant's Rival: The USSR and Latin America*, Pittsburgh: University of Pittsburgh Press, 1983, which is still useful and W. Raymond Duncan, *The Soviet Union and Cuba*, New York: Praeger Publishers, 1985. David Albright continues to follow Africa, and particularly useful are his *Communism in Africa*, Bloomington, IN: Indiana University Press, 1980, and "The USSR and the Third World in the 1980s," *Problems of Communism* (March–June 1989). S. Neil MacFarlane's "The Soviet Union and Southern African Security," *Problems of Communism* (March–June 1989) is both timely and trenchant, and Peter Clement, "Moscow and Southern Africa," *Problems of Communism* (March–April 1985)is an excellent analysis of Gorbachev's inheritance in Africa.

Other useful regional studies are Bruce Larkin, *Vital Interests: The Soviet Issue in U.S. Central American Policy*, Boulder, CO: Lynne Rinner Publishers, 1988; Douglas Pike, *Vietnam and the Soviet Union: Anatomy of an Alliance*, Boulder, CO: Westview Press, 1987; Carol Saivitz (ed.), *The Soviet Union in the Third World*, Boulder, CO: Westview Press, 1989; and Robert G. Patman, *The Soviet Union in the Horn of Africa: The Diplomacy of Intervention and Disengagement*, Cambridge: Cambridge

University Press, 1990. Andrzej Korbonski and Francis Fukuyama, eds., *The Soviet Union and the Third World*, Ithaca and London: Cornell University Press, 1987, places Soviet action in a broader context of Soviet policy. Galia Golan has written perceptively on a variety of Middle East issues, including "Gorbachev's Middle East Strategy" in *Foreign Affairs* (Fall 1987), and her *The Soviet Union and National Liberation Movements in the Third World*, Boston: Unwin Hyman, 1988, which is extremely useful.

It is difficult to obtain timely and accurate information on Soviet military and economic assistance efforts for the Third World, but the task would be virtually impossible without the unclassified publications of the Central Intelligence Agency and the Congressional Reference Service of the Library of Congress. The CIA previously made available such research guides as *Communist Aid Activities in Non-Communist Less Developed Countries* and *Soviet Economic and Military Aid to the Less Developed Countries*. Richard Grimmett of the Congressional Reference Service annually produces *Trends in Conventional Arms Transfers to the Third World by Supplier* and Ruth Leger Sivard regularly presents *World Military and Social Expenditures*. The Arms Control and Disarmament Agency annually produces *World Military Expenditures and Arms Transfers*, which understands the essential differences between arms transfer deliveries and agreements. The *World Military Balance*, an annual study by the International Institute for Strategic Studies in London, and *Warsaw Pact Economic Aid to Non-Communist LDC's*, previously prepared annually by the Department of State's Bureau of Intelligence and Research, are essential to an understanding of the flow and direction of Soviet military and economic assistance efforts.

Insufficient attention has been given to the limits on Soviet power and influence in the Third World. Yaacov Ro'i's *The Limits to Power: Soviet Policy in the Middle East*, London: Croom Helm, 1979, made a useful start in this direction with a handful of American and Israeli scholars but, until recently, the field has been ignored and, as a result, Western literature has tended to exaggerate Soviet power and capabilities in the Third World. More recently, Professors Daniel Nelson and Rajan Menon edited an interesting work on *The Limits to Soviet Power*, Lexington, MA: Lexington Press, 1989, and Andrzej Korbonski and Francis Fukuyama edited *The Soviet Union and the Third World: The Last Three Decades*, Ithaca, NY: Cornell University Press, 1987, which addressed the limits on Soviet power projection in noncontiguous areas. Mark Katz, *The Third World in Soviet Military Thought*, Baltimore: Johns Hopkins University Press, 1982, remains a very useful study of growing Soviet pessimism about the ability of the USSR to achieve and maintain its foreign policy goals in the Third World through anything less than costly long-term military commitments. Conversely, Stephen

T. Hosmer and Thomas W. Wolfe, *Soviet Policy and Practice Toward Third World Conflicts*, Lexington, MA: Lexington Books, 1983, uses the Soviet invasion of Afghanistan as a paradigm for increased regional Soviet involvement.

The "Soviet Daily Report" of the *Foreign Broadcast Information Service* (U.S. Government Printing Office) is invaluable, particularly for its timely coverage of Soviet statements and articles. Some of the more important documents in recent years include Mikhail Gorbachev's "Political Report of the CPSU Central Committee to the 27th Congress of the Communist Party of the Soviet Union" (February 1986), and his "Political Report of the CPSU Central Committee to the 28th Congress of the Communist Party of the Soviet Union" (July 1990). Gorbachev's Seventieth Revolutionary Anniversary Speech (November 1987), speech to the Central Committee Plenum (February 1988), and seminal speech to the United National General Assembly in December 1988 are extremely useful for documenting his views on Soviet policy in the Third World. His speeches in Vladivostok (1986) and Krasnoyarsk (1988) outlined Moscow's approach to policy in Asia for reducing regional tension and lowering the level of military activity.

Key statements by Foreign Minister Shevardnadze include his speeches to conferences of the Ministry of Foreign Affairs in August 1987 and August 1988. These speeches provided the first indications of the legislative constraints that would be placed on foreign and military policy as well as the end to ideological constraints on policy with the noncommunist world. His remarks endorsed the end to class struggle as an element of international relations. Many of Shevardnadze's themes have appeared in articles by Vyacheslav Dashichev, head of the Department of International Relations of Socialist Countries in the Institute of the Economics of the World Socialist System, particularly in *Literaturnaya gazeta* (*Literary Gazette*) and Aleksandr Bovin, *Izvestia* political observer. Their articles have been extremely critical of Brezhnev's policy in the Third World, particularly the effect of those policies on East-West relations.

Index

ABOUT THE AUTHOR

Melvin A. Goodman is Professor of International Security Studies at the National War College in Washington, D.C., and he has served as a Senior Analyst for Soviet Affairs for both the Central Intelligence Agency and the Department of State. He has published articles in *Middle East Journal*, *Journal of Northeast Asian Studies*, and *International Journal*, and has contributed chapters to three books on the Soviet Union.